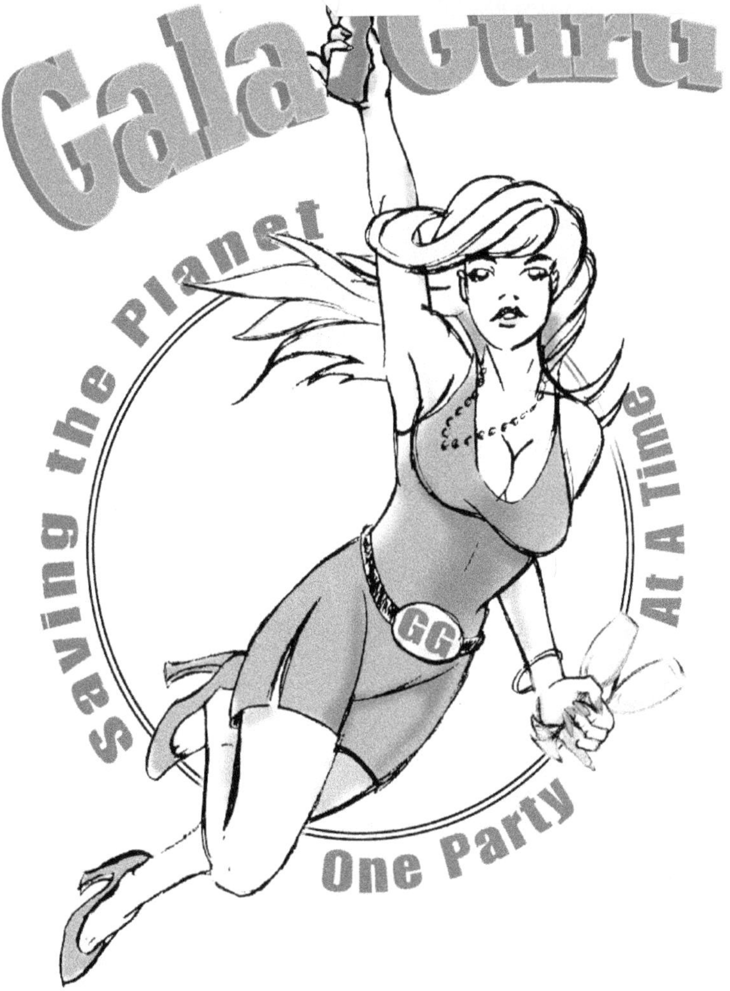

Donna Vessey

www.thegalaguru.net

© 2025 Gala Guru Press, LLC. Printed and bound in the United States of America. All rights reserved. No part of this book may be reproduced or transmitted in any form or by any means, electronic or mechanical, including photocopying, recording, or by an information storage and retrieval system—except by a reviewer who may quote brief passages in a review to be printed in a magazine, newspaper, or on the Web—without permission in writing from the publisher. For more information, please contact "The Gala Guru" at www.thegalaguru.net

This book is a work of fiction. Names, characters, places, and events are prod-ucts of the author's imagination or are used fictitiously. Any resemblance to actual events, locations, or living or deceased persons is purely coincidental. We assume no responsibility for errors, inaccuracies, omissions, or any inconsistency herein.

The trademarks used and characters referenced in this book are the property of their respective owners and are used without their sponsorship or permission.

Cover art by Dave Vanderkolk
First printing 2012
Second printing 2025

eBook ISBN: 978-0-9852893-0-0
Paperback ISBN: 978-0-9852893-1-7
Ingram Spark ISBN: 978-0-9852893-3-1
Library of Congress Control Number: 2024927554

ATTENTION CORPORATIONS, UNIVERSITIES, COLLEGES, AND PROFESSIONAL ORGANIZATIONS: Quantity discounts are available on bulk purchases of this book for educational, gift purposes, or as premiums for increasing magazine subscriptions or renewals. Special books or book excerpts can also be created to fit specific needs.
For information, Contact "The Gala Guru" at www.thegalaguru.net

www.thegalaguru.net

FOREWORD

This book is dedicated to all the event and conference planners I have ever worked with. "Gala Guru" is an affectionate title I assigned to all the men and women who sit on committees and volunteer their time and talents for galas, parties, fundraisers, and events. The job of these individuals is to plan the next event they have signed up for. They are the people who attend parties and charity fundraisers and are often seen in the society column of newspapers and elite magazines. They are in charge of picking out linen colors, deciding on menus, collecting silent auction gifts, determining the layout for a program, and securing advertising for their events. Their organizational skills are unsurpassed. I have enjoyed knowing them all.

The situations and characters in this book were inspired by my years and experiences as an event planner. *Adventures of a Gala Guru* is a work of fiction. Everything you read here—the people, places, and events are all figments of my twisted imagination. Any resemblance to actual events or persons, living or dead, is purely a matter of coincidence. All the cities, states, hotels, and restaurants are used fictitiously.

Here's to anyone planning an event: may all your parties be spectacular!

CONTENTS

CHAPTER 1
WAKE UP CALL 9

CHAPTER 2
KARMAGEDDON 23

CHAPTER 3
IF IT'S NOT ONE THING, IT'S YOUR MOTHER 33

CHAPTER 4
EVERYTHING'S BIGGER IN TEXAS 77

CHAPTER 5
HO, HO, HO 115

CHAPTER 6
SOMEONE BORROWED, SOMEONE BLUE 133

CHAPTER 7
THERE'S NO BUSINESS LIKE HO BUSINESS 143

CHAPTER 8
DANCES WITH DONKEYS 151

CHAPTER 9
LIVIN' LA DIVA LOCA 163

CHAPTER 10
MINOR PROBLEMS 173

CHAPTER 11
LITTLE MALL OF HORRORS 185

CHAPTER 12
MEMBERS ONLY 203

CHAPTER 13
UNDER THE BIG TOP 213

CHAPTER 14
YOU CAN'T BUY HAPPINESS 227

CHAPTER 15
A WALK ON THE WILD SIDE 247

For David, without whose incessant encouragement, patience and culinary skills I would never have survived long enough to write this book!

CHAPTER 1

Wake Up Call

"Cut!" Shouts Jay, our director. "Everybody back to one! Makeup, can we do something about the shine on her nose? It's going to blind somebody if we don't do something about it soon. And Donna, this time can you make your cheeks puff out a little more when you grab your stomach? And you," he says, pointing to the boom mike operator, "do you think we could keep the microphone out of the shot for once?"

The fact is, I'm not even saying anything, so why do we even have a boom mic on this shoot? I'm supposed to act like I have an earthquake going on in my guts, grab my belly, and puff out my cheeks. How hard can this be? But Jay is a perfectionist, and you know what they say about perfectionists: They are frequently disappointed. Betsy, our makeup genius, comes over and studies my nose like it's something from a different planet.

"We could take him if you wanted to," says Betsy with gleeful grin. "I don't think a person on this set would testify against us if we got caught."

"But what would we do with the body?" I ask.

"We could chop him up into little bitty pieces and feed him to the raccoons," she says matter-of-factly.

"This is an antacid commercial for cryin' out loud! How many takes are we going to do on this shot?" I ask in desperation.

"You know, I think he might be going for an Oscar on this one. We might
be here all night." Sam, my best friend and favorite tall person, sidles up

next to me. She's in charge of wardrobe on this gig, and she is doing her best to look like she's adjusting my outfit.

"Ya know, Doll, if you knew what you were doing, we'd have been out of here four hours ago," she says.

"Don't make me laugh—I don't want my makeup to crack," I say through clenched teeth while jabbing a finger into her bony ribs, hoping against hope I can inflict some pain.

"Remember that little Jamaican restaurant we ate at in Denver a few weeks ago?" she asks.

"Oh my God, yes," I answer, cringing at the intestinal distress it put me through.

"Okay, just remember that during your next take." Betsy shoos her away and goes back to powdering my nose.

"Okay, quiet on the set," shouts Jay. "And action!"

GONE WERE THE days when I was cast as the young ingénue who would wake up on a studio set in her flowing silk nightgown with her hair and makeup somehow looking perfect. Like that ever really happens. They could actually do close-ups with me back then.

"I just got a great night's sleep on my new Puffy Cloud mattress, and now I'm ready to face the day," I'd whisper into the camera. Those were the days. Now, I'm hawking remedies for constipation, heartburn, and that "nagging" back pain. The first time my agent sends me on an audition for adult diapers I'm going to snap like a twig.

The drive home offers little in the way of relief from a hard day of trying my best to look bloated. It's already dark, and traffic is out of control. The road ragers are out in force, and evidently, I'm getting in everyone else's way.

As I trudge through the lobby of my condo building, I stop and grab the mail. I make my way to the front door of the condo, weighed down with a wardrobe bag, a duffel bag full of shoes, and my purse. It's going to be dark and lonely once I open the door. My husband, a.k.a. David, is on an extended road trip. He's a photographer and takes off for weeks at a time to do his thing all over the Rockies. Sam has a date tonight, so I couldn't get her to come over and keep me company. Everybody else has family they had to get home to. At least I have Rufus, our big calico cat, and he'll be glad to see me. Okay, a little reality check here—he'll actually be a little miffed that he's had to wait so long for dinner.

I open the door, turn the lights on in the foyer, and the first thing I see is the hairball that my darling cat has coughed up on my new rug. I drop all of my baggage right there at the front door and step out of my heels. God, my feet are killing me. As I slog through the living room, I shed my skirt and blouse. I don't even think to make sure the curtains are closed. I flop the stack of bills onto the dining room table on my way to the kitchen. I clank a handful of ice cubes into the blender, add some margarita mix and a five-second pour of tequila, flip the switch, and hold the top on for dear life. I slip on an extra-sexy pair of yellow rubber gloves and head back out to the foyer to clean up the present that Rufus has left me. I catch a glimpse of my reflection in the patio doors. Me in my knickers, camisole, and yellow rubber gloves. I am a goddess!

"Rawr," says an impatient Rufus as he does a figure-eight around my ankles.

"Okay, okay, wait your turn," I say as I deposit the bezoar in the trash and take off the rubber gloves. I switch off the blender and pour the concoction into a large glass. I grab a can of cat food out of the cabinet and open it with the electric can opener.

"Raaaawr," he says, this time a little louder.

"You're lucky you're getting anything, you little shit. Did you really have to do that on my new rug?" I ask. With a splat, I empty the contents of the can of cat food onto a plate and slide it across the floor. Rufus goes running after it. He starts gobbling it down before the plate comes to a stop and then will ignore me for the rest of the evening. I grab the pile of mail and stand over the trash can in the kitchen. Bill, bill, trash, bill, trash, magazine, trash, trash, bill, ooh, I may have won a million dollars, catalog, trash. After a nice hot bath and another glass of liquid therapy, I collapse on the couch and fall fast asleep

The ancient Chinese man seated across the table from me tries unsuccessfully to insert the acupuncture needles into my fingers. He tries again and again, but they just won't go in. He puts them aside and takes an emery board and gently rubs it across the back of my hand. He seems like a nice old man, but why is he purring? And why is my third-grade teacher here? My eyes flutter open, and in my half-wakened state I see Rufus nudging my hand with his wet nose. I shield my eyes from the sunlight streaming through the den window. Sometime during the middle of the night I curled up on the couch and pulled the afghan down over me.

"Mmmf," says Rufus half-heartedly, without opening his mouth.

"What are you trying to tell me?" I ask.

"Mmmf," he says again. I sit up, and he takes off like he's been shot out of a cannon. I hear him scream at me from the kitchen.

"Okay, okay, I'm coming," I tell him. I guess it's time to eat again. As I shuffle through the living room, I check the time on the wall clock over the fireplace. Ugh, ten 'til ten. I never sleep this late. I must've really needed to recharge my batteries. I grab my cell off the dining room table where I left it last night. I better plug it in before it runs out of juice. The blinking red light lets me know I've missed a call. I dial my voicemail and wedge the phone between my ear and my neck. I grab a can of cat food and cram it into the opener. Rufus is screaming so loud now I can barely hear the phone.

"Stop already! Geez."

"First message, left at 5:33 a.m.," drones the computerized voice.

"Hey, Doll, just passing through a little town outside Glacier National Park. Thought I'd check in while I have cell coverage. I love you, and I'll try again later," says my husband. He must've been out getting sunrise photos. Surely he's slipped into some sort of dementia. He can't seriously have thought I'd be up at that hour.

"Next message, left at 9:29 a.m."

"Good morning, Sunshine. I know you're moping around the condo with nothing to do since your hubby's gone. I'm picking you up at noon to go to a, uh, party," Sam hesitates. "You'll know lots of people there, so throw on something semi-nice and don't even think about wearing flats. Ta-ta," she says in a sing-song voice that's just a little too chipper for me at the moment.

There's nothing quite like the smell of cat food in the morning. I pick up last night's plate and replace it with this morning's selection. Rufus is chowing down before the dish hits the floor.

AFTER A NICE hot shower to help steam the wrinkles out, I stand in front of my closet full of absolutely nothing to wear. I glance over to the full-length mirror and am amazed that, as I stand there in my birthday suit, I see how well gravity has pulled a few body parts a little out of place, some more than others.

"Oof, you gotta get in shape," I mutter to myself. I *really* don't feel like going out today. Maybe I can suddenly be afflicted by some horrible disease. Maybe that would get me out of this. I shuffle into the bathroom to blow dry my hair and put on some makeup. I'm halfway through my facial restoration project when the doorbell rings. I pick up my phone and dial Sam's number.

"Hello?" she answers.

"Is that you at my front door?"

"Yeah, come open up."

"I'm not going."

"Wait a minute—you love going to parties. Why don't you want to go?"

"I've got lymphatic filariasis. I can't go."

"You've got what?!? Just open the door."

"It's open," I say and hang up.

I hear the front door open and shut. A moment later I hear, "Where are you?"

"I'm in my bathroom," I yell back at her.

She pops her head in the door and says, "Whoa, you might give me some warning that you're naked."

"I told you that I'm in my bathroom. Didn't you think that might be a possibility?"

"Okay, what's this hideous disease?—and don't even think it's getting you out of going with me."

"Lymphatic filariasis. You get it from mosquitoes, and it causes elephantiasis. Just look at my ass."

"Wow, you're right," she says as she surveys my derrière. "It's in its advanced stages. How much time do you have left?"

I try to find something to throw at her, and, finding nothing, I just give her a dirty look.

She flinches and says, "I have to admit, that's a very creative excuse, but you're still coming with me. Do you have any coffee made?"

"You know I don't drink that stuff," I say as she disappears from the doorway.

"Oh, great, I suppose I have to drink dried grass clippings?" her voice fading as she gets farther away.

"It's called green tea, and it's good for you," I yell.

I can barely hear the "What ev" she gives in reply.

Moments later, I hear her rifling through my closet. I poke my head out of the bathroom and ask, "What are you doing?"

"Finding something for you to wear. Have you ever thought of donating any of these to a museum?" she says as she furiously flips through my wardrobe. "Have you actually bought any new clothes in the last decade or so? Where's that purple thing that David bought for you in Taos? You are so lucky he has good taste. How do you dress yourself when he's not here?"

"It's in there. You just have to look. And I thought you said 'seminice.' You look like you're going to a formal garden party. Where are we going?"

"Oh, you'll see," she says in a really annoying sing-song voice. I get done with my hair and makeup and find that Sam has laid out the outfit she thinks I'm going to wear today. It's actually pretty nice, but I can't let her know that.

"You don't think I'm actually going to wear those heels with that dress, do you?" I ask. Sam stands there, arms crossed and leaning against my armoire, staring at me blankly.

"If you were normal and had more than six pairs of high heels, we could find something better, but this is all we have to work with. Now, for the love of God, quit complaining and put some clothes on!"

I STILL DON'T know what the occasion for this party is all about, but I find myself getting in the mood to mix and mingle. Some people don't like crowds, but not me. I'm like my crazy Aunt Sally at a free buffet. Besides, Sam has promised me that a lot of our theater friends will be there! I've had the pleasure of working with most of the actors in this town, and when you work for weeks on a production, rehearsing and performing with them, you form a special bond. It's like a second family. I can't wait to see them. Well, most of them anyway.

As we pull onto the side street in the old neighborhood on the west side of town, I see that we'll have a hard time finding a parking spot. Both sides of the tree-lined street are crammed with cars, and there are groups of people, arm in arm, walking toward one particular Victorian house in the middle of the block. I then notice young men running up and down the street with white jackets on emblazoned with "Valet" on the back. Wow, this must be some kind of shindig to have valet parking. I'd ask Sam about it, but I'm still trying to refrain from talking to her. I'm still mad that she's making me wear the most uncomfortable heels on the planet and won't tell me what this is all about. We pull up to the front of the house, and two young gentlemen open our doors. Sam unfolds herself from her Mercedes and adjusts herself to make sure everything is in place. She reaches into the backseat and produces a hat you wouldn't normally see anywhere but a royal wedding.

"You aren't really going to wear that, are you?" I ask incredulously.

"Hey! You have no room to talk about my taste in fashion. I've been waiting years for the opportunity to wear this." Sam, all six feet of her, peers at her reflection in the windows of her white Mercedes and makes sure her chignon and hat are perfectly in place. She is a vision to behold.

With her white dress with black polka dots, long legs, four-inch red heels, and a few colorful feathers sticking out of her hat adding to her stature, she towers head and shoulders above everybody else and, since I'm vertically challenged, my standing next to her only serves to make her look even taller. I know I won't have any problems finding her in a crowd today.

"Oh, look! It's the Wicked Witch of the West and our favorite Munchkin!" says a voice from out of nowhere." Sam and I turn to see two of the neatest people on the planet, Charles and Robert, walking up the sidewalk.

"Oh, Robert, how nice to see you," says Sam, leaning down to plant a kiss on his cheek while completely ignoring Charles, who had uttered the offending remark. "I thought I heard Chuck. Did you bring him with you?" she asks while looking everywhere for him as he fumes right under her nose. Charles is the same height as I am, and since I'm wearing three-inch heels, he is the shortest of the four of us. Except for his stature, Charles is a great-looking guy. It's a crushing blow to women when they find out that he shops from the same aisle as they do. Robert is a tall, distinguished-looking gentleman with salt-and-pepper hair, always impeccably dressed. Today is no different. I give Robert a hug and a kiss on the cheek.

"How are you doing?" Robert asks Sam with some concern in his voice.

"Yeah, I'm doing fine. Thanks," she says. Sam had lost the love of her life a little over a year prior. It took a while, but she had finally pulled herself out of her funk and gotten back to being a functioning human being. It left a huge hole in her heart, and I was really worried that she would never recover.

"What the hell is that on your head? I hope nobody from PETA is here today," says Charles, trying again to get a rise out of Sam.

"Where is that annoying voice coming from," says Sam, still actively searching for Charles. He probably had no idea that his impish behavior would backfire so quickly. Finally, Sam looks down and, acting overly astonished, declares, "Oh *there* you are! I was looking all over for you! How are you, my little darling?" She bends down, gives him a peck on the cheek, and tousles his hair. By now his head is about to pop off. If you didn't know any better, you'd swear these two were mortal enemies. The truth is, they are great friends and have known each other forever. It was, in fact, Sam who introduced Charles and Robert. They both do interior design work and also design sets for local theater productions. That's how I got to know the two of them. Sam started calling him Chuck just to raise his blood pressure, and it just kind of stuck. Sam and I are the only two people on the planet who can get away with it, though. Charles is about as far from a "Chuck" as one can get. Robert felt a little left out, so we started calling him Bob to make him feel more comfortable.

"So, Donna," says Bob in a slow, thoughtful manner, "I don't ever remember you working with Toby."

"Toby?" I query.

"Yeah, Toby McIntosh. The reason we're here," adds Chuck. I look at Chuck and Bob with a deer-in-the-headlights look and then catch a glimpse of Sam shaking her head furiously and giving them a shut-the-hell-up look. I'm obviously being kept out of the loop on something and am starting to get a little impatient with Sam over the whole mystery.

"I know you've heard of him," says Sam as she slips her arm through mine and guides me toward the house. "He made a name for himself in an indie film that won a ton of awards at Sundance, Sydney, and Cannes. But he bought all of this," she says with a Vanna sweep of her hand, "with diarrhea." Chuck and Bob chuckle at her.

"Diarrhea?" I ask and scrunch up my face.

"Yeah, he did a whole series of national ads for one of those upset tummy remedies a few years back and has been living on the residuals ever since." I think back on all the bloating I had to fake yesterday. How come I'm not getting residuals on that? Note to self: have serious talk with agent. As we approach the front door, I notice several groups of people, arm in arm, singing "Good Riddance" by Green Day. Good song. Odd choice for a party, though. There seems to be a lot of togetherness going on here. Most of the people we run into seem to have had a bit to drink already, and it's just past noon when we arrive. As Sam pushes her way through the crowd, we finally make it through the front door. I love these old Victorian houses. This one was painted yellow with white trim.

I adore the hardwood floors, the rich texture of the walls, and the tin ceilings. I guess I should say I love them, but I'm glad I don't have one. Way too much work—and neither David nor I am the type to work in the yard. We are definitely condo people.

The first thing we come to is a full bar mobbed with very thirsty people and bartenders desperately trying to keep up with the orders flying at them from all directions.

"What do you two want to drink?" asks Bob.

"I'll have a double Bloody Mary, extra hot," says Sam without hesitation.

"Just get me water, please," I say.

"Nope, no way," says Sam.

"Yeah," says Chuck. "You need a little something."

"Okay, get me a Mimosa."

"Well, that's almost a drink. I guess we'll let you get away with that," snaps Sam. Bob smiles and winks at me. I begin to notice what a huge production this is. Valet parking, two full bars (I find out later there's one in the backyard as well), and everywhere I look there are tables laden with food and a full staff replenishing all of it. There are flower arrangements everywhere, and I'm overwhelmed at the thought of what the host and hostess must have gone through to put on an affair like this. With all the stories and anecdotes being told about our host, I figure this must be his birthday or the host's anniversary. We make our way from the large foyer into what I imagine would normally be the living room. All of the furniture had been removed except for tables heaped with every imaginable type of finger food lining the room. I've been to countless cast parties with most of the people here, and I can never recall the camaraderie that's on display today. Bob manages to find us and hands Sam and me our drinks.

"Don't go anywhere—I'll be right back," he says as he disappears into the sea of people to retrieve Chuck's and his drink. While the three of us stand there waiting for Bob, we greet a steady stream of friends making their rounds through the room. Finally, Bob makes it back and raises his glass to toast Toby, our host.

"To Toby," he says and downs half of his dirty martini.

"To Toby," we respond in unison. Chuck and I take a sip from our drinks, and Sam gulps down most of her Bloody Mary.

"Okay, enough of the mystery," I state flatly. "When do I get to meet the guest of honor?" Chuck and Bob look at me, then at Sam, and back at me. Sam puts her arm around my shoulder and gives me a squeeze.

"I think he's right over here in the middle of the room," she says while pointing the way with what's left of her drink. Suddenly, we're in a line moving at the speed of a postal worker. Bob leads the way and makes a detour to one of the tables of food. With David being gone, yesterday's marathon shoot, and getting ready for this party, I realize I am *really* hungry. I finish my Mimosa, set the glass down on a nearby bus tray, and grab a plate. As I pass the table, I fill it with a couple of spanakopita's, a few baby carrots, some dip, and a few crackers. With Bob in front of me and Sam and Chuck pushing me from behind, we arrive at the center of the room.

The crowd parts, and there before me is a large table beautifully decorated with flowers and cards. Right smack in the middle of the table is Toby, our guest of honor, laid out in all his glory and dead as a doornail. My jaw and the spanakopita I was holding in my hand drop. I hear my hors d'oeuvre splat on one of Sam's Jimmy Choos and see my napkin float down lazily behind it.

"Really? Did you have to drop that on my shoe?" Sam asks before realizing I am in a state of shock. "Sweetie? Hello? Is anyone in there?" she asks while giving me a shake.

"Wait a minute! You didn't tell her this was a wake?" asks Chuck incredulously. I notice that even Bob gives her a look hinting at disapproval.

"Of course not! I have a hard enough time getting her to come out of her cave when David's not here. She'd never have come had she known," says Sam while contorting herself in a manner that allows her to wipe the spinach and feta cheese off of her favorite shoes.

Meanwhile, my world starts to spin. I look at the dead guy on the table and all of his friends singing, laughing, and drinking. I grab onto Bob's arm and stagger a little bit. Sam is right behind me, rubbing my shoulders.

"Now, take a deep breath. This is all for your own good, sweetie," she says.

"It's an intervention of sorts. You have such a fear of anything to do with death. Look at this crowd. It's a celebration." Toby appears to be wearing what I am sure is his best kilt.

"Hey, let's see if what they say about what they wear under their kilts is true." I recognize the voice of my dear friend Betsy. I whip around and see her delightfully evil grin. I throw my arms around her, not so much to give her a hug but to keep from falling down. My knees still feel a little weak from the shock.

"Hey, hey, hey!" she says while trying to peel me off of her. "I'm glad to see you too, but, jeez, people will start to talk!"

"Ah, Tinker Bell just had a bit of a shock to her system," says Bob sympathetically while helping me unwrap from my embrace. Betsy gives him a confused look. "Seems that Sam neglected to tell her that she was coming to a wake."

Betsy chuckles and says, "Wow, that's even a little too twisted for me."

"Oh, you guys can just kiss my butt," says Sam with crossed arms and a stern look.

"Ya know?" Chuck says wistfully. "He always did like to be the center of attention."

"He does look rather peaceful," I say. My group looks at me as if I had just come back from the dead.

"Yeah, but I still want to take a peek," says Betsy, evoking some giggles from the people around us. "I'm going to the bar. Who's with me?" asks Betsy, snapping the mood back to its proper attitude.

"I am."

"Me too."

"Count me in."

"Well, okay," I add and follow the mob.

As we barge through the crowd, Bob comes to an abrupt halt, causing a chain reaction collision that rivals any Three Stooges movie.

"Estelle, this is my good friend Donna. Donna, this is Estelle, the wife of the centerpiece."

"Donna, it's so good to meet you. I've heard so much about you. Thank you so much for coming," she says with a gracious smile. We all hug her and pay our condolences. "Well, most of you knew him, and you all know this is exactly what he would want."

On the ride home, I stare out the window and think about the wonderful party we were privileged to be a part of. A light bulb comes on over my head. This is no little bitty light bulb. This is a glaring, white-hot light that illuminates a great idea. I've been looking for something to do with my life—and now I've found it.

My cell rings. I check the caller ID and see it's David.

"Hey," I say into the phone.

"Hey back. How are you?"

"Good. Where are you?"

"I'm still up at Glacier. I thought I'd spend the night in a hotel. Take a shower and get some laundry done. How was your day?"

"A little surreal. Sam dragged me to a party and didn't bother to tell me it was a wake."

"No way," he says with a chuckle.

"Way! It wasn't so bad. I got to see a ton of people I hadn't seen in forever, and it was a great party."

"Who was it for?"

"Toby McIntosh. Another actor here in town."

"Oh yeah, I've heard of him. How'd he die?"

"I don't know—I didn't even think to ask."

"Did they have him laid out on a table and everything?"

"Yeah, wearing a kilt and all."

"Who peeked?"

"Peeked?"

"Yeah, up his kilt. I know that crowd. Somebody had to peek."

"Betsy really wanted to, but she managed to control herself."

"Wow, that must've been a trip."

"Yeah, it was. David, I've been thinking."

"Um, okay. Remember the last time you said that it cost us fifteen thousand dollars to redo the kitchen cabinets."

"No, no. This is different. I want to make a change…"

THAT DAY WAS more than just a lesson in facing death and celebrating a man's life. It was a crossroads in my life. Later that night, after a bit of brie and a couple of glasses of wine, I made a life-changing decision. I was destined to be an event planner. What better path can I take than that of making people laugh and helping them find happiness in the face of all of life's significant moments, joyful and sad?

Five years later, after a successful event, a client asks me what inspired me to get into this crazy business. I simply reply, "A corpse whispered in my ear."

CHAPTER 2

Karmageddon

"Hi Mom, it's..." is about all I can say before she blurts:

"Colorado is going to get ten inches of snow tonight!" Ever since my parents moved to Arizona, they've become weather experts. They love informing me how bad our weather will be compared to theirs, especially when we have snow on the way. They've gone completely 'round the bend, and it's particularly funny when they report that it will be one hundred ten or one hundred and fifteen degrees there.

"Huh," I respond flatly.

"It's getting up to ninety-six here today," she reports with glee.

"I'm sure we'll survive. The pantry is well stocked, and if worse comes to worse, we have lots of cat food. If Rufus doesn't mind sharing, we can last a few weeks." The silence on the other end of the line indicates she doesn't see the humor in this. "Momma, I'm kidding! Most of that will be in the mountains. We'll be fine here."

"Well, just be careful. You know, there's a nice two-bedroom house down the street from us. You'd love living down here."

"Um, no, I'm not sure that's true. It gets way too hot down there for me. I mean, really, a hundred and fifteen in the summer? That's not natural." I say hoping to get off this subject as quickly as possible.

"Oh, now, you know it's a dry heat. You can get used to it," she says as convincingly as she can.

"No, Momma, it's like breathing in a blast furnace. You don't get used to that!" This is a replay of most of the conversations I've had with my mother since they moved a few years ago. We have to get this out of the way before we can move on to other, more newsworthy things. "I actually called to tell you something," I say, trying to move on.

"Is everything okay?" she asks, switching to her concerned mother mode.

"Yeah, everything's fine. I'm starting a new business."

"Really? What kind of business?"

"Event planning—I'm going to become an event planner," I say with more than just a hint of enthusiasm.

"Are you sure? That's a pretty big switch. What about your acting? Are you still going to do that?"

"Depends. If the right thing comes along, I will, but for now I think I need to take a break from that."

"What does David think about this?" she asks skeptically.

"He loves it. He's the one who pointed out I've been doing a lot of that for the clients I do the murder mysteries for." And it's true. I had been doing murder mystery improv for the last few years, and the more and more I did it, the more the clients had started asking me to handle other parts of their events. I had started to compile a pretty extensive list of caterers, bands, and décor companies.

"It's a lot of work, you know," she says, trying hard not to be too negative. "I've put on a few parties in my time, and there are tons of details you have to keep track of." To say that she's put on a few parties is a titanic understatement. My dad was an officer in the military, and she threw her fair share of teas and parties when I was in my formative years. But it wasn't until they retired that she became the sovereign of soirees, the empress of events.

"Yeah, I know. But it's something I think I can really sink my teeth into," I reply.

"Take it slow at first. It shouldn't be hard to start out—you know everybody in that town. Just don't bite off more than you can chew."

"Thanks, Mom. I'll do my best to remember that."

"Well, I just know that you don't know how to say *no* to anybody."

"I don't think that's really going to be a problem. It will be hard enough to get other people to say *yes!*"

"Okay. Keep us updated."

I didn't really have to worry about taking it slow at first. Most people needed to be convinced they needed an event planner. I used the pitch that their lives would be much easier if they hired me to do the hard part; that way they could show up and actually enjoy their parties. For businesses, I told them that their secretary was already too busy to find the best bands and caterers and that they were unfairly increasing her workload by dumping the company's holiday party in her lap. It was hard though to convince them of this when I hadn't really done this before. I kind of fudged on the experience when asked about it. I used some of the theatrical and murder mystery experiences to pad the résumé until I got a few real events under my belt. The trust factor was a big deal at first. I was thrilled when I got my first gig. It was for a solo western guitar player at an open house for a new housing development. The problem was, I didn't know any guitar players, much less any who knew all the old cowboy standards. I enlisted David to help me track one down.

It was like that for the first few years I was in business. Just as soon as I thought I had all the bases covered, somebody would call and ask for something I had never thought of. David and I share an office, so he could hear the conversations I was having on the phone. As soon as he would hear me say that, sure, I could provide trained flying squirrels for a six-year-old's birthday party, he'd be on the Internet trying to find them.

My second gig was a big step forward. I was contracted to provide a clown *and* a face painter for a graduation party for a group of kindergarteners. Over the next few months, I had worked my way up to providing a band for a fundraising event. I don't think I'd ever been so nervous in my life. It was a four-piece country band. Four people to worry about! Will they all show up on time? Will they be good? Their demo was good, and I had checked out their references, but this was a huge deal. I found out that I was a world-class worrier. Of course, I didn't sleep a wink the night before. I had contracted with the organization to provide the entertainment for their annual fundraiser. I had contracted with the band to show up and play. The organization had paid me. I had paid the band half, with the other half to be paid when they went on stage. But this was all overwhelming for me. I lay there all night thinking of everything that could go wrong, and let me tell you, I was very creative. I thought of things that would put the best disaster movies ever made to shame.

The following day I showed up two hours early and waited. The band showed up, they played, and everybody had a good time. I was so relieved I almost cried. While the band was tearing down after the event, I visited with the musicians. The drummer, Phil, said that if I ever needed anybody to help with running an event, he'd be more than happy to assist. He was a nice enough guy and seemed to know an awful lot about bands and equipment. I thanked him and took his contact info. I didn't have the heart to tell him I wasn't anywhere close to needing help with my teeny events. But I was thinking positive, and one day, hopefully soon, I would be able to call him.

A few weeks later I was asked to find an oldies band. I was having a hard time finding one, so I called Phil to see if he knew any. Turns out, the band he was playing in at the fundraiser could also do oldies. I hired them for that job, too. This was an outdoor event under a big tent. I had been contracted to provide the tent, band, catering, a public address system, and a generator to run it all. The day of the event came, and everything was delivered and set up. As the start time for the event approached, I panicked at the realization that the lights for the inside of the tent hadn't been connected to the electrical outlets, the generator hadn't been turned on, and the PA system hadn't been checked out. The tent, the lights, and the PA system were all rented from different companies, and I realized I hadn't made it clear that they needed to coordinate with each other to make sure everything was working before the crews left. I noticed that Phil had set up most of the band's sound system, so, out of desperation, I sheepishly asked him to help me out of my dilemma.

"Um, Phil?"

"Oh, hi, Donna. How are things?" he asks, looking up from some sort of electrical gizmo.

"Well," I say and let it float in the air for a moment. "They could be better."

"Why? What's up?" he asks.

"ThelightsandthePAaren'thookeduptothegeneratorandIhavenoclue howtoturnthegeneratoron." I tend to speed talk when I'm panicked.

"Uh, could you run that by me one more time? This time try to breathe," he says with a wide grin. I take in a huge breath and start again.

"Okay, the lights for the inside of the tent and the PA aren't plugged into the generator and wouldn't matter if they were because I have no clue how to turn the generator on."

"Ah, well, that shouldn't really be a problem. Lemme take a look," he says while looking around the tent and trying to figure out where to start.

He was more than happy to help. He hooked up the lights, checked out the PA system, got the generator running, and generally made me look great in front of my clients. Everybody needs a Superman, and that day Phil was mine. I can't think of too many events I've done since that day where he wasn't there to make sure everything was running smoothly.

I SPENT MANY boring days waiting for the phone to ring in the early days of my venture. I did everything I could to drum up business. I spent a small fortune taking people to lunch or coffee. One of the ladies I knew from my acting days called me to help her find an actress who could help her out. She wanted to play a prank on her son, who was about to turn the big three-oh.

That afternoon, I meet Gwen at a nearby coffee shop. She's the quintessential mom. She is not a tall woman and practically has to use repelling ropes to descend from her enormous SUV. For her son's event, she's rented a 1,500-square-foot suite in the finest hotel in town, but a room is just a room until you put something in it. She needed help with all the basics: catering, décor, and theme.

"What does he love most in the world?" I ask her.

"Women," Gwen replies with a sigh, handing over the guest list. There were about seventy-five guests on the list, most with names like Ashley, Caitlin, Missy, and Brittany. It was a litany of cute and sexy.

"Are any of these his better half?" I ask with a grin.

"Many of them have been," she said. "His only regret is that he has but one better half to give to womankind." She glanced wistfully at a couple a few tables away who were obviously in love.

"A couple of dates, and he tells them they are 'growing apart,'" she continues. "That's not even enough time to 'grow together'! I love my son, but how many 'wild oats' can one man sow? I feel bad for all those poor girls, too. Not to mention that, at this rate, I'll never be a grandmother!"

And so, A Theme Is Born (sounds like a movie title, huh?). Armed with all the info Gwen could provide and my team of Merry Pranksters, I am prepared to make Don Juan's thirtieth an event he will never forget, no matter how hard he tries. Planning the party takes months of preparation. In between working with the caterer and sending out invitations, I continue to pick Gwen's brains about Don Juan's lifestyle. His favorite vacation spot is Cabo San Lucas. His favorite hotel is The Mango Moon. His favorite drink is a Tequila Sunrise. He favors tall, leggy blondes. He was last in Cabo eight months ago. A light goes on in my head. I figure it's time to put in a call to a friend who runs one of the local modeling agencies. He sends over a stack of head shots, and I pick out a few and call him back.

"What kind of project is this?" asks Chris, the owner of the agency. "Is this film, video, or still?"

"None of the above," I respond. "It's a small acting job.... Who's the most personable one out of these three?" I list off the names of the girls I had culled from the stack.

"Oh, Lily, by far. She's a sweetheart."

"Okay, I want to meet her first, but go ahead and fax me over a contract."

LILY IS A wonderful person with a great sense of humor—but an actress she is not. So, I spend several weeks coaching her. I feel like Henry Higgins in *My Fair Lady*. My efforts pay off. I defy any Julliard professor to do better. Lily has been molded into the perfect jilted ex-girlfriend. Correction, *pregnant* ex-girlfriend. I borrow a theatrical foam belly from Sam for the pièce de résistance, and we are ready to roll.

I decide on Mexican food, and Chuck and Bob transform the bland hotel ballroom into a "fabulous" tropical wonderland.

"All it lacks is Carmen Miranda and Cesar Romero dancing the Merengue," says Chuck, admiring his handiwork.

"You're just dying for a chance to wear that fruit salad headpiece you made," Bob retorts with a roll of his eyes. I instruct the bartender to hand our "bad boy" a stiff drink when he arrives. God knows he is going to need it. As Lily and I take our seats, I have her slump over and rearrange a tablecloth to hide her belly. I am wearing a dark suit with my hair pulled back severely and almost no makeup. I have a briefcase by my side. My role (one I have played a time or two before) in this little melodrama is that of the pit bull lawyer.

Right on time, Don Juan strolls in like he just stepped off the cover of *GQ*. He shakes men's hands and hugs several women. He is in his element. The men admire him, and the women long for him. Suddenly, he spots Lily. Momentarily, he is perplexed. How could there be a gorgeous woman in the room that he does not know? He immediately snaps back into his Don Juan mode and, flashing a grin (I swear I saw a sparkle of light bounce off his teeth), approaches our table. The fish has taken the bait.

"I don't believe I've had the pleasure," he says smoothly as he extends his hand. Lily goes into the shocked look she has rehearsed so many times over the last few months. "You go girl," I think to myself.

"You don't remember me?" she says, staring at his hand as though it were a claw.

"I, uh, I just got new contacts," he says, pulling back the offending hand. "Yeah, that's it…new contacts, and I'm having trouble adjusting to them. I'd never forget meeting someone as charming as you. When did we…"

Lily does not let him finish. She slams her menu down and lashes out at him furiously.

"Cabo? Eight months ago?" she almost spits it out at him. "We were soul mates? I was the one you had been waiting for all your life!" And then, she stands up. There is no mistaking her "condition." "You said I was the most amazing creature on the planet!" she says in a tone of voice that is somewhere between a whisper and a hiss. She's doing better than I expected. She's even managed to work up a few tears. The whole room is quiet. Everyone is staring at her and Don. Several women are wiping away tears. Others are looking at Don with a "He's finally getting what he deserves" look on their faces.

"The most amazing creature on the planet," she repeats, sniffing and dabbing tears away with her napkin. "It was such a beautiful night…a warm breeze was blowing on the patio of The Scarlet Macaw. We danced, sipped tequila, and then went to your room at The Mango Moon."

At this point, as rehearsed, she places her hand on her belly and rubs it almost fondly. "It was the most incredible night of my life, and you…" she says and dissolves into tears. I gently urge her to sit back down.

Don's in shock. You can see him cataloging years of women as he tries to find any glimmer of recognition.

"I, uh, have one of those faces, you know," he says as he takes a step or two backward. "Right, Mom?" He looks over at Gwen as if she can save him from this predicament. "People are always mistaking me for someone else," he laughs halfheartedly. Gwen just shrugs and examines the nails on her perfectly manicured right hand. Now it's my turn.

"Why don't you sit down?" I coax as I pull a manila envelope out of my briefcase and introduce myself as Lily's lawyer. "This is a court order for a DNA test to prove you're the father." I say, "Given your reaction, I believe we'll need that proof." Don is speechless and white as a sheet. I almost feel sorry for him. He opens the envelope and pulls out a large card that reads, "Happy Birthday! You've been had." The room explodes with laughter.

Gwen rushes up and hugs her son.

"The best gift I can give you today is that you're not going to be a father," she says, "But I hope you will be someday. You've just got to stop being afraid of relationships. You're thirty now, and it's time to reexamine where you're headed."

My biggest fear was that he would get angry and lash out at all of us, but he turned out to be the good-natured guy with a fine sense of humor his mother said he was. Amid the flashing of cameras and applause, he looks over at Lily and me and says, "You deserve an Oscar for that performance." Moments later, Lily emerges from the ladies' room clutching her maternity suit.

"I feel thirty pounds lighter," says the newly-born actress. Her adoring public laughs heartily. She glances up at Don and, with a shy smile, says, "I was hoping you wouldn't disapprove of my drinking a martini and endangering our baby's health."

Two days later Lily calls me to tell me that Don has asked her out. One year later, I receive a wedding invitation along with a thank you note from Gwen. Lily and Don get married on the white sands of Cabo with just family and a few friends in attendance. I guess Don got over his fear of commitment and need for attention.

AND THAT'S HOW theatricality and humor became my trademark. Thanks to referrals from Gwen and my friends, I was on my way. It really helps to be an actress. After all, Shakespeare said, "The whole world is a stage." Or something like that.

CHAPTER 3

If It's Not One Thing, It's Your Mother

My first event was the marriage of Anna Marie Morgan Huntington to a guy whose name escapes me. I never saw him till the day of the wedding. Let's refer to him as Poor Sap. My friend Gwen recommended me to Anna Marie's mother, Abigail, because of the success of her son's birthday party that we did a year earlier. I've done a few weddings with excellent results so far, so I figured there would be no problems with this one. It would be the same just bigger, right? Besides, at this point I had assembled what I considered to be the A-Team of event planning. "Are you sure this is a good idea?" my husband, David, asks as he removes our rather hefty cat, Rufus, from the kitchen counter. "I mean, as I recall, weddings can be a real pain. This event has over five hundred guests and a lot of details to arrange. Shouldn't you start off with something a little less daunting?"

RUFUS AND I glare at him. "This is a chance to jump several steps ahead in this business." I tell him. "Sam's going to be taking care of the bride, Phil's agreed to be my event manager, Chuck and Bob are doing the décor, and we've got Nelson, the best caterer in the state." Nelson started out as a short order cook in a diner in Oklahoma. He worked all over the world and rose up through the ranks to be a chef at a five-star hotel when he got the itch to be in business for himself. His birthday present to himself on his fiftieth birthday was the grand opening of a catering business. Nelson is the stereotypical vision of a chef. He has sampled a little too much of his own great cuisine, and when not in his crisp chef's whites, he prefers shorts and Hawaiian shirts. Although he does a few gigs for other people, most of his business is done for me. "We can't lose." Rufus turns his back on David to add emphasis to my rebuttal. It's two against one—majority rules.

Besides, I am thinking to myself, event planning is a whole lot better than chasing after roles in commercials. I land about one out of ten, and they're not calling me for the energetic young housewife parts any more. I made the big switch so I wouldn't have to play the woman in the erectile dysfunction ads. The next acting career step is doing the ads for laxatives and bladder protection pads. Better to move on with my dignity still intact.

SAM AND I finally meet Anne Marie and her mom, Abigail, on a cold January day at their home in Denver. She seems a little aloof, but it's not the first time I've dealt with brides with attitudes. Not to be unkind, but the photographer will have to use some tricky angles to make her look good. As we talk, she plays with fringe on her leather jacket, which I am sure cost more than my mortgage and car payment combined. Try as I might, I can't draw her mother into the conversation. We talk about the wedding in broad strokes. No sense in getting into too many details this far ahead of the date. Anne Marie seems to be excited that the ceremony will be held at their house in Aspen and that the reception will be in the backyard. They have a few photos of their house: This isn't your normal house or backyard. The house is located along Castle Creek, just south of town, with a spectacular view of the valley. The great room is more than big enough to hold the one hundred and fifty guests who will be invited to the "small" ceremony, and the backyard will easily hold the tent for the reception, for which five hundred invitations will be sent.

"Just something really simple. That's what I have in mind," Anne Marie says wistfully.

I'm picturing understated, elegant décor, and a simple dress that Sam can accent with some bling or something. Sam and Anne Marie make a date to meet a month later in Denver to start the dress selection process. I make a date for the rest of the crew and me to meet with Abigail and her husband to discuss everything else. Chuck and Bob are a big hit with Abigail. The husband? Not so much. I manage to get Dad out of the room and talk about contracts, prices—and then hand him off to Phil to talk about logistics. Meanwhile, Mom, Chuck, and Bob talk about everything from linens and flower arrangements to Judy Garland and Liza Minnelli. It's odd that Anne Marie is nowhere to be found while the mom, Chuck, and Bob discuss flowers, décor, and colors. A bride's colors make a wedding her signature event.

Our Mom makes it clear that Anne Marie has neither the desire nor the imagination to pick out her own colors. "She didn't get any of my creativity," she says while exhaling an extra-long drag of her cigarette.

THREE WEEKS AND eighteen bridal shops later, Sam is hardly speaking to me.

"Oh, come on, Sammy," I say as I pick her up in front of Something Borrowed, Something Blue, where she collapses into my car. "It can't be that bad," I say.

"She wants to add sequins to a Vera Wang…a Vera Wang!!" she says with just a touch of hysteria. "The train is so long, if it were plastic, it would be a Slip 'N Slide!"

I adjust the side-view mirror and clear my throat. "Okay, well, let's go see what's up with Nelson. He left me a message about a meeting he has to have with Abigail."

Sam sighs, wraps her hair into a chignon, and continues, "And she wants a blusher veil." Sam cannot let go. She's like a dog with a sock.

"So, let her have it," I say with a shrug as we merge into traffic.

"A blusher veil denotes innocence, okay?" she says, her hysteria rising by a notch. "Innocence, my ass. Have you noticed how the little troll acts completely different with her mom, dad, and fiancé? Last time I saw them all together, I thought I was watching a reenactment of *Three Faces of Eve*! She's playing them all for fools, and the poor groom has no idea what he's getting into!" She lost the power of speech at that point and fumed a little while staring out the window.

Sam is my best friend, and since the love of her life died of a heart attack six years ago, I guess I've been a little overprotective of her. She's getting better, though. However, she has vowed to herself that she will never fall in love again. So, her attachments (once she started dating again) are brief and superficial. Dinner, a movie, possibly a sleepover, and then, bye-bye forever. Her relationships are the romantic version of a drive-by shooting.

"Didn't you have a date last night?" I said, trying to change the subject.

"First and last, as usual," she says with a sarcastic grin. "Maybe I should put a revolving door on the front of my house."

NELSON IS DRESSED in his best khaki shorts and one of his nicer Hawaiian shirts. His hands are folded in front of him, and he is smiling and nodding politely. Pacing in front of him is Abigail, looking like she's about to pop a gasket.

"I can't tell you the number of times I've been to a party in this state and had dried-out or half-frozen shrimp! Nothing ruins a party faster than bad shrimp. The shrimp you get here in Colorado might be good enough for your other clients, but I want these flown in fresh, from Louisiana. And for the love of God, can we please do something a little more creative than spanakopita? If I never see one of those again, it will be too soon!"

Nelson notices Sam and me coming to his rescue, and his expression changes from feigned politeness to utter relief. Abigail whips around and, now that she has a bigger audience, manages to ratchet up her ire a little more.

"There you are! I've been trying to get your *chef* to realize you can't get real fresh seafood in this God-forsaken state," she announces with as much flair as she can muster. The added little emphasis on "fresh" gives me a good indication that the mother of the bride is halfway to being pickled. And it's barely ten o'clock in the morning. "Every time I make even the simplest little request, it turns into a huge debate. Is it too much to ask to have everything go like I want it to? I can't have the people coming to this thing thinking I don't know how to throw a party!"

As I slide my arm around Abigail's waist to, hopefully, guide her into the living room and more comfortable surroundings, I notice my two cohorts bolting for the door. I guess that's what you get when you're the boss. I pat her on the arm and attempt to be as reassuring as possible and say, "You can rest assured that Nelson will get your shrimp flown in from the best seafood market in New Orleans."

What mom doesn't realize is that every shrimp that gets eaten in the state of Colorado is flown in from *some*where, and most of them are frozen solid for the journey. But, to make her happy, we will fly in a special batch of shrimp just for her, and we'll even show her the box from The Cajun Cabin when they get here. She manages a very sharp "Whatever" and then adds, "I don't give a shit how much it costs; I want those shrimp delivered the day of, not the day before, not two days before, the day of the reception. Is that too much to ask?"

"No, ma'am," I respond as chipper as I can be. We will not, however, have them delivered the day of the wedding. That's just asking for a disaster. They will be here a day or two in advance with enough time to thaw out before Abigail gets to inspect them and enough time to make an emergency run to Denver in case they get lost in transit. I've ordered shrimp from the Gulf Coast before, and I'm quite sure she will be thrilled with her little crustaceans.

"Is there anything else we can do for you?" She doesn't bother answering as she disappears up the grand staircase.

No sooner is she out of sight than her husband stomps through, pausing only long enough to ask, "Have you seen my wife?" I point toward the stairs where she just flew off on her broom and, before I can utter a word, he's off in hot pursuit.

The tone and volume of their conversation are just heating up as I let myself out the front door.

I'm working on my laptop at Little Ollie's, waiting for my Veggie Delight, when Sam plops down in one of the seats across from me.

"Will you come visit me in prison?" she asks.

I try to discern whether she's serious or not.

"You really don't want to go to prison," I respond dryly.

"It'll be worth it," she retorts.

"Whatever it is, it's really not worth it," I say while I'm perusing my email, trying to ignore her mini hissy fit.

"Why not?" she whines.

"Poopin' in public," I say, suppressing a grin.

"What?!?!" Sam demands, almost spewing the mouthful of water she just took in.

"Yep, poopin' in public. You have a hard enough time with me seeing you naked when we share a room on these road trips. Just think what it'll be like having to do your business in front of the whole prison population. And, by the way, their private suites are called solitary confinement. So, whatever it was you were thinking of doing that was going to land you in the big house, you might want to reconsider."

With her skinny elbows on the table, she rests her chin in her skinny little hands and pouts. "I really could have snapped her little neck today."

"What now?" I ask.

"Well," she starts, taking in a deep breath, "Daddy is with her when I meet her at the dress shop. Now, she's acting like a perfect little angel, not the devil spawn she is when she's around her mother. Guess which dress Daddy picks out."

"I don't know. Which one?"

"The very first dress we looked at when we started all of this. That fabulous A-line by Vera Wang that her mom so desperately tried to get her to go with."

"No way!"

"Yes way!"

"You know, they make a really good Mojito here," I say, trying to get her out of her murderous mood.

"Do you have any idea how much time I've wasted with that little…"

Just then the waiter delivers my Veggie Delight.

"Ooh, that looks yummy," she says, eyeing my lunch. She looks up at our waiter, smiles, and says, "Dirty Martini please, three olives."

"Ouch," I think to myself. This could be a long afternoon.

Phil and Nelson join our impromptu lunch gathering, and we discuss everything about this wedding down to the smallest detail. Tents, tables, chairs, linens, chair covers, floral arrangements, décor, lights, photographer, videographer, menu (including shrimp delivery), bar setup, champagne, and on and on and on. The list of things that have to be just perfect for our bride seems endless. Each one of us has a list of our specific responsibilities, and we rack our brains to make sure we haven't left anything out.

Phil chimes in, "We have a couple of months before this shindig, so I'm sure we can make sure we have all the bases covered once we get back to the office."

"I think we need to have a discussion about our bride and her family," he adds while setting his beer down gently on the table.

"Oh great," I think to myself. I just get Sam scraped off the ceiling and now this? I can see her hackles rise at the very mention of the family.

"Okay," I say inquisitively, "what now?"

"I'm just concerned about the family dynamics and how that's going to play out on the big day," Phil says in a way that seems like he's strategizing for a football game.

"They certainly put the 'fun' in dys*fun*ctional," adds Nelson.

Sam spits out a venomous, "Don't *even* get me started."

"I think, at the very least, we will have to put the bartenders on alert and maybe get them to water down her drinks," I propose while I'm sipping my very own Cosmo.

"That's not going to stop her. She has a stash in every room of that house. And it's a big house! Have you seen the pictures?" asks Nelson with a chuckle.

"Yes, I have, and I'm not sure there's anything we can do about the family; all we can do is make sure we have everything ticking like clockwork on the big day. If it turns out to be an episode of *Family Feud*, then at least we'll get some entertainment out of it."

"Our bride is a master at playing one parent against the other," Sam says while shaking her head. "I've never seen anything like it. When Mom isn't around, she treats her dad like he's her manservant. When all three of them are together, she acts like Daddy's little girl, and it just sends Mom up a wall. Then, when Mom goes volcanic and stomps out of the room, she goes back to treating her dad like dirt. I see the gleam in her eye. She's pure evil."

"Has anybody noticed that the groom is nowhere to be found during all of this? Do we even know his name?" asks Nelson.

"Bart," says Sam. I think she's the only one to have actually seen him in the flesh.

"Bart?" we ask in unison.

"Yeah, short for Bartholomew," she adds.

"It's probably best that he doesn't see his fiancée acting like Bride of Chucky," I interject. "He'd have called the whole thing off long ago, and we'd be out of a job."

"That's pretty mercenary of you," Phil adds with a dash of mock astonishment.

"Yeah, well, I've got overhead, and I have to pay you ne'er-do-wells," I snap back with my best Scrooge impression.

They all shake their heads in agreement, and the conversation dies while we finish our lunch.

THE MONTHS SEEM to drag as we make it through the first quarter of the year. It's usually a time to take a vacation and recharge our batteries after a hectic fourth quarter of the previous year. We manage a few corporate events, do some planning for annual events that will happen later in the year, and make some sales calls. What takes up most of our time this year is the big wedding. After a few more meetings with MOB (mother-of-bride) and BOF (bride-of-Frankenstein) and a couple of trips up to the house in Aspen, we finalize everything and get Dad to sign both contract and deposit check. With all the details confirmed and all the contracts and deposits sent out to our vendors, all we have to do is wait. Every once in a while, somebody has a panic attack: "Oh, my God, did anybody remember to…" Out comes the massive three-ring binder, and we look through a ream of checklists, documents, and contracts to confirm that, yes, we indeed "remembered to…"

About a month before an event, we have what we commonly refer to as our "What if?" meeting. As meeting planners, it is easy to have Plan A in place, but, as the wise philosopher Mike Tyson once said, "Everyone has a plan until they get punched in the face." An important part of our job is to have Plans B, C, D, E, and F in place as well. We always have our own internal "What If" meeting. If it's a large corporate event or an important private affair, we have one with the client as well to cover the big "ifs." We never, ever have one with a bride, her mother, or anybody else associated with a wedding. The possibility of something not going perfectly as planned is unthinkable for a bride. A wedding is a once-in-a-lifetime event (hopefully). Most young ladies have been dreaming of their weddings since they were little girls, envisioning in their minds exactly how it will be. However, when the big day does arrive, they have to make real decisions about how things will actually be in the real world. If they expect the fairy tale perfection of their girlhood dreams, they are setting themselves up for disappointment. At this point, Phil, Chuck, Bob, and I have been to Denver and Aspen a few times, working out every tiny detail with the bride and her family. Weddings are in a class all by themselves as far as events go.

"Okay, what if it rains? How do we get people from the house to the tent?"

"What if the generator quits?"

"What if the shrimp aren't delivered on time?"

And on and on, ad nauseum. I'll never forget the first time Phil and I did one of these with a client. It was for a huge annual fundraising dinner, for which we were contracted to bring in an "A" list comedian for the evening's entertainment. I prefaced my first question to their board of directors and the planning committee with a warning that this is not an easy discussion to have, but it is, nonetheless, very necessary. "What happens if your $150,000 comedian can't make it?"

The uproar was immediate and intense: "What on earth do you mean?" "Don't even think that!" "Why would you even ask a question like that?"

"Well," I continue, "what happens if she comes down with a case of laryngitis or something else that lands her in the hospital? What happens if the weather prevents her from getting here? What happens..."

"Okay, okay, you're right," the executive director interrupts. "So what do you suggest?" That's when we lay out plans B, C, D, E, and F. And that's why we get the big bucks.

TWELVE DAYS TO go. This is when all the checklists come out and the A-Team really kicks into high gear. Every one of the vendors is called to check and double-check every order. Some vendors bristle at these calls, but we catch enough little mistakes to make it worth our while. It's the best way I know of to prevent any major screw-ups from happening. Besides, we've worked with most of these companies several times, so they know my calls are just the way we do business. The seafood market in New Orleans must think Nelson is out of his mind. By now he's on a first-name basis with one of the customer service managers, and she has assured him that she will personally handpick every shrimp for his order. Most good event and wedding planners are your typical type-A control freaks. They have to be. There are too many critical details that have to be chased after to have any other personality type in charge of them. After sending a couple of reminders to the dad, we get the check for the balance of our charges for the wedding. That's a huge load off of my mind and a relief for our accountant.

Have you ever ridden on a roller coaster? You know how, when you first start out, it usually ratchets you up this big long incline? That's what the week leading up to any event is like for us. Then, the day or two before we get to the top—and the fun begins. Hold your hands up in the air and scream like an idiot. The twists and turns over the next few days will be a thrill.

The grounds of the house are a beehive of activity. It's the day before the wedding, and the biggest job going on right now is decorating the tent, which was erected, along with the smaller catering tent, the day before. The tent is massive. It takes a crew of fifteen to raise it and then lay the floor. After that, they have to carpet the whole thing, and then the décor company and the audiovisual crews take over. They work side by side with the equipment rental company, which is setting up tables and chairs at the same time. The audiovisual company has to work hand in hand with the décor company so all the wires for the lights and the sound system are out of sight when everything is done and in place.

The voice comes out of nowhere:

"How are things going?"

I recognize the voice as that of the father of the bride, though I've never heard him so cheerful. "Very well, thank you," I say as I turn to greet him. We shake hands, and he takes in the commotion. "We are ahead of schedule, and if the weather cooperates, we'll stay that way," I report.

"Well, both of us have lived in Colorado long enough to know that Mother Nature has a way of screwing up even the best laid plans," he says, maintaining his cheerfulness. It is a glorious day, and it would be hard for anyone to be anything but cheerful. "Have you seen my wife?" he asks with a noticeable dip in enthusiasm.

"I haven't. I thought she was still in Denver," I respond.

"No, she wanted to come up and see what was going on here." Reading between the lines, I guess we will have her looking over our shoulders during the rest of the setup. No worries—if she isn't here in the next couple of hours, she will have missed the whole thing. I don't recognize the car pulling into the gate at the end of the long gravel driveway. The black Mercedes with dealer plates skids to a halt halfway to the house, and out pops a red-faced Anne Marie. I'm guessing somebody got a wedding present a little early.

She stomps over to where her dad and I are standing and shrieks,

"What is this?" pointing at the tent.

"What do you mean, sweetheart?" queries her doting father.

"That," she spits, pointing at the gleaming white tent.

"It's the tent for your reception. Why? What's the matter?"

Okay, here comes the first long descent on our roller coaster ride.

"I specifically told Mom I wanted a clear tent!" she says while—and I'm not kidding—she stomps her foot. "What good does it do to have a reception in our yard if nobody can see the scenery?" she asks rhetorically.

"Do they even make clear tents?" Dad asks inquisitively, looking to me for an answer.

"Yes, they do, but this is the one Abigail picked out." Opening my three-ring binder and flipping to the "Tent" section, I say, "Here's the photo and Abigail's initials where she approved it."

There was never any discussion about a clear tent in my dealings with Abigail. Mom wanted a white tent with the high peaks for the center poles. She liked how they looked like the main terminal at Denver International Airport. Anne Marie stomps her way over to the tent and tries her best to rip the main door off its hinges. The door closes behind her, and I can feel the pressure rising in the tent. Waiting, waiting, waiting…

"Where's the yellow?" she shouts.

I look at Dad. His face is full of exasperated helplessness, and I see his cheerfulness evaporate into thin air. We both hustle over to the tent with very different motivations. Dad, I'm sure, wants to tend to his daughter, who is about to go volcanic, and I want to make sure she isn't terrorizing any of the tent or décor crew. As we enter the tent, she is there, hands on hips, eyeing every corner of the tent for something that even resembles the color yellow.

Not finding anything, she whips around and launches a verbal barrage that would make a Marine drill sergeant proud. "How old am I? How long has yellow been my favorite color? Whose wedding is this? Did I miss something here?" she fumes while pacing back and forth in front of her father and me. She then directs her venom toward her dad: "I told Mom there were only two things I cared about with this wedding, a clear tent and yellow."

I flinch as she suddenly points a chubby little finger at me and says, "Yellow décor and yellow flowers! There's nothing yellow here. This is all white and silver!" her index finger punching the air to add emphasis to just about every word that comes out of her mouth. With her face reddening as the volume and pitch of her voice are going higher and higher, I'm afraid she's going to be shattering glass at any moment.

At this point all activity inside the tent has ceased. Everybody, the whole tent, décor, and A/V crew are looking at me for some hint of what to do. Even Phil, Chuck, and Bob, who are there overseeing every detail, have stopped in their tracks. I nod my head toward the service entrance, and the place empties in a matter of seconds. Suddenly, it's just Anne Marie, her dad, and me. Phil, Chuck, and Bob remain but do their very best to be invisible while sticking around, just in case I need them for backup. Before Dad even thinks to ask, I have my three-ring binder open to the décor order where Abigail had initialed all the specifics that she had ordered with Chuck and Bob.

"I don't know what to tell you, Sweetheart. Your mom will be here soon, and we'll do what we can to make it right, okay?" Dad says to his daughter, who is now so mad she's visibly shaking.

"You know as well as I do what this is all about…" says our bride.

"Whoa, whoa, whoa, calm down now," her dad says with a commanding presence that has been missing up until now. "Donna?" he says, and I already know what answers he's looking for.

"Well, there's nothing we can do about the tent. We don't have enough time between now and the wedding to take this one down and get a clear one up here, and there's no guarantee we could find one on such short notice anyways. Besides, the whole décor package is built around this kind of tent. We can get clear sides for this tent, and the LED lights on the inside of the tent liner can be programmed to be any color you want. So, if you want yellow, we can set the lights for yellow and leave it at that."

At the mention of yellow lights, Bob gives me a bug-eyed look and shakes his head furiously in dissent. I look at him quizzically, and he mouths the word "Later." At that I flip to the floral section of my book to find that Mom has ordered everything but yellow flowers.

"Chuck, can you call the florist and see if we can get some yellow in the centerpieces?"

With that Chuck is out the door and on his cell. Anne Marie has calmed down to a slow simmer, and her dad is trying to make the best out of a bad situation.

"You have to remember, Sweetheart, it's going to be dark for most of the reception, so having a clear tent wouldn't have been that big of a deal."

"Yeah, well, would somebody please remind my mother that this is *my* wedding—and this is one day that it doesn't have to be all about her!" she seethes and stomps out the door.

Dad looks at me and says, "All right, get the clear sides and do whatever else you can think of to make her happy." He thanks me as he exits the tent, and I see him trudge over to the new Mercedes and move it up to the house.

I turn to Phil and Bob and shrug. "Okay, so *that* happened! What the hell else are we going to have to deal with today?" I say while flipping through my event book, looking for anything with her mom's initials on it and wondering what else is going to make our bride go ballistic.

"You know, I thought it was strange when we met with Abigail about the décor," Bob muses. "Every time I asked her about what Anne Marie likes or what she might want, she would be totally dismissive and almost contemptuous. This might be a whole new level of passive-aggressive we're seeing here," he adds.

At that Phil wanders off to the back door of the tent to give the all-clear sign to the setup crew. My look of dejection must be pretty obvious. "You know, Donna, we're doing everything we're contracted to do, and we're doing it very well. There isn't a thing we can do about what's going on between Mom and daughter," Bob says while placing a reassuring hand on my shoulder.

"You're right, but even if we do everything perfectly as planned, if the client isn't happy, it won't be a success in my book," I say, doing my best to hide my disappointment.

"But no one else is going to know the behind-the-scenes drama," Bob adds. "All they are going to see is a perfectly run wedding."

The tent, A/V, and décor team are soon back at work, and it's really quiet in the tent. To break the mood, Remberto, the tent company team leader, says, "You guys remember that bride we had in Greenwood Village?"

At that his whole crew starts laughing and telling stories about a true bridezilla they had the year before.

"This girl is an amateur compared to her, Donna. Don't worry. She'll be fine once she hears the wedding march begin," he says with an immense amount of reassurance. Not to be outdone, the décor team adds a few of their own horror stories. Pretty soon everybody is laughing, and the dark pall that had permeated the room has vanished.

"Okay, so what was that look you gave me when we were talking about the flowers and lights?" I ask, remembering how comical Bob looked.

"Girlfriend, yellow lights are not flattering! You don't really want to make everybody look jaundiced. That might be a good look for Mom, but not so much for everybody else. We'll have to keep it a pale yellow to keep everybody from thinking they need to stop by the emergency room on the way home!"

"Oops, didn't think about that," I say, chuckling at the thought of five hundred sickly partiers. "Well, okay, we can tone down the yellow lights, but you and Chuck have to come up with some more yellow. Now go do that voodoo you do so well!" I say in my best Harvey Korman voice. Okay, it wasn't great, but he got the idea.

We hear the sound of a diesel engine pulling up beside the back door of the tent. "Ah, this must be our heaters," says Phil in an all-too-upbeat voice.

I'm sure he's just happy to get back to what he does best, putting all the pieces of an event puzzle together. The delivery truck's engine goes silent as Phil heads out the back door. I hear the back door of the truck open, and a split second later, I hear an exasperated, "Oh shit!" Those words don't escape Phil's lips very often, so when they do, I know it's not good.

I fly out the tent's back door to find Phil and the delivery truck driver staring into the back of the truck with their mouths agape. "What?" I say before I can get to them.

Phil points and shakes his head. "We can't use these," he says, looking at his watch.

This is no small problem. Yes, it's a June wedding, but at just over eight thousand feet of elevation, it gets quite cool here at night. Heaters are a must. The heaters that are in the back of the truck are patio heaters. I don't think carbon monoxide is on the menu, and if we don't want to kill off most of the invited guests, we'll have to scramble to get the correct heaters here and get them here fast.

"Where did these come from?" Remberto starts grilling his driver.

"Vail," responds the driver, who is now starting to feel the heat.

"Did these come from that event at Beaver Creek Lodge last night?" he continues.

"Yeah."

"Okay, they had some of the big tent heaters there, didn't they?"

"Yeah."

This is pretty much a one-sided conversation, but as long as the driver keeps giving Remberto the right answers, I'm getting the feeling we'll get this worked out.

"Okay, and that all got torn down this morning?"

"Yeah." Bingo, another right answer.

"Who's driving the other truck?" Remberto continues with the interrogation.

"I'm not sure." Bzzzt! Wrong answer.

"Okay, who was the site manager last night?"

"Juan Carlos."

At that, Remberto whips out his phone and speed dials Juan Carlos. Whoever wrote "Spanish Is a Loving Tongue" never heard it spoken like this. The machine gun staccato that flows forth into the phone sounds nothing like the Spanish I learned in high school. Then, as suddenly as it started, Remberto snaps his phone closed and announces that these heaters were supposed to go to Breckenridge for an outdoor concert tonight. And, yep, you guessed it, the crew in Breckenridge had, almost simultaneously, come to the same realization.

There are two ways to get from Aspen to Breckenridge, and both require traversing some tricky mountain passes. I don't like driving those roads in a car. You couldn't pay me enough to drive a twenty-six-foot truck on either route.

"Well, ours will be here sometime tonight, and we can set them up in the morning," Remberto says with a sigh of relief. "I don't think they'll have the patio heaters in time for their concert tonight, though," he says, shaking his head in disappointment. These guys take their job very seriously, and they hate making mistakes as much as we do. I feel bad for the concertgoers, but I am bathed in relief that our attendees will be nice and toasty.

IT'S THE DAY before the wedding, and everything that can be done is all set. And we did it before the mom showed up. That was a huge relief to me and everyone involved. Now, all we have to do is make sure everything that will happen tomorrow morning is perfectly orchestrated. The wedding doesn't start until three in the afternoon, so we can do most of what we have to do fairly leisurely.

Mom arrives, but much later than we anticipated. She parks her car cockeyed in the driveway and enters the house without acknowledging us or the massive tent in her backyard.

"I can take care of everything else here," says Phil. "Why don't you go find Sam and grab some dinner?"

"What are you going to do for dinner?" I ask.

"Nelson's gonna whip up something simple at the condo," he says sheepishly. He is well aware that I know that Nelson never "whips up something simple"; usually, we are all automatically invited to partake. This is Phil's way of saying we've all been spending a lot of time together, and it's a good time to take a break. Normally, I'd have insisted that we all eat together and use the cocktail hour to go through our checklists for the next day, but we've already done that, and I'm so exhausted that a drink, a quick bite to eat, and a long hot bath sound like the makings of a perfect evening. I want to go to bed early and get a good night's sleep, but I know that won't happen in reality. Sleeping the night before a big event is something I've become accustomed to doing without.

"Okay," I relent. "What is he whipping up?" I ask out of curiosity.

"I think we are taste-testing the shrimp," he says, almost under his breath.

"Oh, man, if Sam finds out about this, heads will roll."

"I'm counting on your discretion," he pleads.

"It will cost you big time." I add: "I guess I'll see you in the morning. Oh, where are Chuck and Bob?"

"Last time I saw them, they were both on their cell phones, and they took one of the vans and went blazing out of here with their hair on fire," Phil says with a chuckle.

"I'm sure they are out trying to find more yellow," I say as I head for my car.

"Did I miss anything fun today?" asks Sam with a huge grin.

"Oh, not much, just a mini-meltdown by our bride and a little mix-up with the tent heaters. Other than that, not much," I report. "I'm ready for a drink; what do we have here?"

We rented three condos for our short stay in Aspen. The condos are actually in Basalt, about twenty miles away, and it's about half an hour drive from Aspen, but it's light years away in price. Three vacation rentals in Basalt cost a fraction of what it would cost for the same thing in Aspen.

"Well, we have the standard Australian Shiraz, and we have all the ingredients for a wonderful margarita. Which would you prefer?" she asks, holding a bottle of red wine in one hand and a bottle of tequila in the other.

I really want a margarita, but, like potato chips, you can't have just one, and I don't want to feel like the walk of the living dead tomorrow morning. Red wine would be okay, but… Sam starts humming the theme to *Jeopardy* while I go through my mental gymnastics. "Okay, margarita," I say, adding, "but no more than two!"

"Sweet!" Sam says as she bounces into the kitchen and starts to whip up our drinks. "So, what was the meltdown about?"

"I guess our bride's favorite color is yellow, and when Mom set up the décor package with Chuck and Bob, she didn't include anything yellow."

"What?" Sam asks. "No way, this is too twisted for color TV!"

"What are you talking about?"

"Her favorite color isn't yellow," she says flatly while slicing our limes. "Her favorite color is teal. The only reason she likes yellow is because her dear mother can't stand it!"

"Are you serious?"

"Yep. You get to know some pretty intimate details about a person when you are helping her pick out a wedding dress," she shouts at me over the whir of the blender.

"Shit, shit, shit, shit, shit!" I mutter under my breath as I scramble for my phone.

"Now what?" asks Sam as she hands me my drink.

"Chuck and Bob are on a mission to buy everything yellow within a fifty-mile radius of here. I have to stop them before it's too late."

Bob's phone rings while I take a sip of my drink and wince at its potency. "Did you put anything besides tequila in here?" All I can see is Sam's smiling eyes over the rim of her glass as she takes a long sip and sashays off into the living room.

Bob's phone goes directly to voicemail. I quickly dial Chuck's phone, and his, too, goes directly to voicemail. I leave a frantic "Call me!" on both of their phones, text them both a "Call me 911" message, and toss my phone onto the kitchen table. "Do we have anything here to soak up the alcohol with?" I plead while rummaging through the refrigerator.

"Yeah, we have chips and salsa or cheese and crackers. Salsa and cheese are in the fridge. Chips and crackers are in the bag on the counter." I grab for the cheese and salsa and fumble through the bag for the chips. Just then Sam's phone rings. She lets out a frustrated sigh and says, "Who on earth could this be?" She looks at her phone and says, "It's Phil" while she answers.

"Hey, good lookin', whacha got cookin'," she breathes into her phone. "Yep, she's here." Pause. "Not sure—she just used it to call the Bobbsey Twins." Pause. "Okay, hang on—I'll put her on." She shrugs as she hands me her phone.

"Hey, what's up?" I ask.

"Is your phone on?" he queries.

"Yeah, I think it is."

"Well, Chuck and Bob have a flat, and they're in Vail. They got your 911 message, but they couldn't get through to you," he says.

I pick up my phone to discover that, when I tossed it on the table, I had knocked the battery cover off, and the battery dislodged just enough to shut my phone off.

"What on earth are they doing in Vail?" I ask with a modicum of disbelief.

"They went to the Wal-Mart there to buy yellow fabric."

I groan at the revelation.

"Isn't there a Wal-Mart in Glenwood Springs?" I ask.

"Yeah, but I guess they didn't have what they were looking for."

"Okay, what now?"

"Well, we have roadside assistance on the vans, so I called the insurance company, and they gave me the name of a towing company that will go change the tire for them."

"How long of a drive is it from Vail to here?"

"About two hours."

"Wow," I say. "It's going to be a long night for them."

"Yep," says Phil, "but they are happy they got some yellow stuff for accenting the décor for the little princess."

"They won't be so thrilled when they find out we can't use any of it."

There's a long pause. "Are you still there?" I ask.

"I don't even want to know what that's all about."

"It's a long story, and you're right—you're probably better off not knowing. Where are you now?"

"I'm on my way back to the condo with Nelson."

"Okay," I say. "Enjoy your evening. I'll see you in the morning."

THE FIRST THING I hear when I wake up are the words "TA DA!"

I shake my head to clear the cobwebs and look up to see Chuck and Bob in the foyer and Sam half asleep, leaning against the opened door. They are proudly displaying a bolt of canary yellow fabric and bags of yellow stuff. Sam and I must have dozed off after Margarita number… hmmm, I'm not sure what number we were on when we drifted off.

"Wow, what time is it?" I ask while stretching.

"Eleven-thirty," Chuck announces.

"It took that long to change the tire?" I ask in amazement.

"Oh no, Missy, Bob the tow driver was there in a jiff. We stopped in Edwards for a bite to eat on the way back," Bob adds.

"My, my, my! Did we have a little party here?" Chuck asks, surveying the empty bottles, dirty glasses, and empty bag of chips.

"We didn't," Sam says in a groggy voice. "Somebody must've broken in and did all this while we were sleeping."

"Uh-huh, sure they did," Chuck says, slathering on the sarcasm. "Well, you'll be proud of us! We found lots of little things and this yellow fabric to spruce up the house and the tent so little Miss Anne Marie will be thrilled."

"Um, no, actually she won't," I say as I fight my way out of the overstuffed chair that had swallowed me.

From his outstretched arms Bob drops the bolt of fabric and the bag of yellow stuff on the floor as his expression goes from one of smug satisfaction to utter shock.

"Oh no, no way," he says while waving his hand in front of his face like he's wiping away a bad vision. "I must not have heard you correctly.

Did you just say, and I quote 'Um, no, actually she won't'?" Bob asks as he inches closer to me.

"I think that's exactly what she said," Chuck adds, flopping dejectedly on the couch.

They look back at Sam and find her nodding in agreement.

"Thank you, boys, for going above and beyond the call of duty, but it seems that Anne Marie's love of yellow is in direct proportion to her mother's hate of it. This was just another mom-daughter power struggle," I say as matter-of-factly as I can in my current state of wakefulness.

"Do we still get paid for the wedding if the bride mysteriously disappears?" asks Chuck with a twinkle in his eye.

"Oh no, you don't!" blurts Sam. "Take a number—I get to kill her first."

"Just save the receipt, and we'll take it all back to the store on the way home," I say, trying to steer the conversation away from anything to do with homicide. "Did you have a nice dinner?" I ask, trying to be cheerful.

I KNEW IT. I just knew it. As soon as I crawled into bed, I knew I wasn't going to get even a minute of sleep. I lay there trying to at least enjoy the peace and quiet, but I could only take so much of that. By 3:30 I am up and poring over the event book and mentally choreographing everything that has to happen later in the day. I check a few different weather services for the forecast and am relieved to see that this day will be a carbon copy of almost every day in Colorado between the beginning of May and the end of August: clear in the morning, with a chance of thunderstorms in the afternoon. High temperature around seventy-two, low tonight around forty-five.

In the back of my mind I know that Phil has checked the weather for this day at least twice a day for the last ten days. If anything out of the ordinary was going to happen, I would have known about it. While I sip my tea and cherish the tranquility, I can see the magenta alpenglow in the western sky, and I know that sunrise is not far behind. About that time I hear the buzz of Sam's alarm clock. I smile to myself, knowing that Sam is not a morning person. I also know that the snooze button on her alarm clock will get a workout this morning. Sure enough, after a few seconds the alarm clock goes silent. A few more minutes of peace and quiet pass; then, I hear the alarm clock again, and not long after it goes silent. Again. This will go on at least three more times. I think her record is eight, but that's only when I'm with her. Lord knows how long this goes on when she's by herself. I have witnessed the demise of a few travel alarm clocks when they have been flung across the room and shattered into hundreds of pieces.

Finally, the door to her room opens, and she emerges in all her glory. Her hair looks like a rat's nest, and she has wrinkles on the side of her face she slept on. It will take a while to steam those out! She also has the posture of a limp rag in the morning. She lifts her head up, parts the hair covering her face, and squints at me. Without a word she shuffles over to the kitchen and starts fumbling around for the bag of French roast coffee.

"Good morning, Sunshine," I say in my cheeriest voice.

A low groan is all I get in return. How this woman transforms herself from a limp, lifeless zombie to the immaculately dressed, perfectly coiffed stunner we all know and love is beyond me. But it happens. It takes a little time, but it happens. We love each other like sisters and accept each other for who we are, but I don't think she has ever forgiven me for being a morning person. As she trudges back into her bedroom to begin the miraculous transformation, I hear a soft knock on the front door.

The blast of sunlight that hits me as I open the door is almost overwhelming. I squint at Phil's outline as he greets me with a cheerful "Good morning!"

"Good morning to you as well," I answer back. "Coffee's made if you want some, but I have to warn you, Sam made it," I say as I point to the kitchen.

"Um, thanks, I'll pass. Last time I had some of her tar I didn't sleep for a week," Phil says while he unloads his laptop and event book onto the kitchen table. "Speaking of which, did you get any last night?" he asks immediately, realizing how that sounds. "Sleep! Did you get any sleep last night?" he says, doing his best to recover.

"No," I sigh. "How about you?"

"A little, not much. I'm not worried about anything, but you know Nelson snores like a buzzsaw. I'd have to be in a coma to get any sleep with that going on in the next room."

"How were the shrimp?"

"Wonderful," he answers with a little too much enthusiasm. "They're so fresh, I'm sure a few of the little buggers will get slapped by the ladies at the party."

I giggle at the visual that suddenly appears in my head.

"Where's Aurora, goddess of the morning?" he asks, looking around the living room.

"She's still in her cave. The metamorphosis has just begun."

"Okay, so, I've got the band, the valet parkers. You're handling Mom, Sam has the bride, and Nelson has catering. Chuck and Bob have the floral and table setup." He states matter-of-factly. While flipping open his event book to a map of the grounds, he says, "I think we have everything covered. The only thing we didn't do yesterday was figure out where to put the ambulance. With the ceremony happening in the house and the reception out back and the shuttle busses arriving through the front gate, I didn't see anywhere where we could hide it."

"They have a four-car garage. Can't we put it in there?"

"It's too tall. Wouldn't fit."

With this many people in attendance especially with so many coming from sea level it was imperative that we have EMTs on the grounds. Just in case.

"They aren't supposed to be there until two o'clock," he says while running his finger over the map. "I'm headed out there pretty quick. I'm sure we'll figure something out."

It's barely six in the morning, but I've quit trying to keep him from being on-site so early. It's just the way he works, and nothing's going to change that. Besides, he might say that everyone else has their areas of responsibility, but in truth, he's got his eye on everything.

"What are you doing for breakfast?" I ask.

"Oh, yeah, that's why I came over," he answers with a quick shake of the head to snap him back to the here and now. "Café Nelson is already open. He says come over anytime. He's got some twigs and berries for you. He's making omelets for the rest of us. Chuck and Bob are already over there."

"I WONDER IF any of those planes belong to anybody on the guest list today?" Sam asks while we drive by the Aspen airport. It's always a treat to drive by and see all the private jets parked there.

"I'm sure a few of them do," I answer while remembering how flying on a private jet spoils you forever from flying commercial. I've only had the pleasure a couple of times, but it made me realize that air travel has become a glorified bus service, and flying steerage class is the worst.

"Looks like they got some rain here last night," I say, driving around the traffic circle that is supposed to be our turnoff for Castle Creek Road.

"Weren't we supposed to turn there?" Sam says as her finger follows what should have been our exit from the traffic vortex from hell.

"Yes, it was," I say dejectedly. "You know these traffic circles drive me nuts."

As we whip around the circle, I manage to get stuck in the inside lane.

"Okay, you can get over now," says Sam while scoping out the outside lane. She looks at me incredulously as our turnoff goes whizzing by again. "Donna!" she says out of complete frustration. "It's Sunday morning! There are only three other cars on the road! This isn't rocket science."

At that, I start laughing hysterically. I know this isn't rocket science, but why we've decided that traffic circles are a good thing is beyond me. One more trip around and now there aren't any other cars in sight. I managed to make it out of the circle without any personal injuries or property damage.

SAM GOES INTO ignore mode as she takes in the scenery. I'm hoping it was just a light early morning shower. As I drive farther and farther into the valley, I see that the puddles keep getting deeper and deeper.

"I hope all this dries up by this afternoon," I say while scanning the skies for clouds.

"What?" asks Sam.

"Nothing," I answer with a little bit of annoyance creeping into my voice. Just to be a little vengeful, I reach down on the center console and turn the bun warmer on her seat on "High." It will take a few minutes before she realizes her butt is roasting, and it brings a smile to my face. It's the little things in life, ya know?

As I turn onto the grounds and through the gate, I realize that this is one big, muddy mess. I know I have the best event planning crew on the planet, and we can do things that other people won't even attempt, but one thing I've never been able to do is control the weather. Try as I might, Mother Nature never listens to me. I gave up trying a long time ago. But now, we will have to scramble to see how bad it is.

"Did you bring anything to wear besides those Jimmy Choo's?" I ask Sam.

"Yep, you know I did," she says while digging through a purse that wouldn't pass the size restrictions for carry-on luggage. She produces a pair of glittery pink-and-silver running shoes. I look at them, then at her, and back at the shoes.

"You're kidding, right?" I ask.

She ignores the comment and goes about changing her shoes.

"Donna!" Sam blurts out as she tries to levitate her scrawny little butt off her seat. "I swear, sometimes you're worse than a little kid!"

I scrunch up my face and give her an impudent little smile.

I see our two vans parked behind the catering tent and out of sight, just enough to be inconspicuous but still visible enough for everybody to see our logos. There's nothing quite as good as a little free advertising! I pull up behind them and slide to a stop in the mud. I reach behind Sam's seat and grab a pair of Sorels and change my shoes before climbing out of my SUV.

"I've already talked to Dad," reports Phil as he exits the tent to greet us.

"He says this will all be dry by this afternoon." His smile is enough to let me know that that is one less thing we have to worry about.

"I put down a few extra mats by the backdoor so we don't track mud into the house. That seemed to make him happy," he adds.

"Good," I say. "Let's keep the guy who's signing our check happy. Any sign of Mom or the bride yet?"

"Nope, not yet," he says, still grinning. He's in a jolly mood because he knows he won't have to interact with either of them at all today.

Just then, three large trucks drive up the long driveway and pull in behind our vans. It's Nelson and his crew. People start spilling out of the trucks' doors like clowns out of a VW Bug. They barely stop to say hello before flinging the doors open, and, like an army of ants, they start unloading all the food and beverages into the catering tent.

"Word of warning," Phil announces to everyone in earshot. "It would probably be in your best interest not to use the word 'yellow' around Chuck or Bob today."

"Good safety tip!" I add. "That probably goes for Mom and the bride as well."

"The two-way radios are on the first table in the tent. They are all charged and ready to go. Donna, yours is one of the ones with a headset. Sam, there's one in there with a headset for you as well. Leave the third radio and headset for the photographer. Chuck and Bob already have theirs, and I'll take one to Nelson." And just like that, Phil has switched into "'Event Mode,'" and he will be like this until the newly married couple has departed and the last guest has been shuttled back to his or her hotel.

I step into the main tent and see Chuck and Bob busy with their setup. The sunlight is hitting the east side of the tent and providing a warm glow to the interior. I grab Sam's and my radios and slip out without disturbing the décor team.

Sam and I make our way to the house and hang out in the kitchen until we hear signs of life in the other parts of the house. This is a beautiful modern house built of rough-hewn logs and stone. The floors are all bare hardwood, and there are vaulted ceilings. Large windows let in the light everywhere, and most of them extend from floor to ceiling, taking full advantage of the spectacular scenery this valley is blessed with.

The first one to appear is Abigail. I must say she seems awfully chipper and sober this morning.

"Good morning, Abigail. Today's the big day!" I say, realizing halfway through my sentence I should probably tone down the chipperness in my voice.

"Yep," she says. "It sure is."

"Is Anne Marie up yet?" asks Sam.

"I don't know," answers Abigail with her back to us, looking for something in a cabinet. "I haven't seen her since I got here yesterday."

I steal a glance at Sam just in time to see her roll her eyes. I furrow my brow and nod toward Mom, trying to warn Sam not to get caught.

"Well, when you get a moment, I can take you out to the tent and show you the setup. Chuck and Bob will be in to finish the décor in the great room anytime now."

"Uh, yeah, whatever," says Mom while still digging through the cabinet.

"Can I help you find something?" offers Sam in a helpful voice.

"No, that's okay," she responds and closes the cabinet doors.

I hear the back door open and see Dad enter the mud room. He sits down on a bench by the door and takes off his boots. He looks up at me and grins.

"How was your walk?" I ask.

"Great!" he says in a booming voice. "Gorgeous morning, absolutely gorgeous. Not a cloud in the sky and a nice, brisk breeze coming up the valley."

"I agree—it is a glorious morning," I say, catching myself before I add, *"Let's hope it stays this way."* No sense in tempting fate.

As he enters the kitchen, he notices his wife and says, "Ah, good morning, darling—how are you?"

"Fine," she says with no discernable emotion. "Just trying to find something to eat."

"Do you want to go into town and grab a bite somewhere?" he asks with some enthusiasm.

"Mmm, no, I'll just have a piece of fruit and some coffee here. Besides, Donna's going to show me what's going on out in the yard," she says, surprising me since not five minutes ago she showed no interest whatsoever in taking the tour.

"Well, okay. I'm going to work out for a little bit and take a shower," he says, giving his wife a kiss on her cheek as he passes her by.

I can tell nothing is going to spoil his mood today. There's an awkward pause after Dad leaves the kitchen, and Mom, Sam, and I are left standing, not knowing what to say next. Sam's cell phone breaks the silence, and she answers the impatient buzzing.

"Hi, this is Sam," she says. "Yep, I'm down in the kitchen." A few seconds pass and then she says, "Yep, mmm, hmm, yep. Okay, I'll be right up."

With that Sam is off, and I can tell she's not at all sad about leaving me alone with Mom.

"Well, okay, let's go see how everything is going out in the great outdoors," says Abigail.

"Okay," I say and then look down at her big, fuzzy slippers, "but you might want to put something else on. It's a little wet and muddy in spots out there."

She wasn't paying attention to a word I said. She breezes past me and out the back door. I rush to catch up with her and look at my clipboard to make sure I cover everything that might be of interest to her. She slogs through the mud puddles, and I'm not completely sure she is aware her feet are now soaking wet.

"What's this small tent for?" she demands.

"It's the catering tent. That's where Chef and his staff will be preparing and plating all of the food," I answer, trying to control the tone of my voice.

She should know very well what the hell this tent is for. We talked about it at length during the planning stages of the wedding. She couldn't get her head wrapped around the idea that the catering and wait staff would need their own tent to accomplish their appointed tasks. It took her husband to finally give us the okay. She pops her head into the catering tent just in time to see Nelson and his staff unpacking all of the shrimp that he went out of his way to get for her. Expecting at least some acknowledgement that her precious shrimp are here safe and sound, we are all floored as she spins around without a word and heads for the big tent. Nelson and I exchange quizzical looks, and I shrug as I run out to catch up with Abigail.

By the time I catch up with her, she is standing in the middle of the big tent, staring up at the ceiling. She is clearly enthralled by the size and height of the center poles. Chuck, Bob, and crew have done an amazing job of transforming the interior of this expansive tent. The tables and chairs are covered with crisp white linens and chair covers, and everything has a contrasting silver sash around it. The tent liner billows down from the two peaks and the top of the tent and attaches at the sides of the tent. It makes you feel like you're in a very big, very comfortable pillow. The centerpieces are all set, and there is a crew of people placing the crystal and silverware on all the tables. Nobody stops to take notice of us as we walk through the tent, least of all Chuck and Bob. As we exit the double glass doors at the main entrance, she points to the two large white metal boxes butted up against the side of the tent.

"What are those?" she asks, clearly not approving of their utilitarian appearance.

"Those are the heaters," I answer.

She whips around and looks at me like I've lost my mind. "Heaters? What the hell do we need heaters for?" she asks while taking a closer look at the offending machinery.

"Well," I start, "we talked about this when we were deciding on this tent. Remember, most of your guests are coming from Florida and California, and it's getting down into the forties here tonight. We didn't want anybody suffering from hypothermia, so we got these to keep everyone warm."

She lets out an exasperated sigh and marches off toward the house. Again, I have to hustle a little to catch up with her. I don't even try to make conversation at this point. It's clear that she's not in a talkative mood. I wonder if she's ever been in a talkative mood. It's people like her who remind me that money certainly does not buy happiness.

As we enter the mud room, I sit on the bench by the door to take off my mud-caked shoes. I guess Abigail can't be bothered with such trivialities and she heads off into the house, leaving a trail of muddy footprints along her way. Being left to my own devices, I take a minute to glance over my checklist and wonder how things are progressing outside.

"Phil?" I ask into my headset.

"Yeah, Donna."

"How's everything going?"

"Just peachy."

That's Phil's way of saying "There are some small problems, but they are being taken care of. Nothing to worry about."

Damn it, now I'm stuck here in the kitchen with nothing to do. My ears perk up when I start to hear voices in the hallway. It's Sam and Anne Marie, and they are headed my way. Hallelujah, some human interaction. Sam enters the kitchen first, followed by the "blushing" bride. The contrast is stark and comical. My dear friend Sam is tall, blonde, and dressed in a black suit with a cream-colored blouse. Our bride, by contrast, in none of those things. She is short and dressed in her pajamas. Her hair is up in curlers of all different sizes, her face is covered in some sort of green-colored cream, and she has large wads of cotton stuffed between her toes to protect her freshly painted toenails.

"Ha!" says our little Martian-looking bride. "Get a load of me!"

"My goodness," I say in return. "I guess there really is a good reason for a groom not to see his bride before the wedding."

"Do you have your camera with you?" Sam asks.

"I think I do. Hang on," I say as I fumble through my soft-sided briefcase. "Yep, I sure do."

"Yesss!" squeals Anne Marie, jumping up and down with excitement. "This is going on the first page of our wedding album."

I take one of her smiling and about three or four more of her in various scary, monster-like poses and one last one of her and Sam. Dad walks in and is startled by the sight of his daughter.

"Has Bart seen you like this?" he asks with an extra dose of horror in his voice.

"Of course he has, Daddy, and he still wants to marry me," she answers, putting on her best diva act.

"Well, it's not a good look for you. I wouldn't push my luck," he says while she pulls his face down to him and gives him a kiss on the cheek.

"Oh, thank you," he says, "now I've got that green…"

"Cream," she interjects.

"…crap," he continues, "all over my face."

"Take another picture, Donna!" demands our bouncing bride.

Dad bends down and put his face beside his daughter's, and I say, "Okay, say green crap."

"Green crap!" they say in unison, and I snap the picture. Just as our eyes are recovering from the flash, Abigail walks into the room.

"Good God!" she exclaims, wincing at the sight of her daughter.

"Oh, goody, another photo!" says Anne Marie, unable to contain her giddiness.

She grabs her mom and pulls her to her side, and I say "Cheeeese!"

Dad and daughter smile. I can't say the same for Mom.

"Lemme see, lemme see!" says Anne Marie, grabbing the camera out of my hand. I punch the little button on the back of my camera to bring up the last photo taken, and Anne Marie says, "That is so cool. How do I see the others?"

"Just run your finger across the screen to scroll though them. Just like your smart phone," I say while swiping my finger across the back of the camera.

She acts like she didn't see Mom's expression in the photo. Of the three of them, hers is not what I would normally describe as "happy." She scrolls through all the photos and stops at one of the B-movie monster poses.

"This is the photo I'm going to print off for Bart to carry around in his wallet!" exclaims our enthusiastic bride, showing the photo to her parents.

"You do that babe," says Dad while Mom rolls her eyes.

As I survey the scene, I notice Dad and daughter carrying on in their merriment and that Mom is decidedly more wobbly and glassy-eyed than she was when we went on the tour of the tents.

"Donna?" Phil's voice in my headset snaps me back into reality.

"This is Donna," I answer back, tuning away from the others in the room.

"Can I see you at the main tent, please?"

I jump at the chance to remove myself from this mini family get-together. "I'll be right there."

While I stop at the door to put my shoes on, I realize that by calling me out to the tent, there's either something very wrong or he just wants to run something by me before he makes a decision. That's okay—anything is better than hanging around the house.

I make my way over to the main tent and spy Phil standing out in the field beside the tent, looking up at the sky and grinning like an idiot. Ever since he had his bypass surgery, you literally can't wipe the smile off of his face. He's a heart attack survivor, and I think it has given him a whole new outlook on life.

He's still smiling when he tells me, "I think we can put the ambulance on the other side of the garage and it will be hidden from everybody arriving through the front gate and also the people going from the house to the tent. Also, I just got a call from the keyboard player in the band. He's stuck on top of Independence Pass with a bad transmission."

"Why is he calling you with this bit of news?" I ask.

"Because he can't get a hold of the rest of the band," he answers and goes back to smiling at the sky.

It takes a minute for that last little bit of information to sink in. "What do you mean he can't get a hold of the rest of the band?" I ask, choking down the panic.

"You know how cell service is up here in the mountains. They're probably just nowhere near a cell site." He turns to me and grins. "It's okay; I stole one of Nelson's minions and sent him in one of the vans to pick up our wayward piano player." He pauses for a moment and answers a question I hadn't thought to ask, yet. "It's only a half hour to the summit of the pass. I suspect he broke down on his way up the other side, so they should be back in a little over an hour."

A little reassurance is better than none, I guess. We both turn and see four vehicles pull through the gate. Two large trucks, a beat-up SUV, and a shiny black Mercedes coupe. Phil looks at me and shrugs, and we both head off to investigate. The first truck is our florist. I call Chuck and Bob on the radio, and they emerge from the main tent to help get all the flowers to where they need to be. The next truck is the majority of our band. They had not yet heard about their stranded keyboard player and were relieved to find out somebody had gone to pick him up. The beat-up SUV belonged to our photographer/videographer team. Kris and Chris are a married couple who do one hundred and fifty weddings a year.

Shoot me now! I do no more than a handful per year, and those are enough to drive me clean out of my mind. They love it, and they have the perfect personalities for the business. He is a huge guy, probably six foot two. She, on the other hand, is tiny. Even in heels, I think she's shorter than I am.

They do most of the weddings we plan, and, oddly, we hadn't seen them until now on this gig. Neither the bride nor the groom wanted a bachelor or bachelorette party, and the idea of a rehearsal dinner was the first thing that got nixed in the initial stages of planning. He does all the photography, and she does the videography. I hand him the last two-way with a headset, and I call Sam on the radio to come get him. She seems to materialize out of thin air to take Chris in to get him acquainted with the house and the bride. Kris begins the arduous process of setting up all the remote video cameras that will record the wedding ceremony from every angle imaginable and the microphones that will pick up everything in the great room.

I always thought it was ironic, if not a little unfair, that Kris has the biggest and heaviest equipment. But they are great at what they do, and I'm sure the division of responsibilities is something they worked out long ago.

After that a minivan pulls into the drive, and Phil recognizes the passengers as the string quartet for the wedding ceremony. I help them get their instruments and music stands into the great room, and Phil parks their van in a spot that will allow them to get out of there when they are done with their duties.

The big mystery for me was the black Mercedes. It screeches to a halt in front of the house, and a very slight, handsome, and very well-dressed African-American male disappears through the front door.

"Sam, over," I say into my headset.

"Sam here," she answers back with some static.

"We seem to have an unexpected guest," I inform her.

A little more static crackles in my headset. "Yes, we've had a slight hair emergency. Nothing to worry about," she says in her most reassuring voice.

I let it slide as I watch Phil direct the band members to where they are to set up and the floral crew distribute the flowers to various parts of the house and main tent.

Not fifteen minutes later, Sam and the hair doctor emerge from the house. "Donna, this is An' Twon. An' Twon, this is Donna. Anne Marie just couldn't get her hair like she wanted it, so we called in the best hair magician in the city," Sam adds under her breath.

"Good lord, yes," snaps An' Twon, "what gave her the idea she could do her own hair on the morning of her wedding?"

Sam gives me a shrug and hands An' Twon one of my cards. "And my heavens, do they ever shut up on her planet?" he asks as he tosses his bag into the car.

"I'm not sure," I say, trying to be noncommittal. "Send me the bill," I say while he approaches the driver's door.

"Oh, Honey, I will," he says—and adds, "My house calls aren't for the faint of heart, but I've been here before for Abby, so it won't come as a big surprise to Daddy."

With that, he pulls the door closed and is off in a cloud of dust. Sam gives me a smile of feigned sanity and is promptly on her way back to her bride.

I'M OF THE mind that if things are going well, you're overlooking something. I grab Phil, and we make the rounds through the catering tent and the main tent. The band is almost completely set up (except for the tardy keyboard player), and all the tables are set. Everything is ticking like clockwork there.

We make our way to the house, and Chuck and Bob have all the flowers and décor set to perfection. Sam has the bride and photographer going through the list of shots they'll need to do, and we make it back outside just in time for the ambulance to show up.

We get them situated beside the garage on the far side of the house, and both Phil and I get a mixed sense of relief and disappointment. Relief because everybody else has everything under control, and disappointment because solving problems is what we do best. If there aren't any problems to solve, we don't have anything to do. This is the longest hour or two of the day for me. It is the calm before the storm. We always have it timed to where everything is in place and all we have to do is wait for the guests to arrive. This gives us a little cushion of time to take care of anything that doesn't go according to plan.

The first cars through the gate are the bridesmaids and the maid of honor. I greet them as they pull up to the front door and help them get their dresses and shoes and point them in the direction of Anne Marie's room. What follows is a riot of squeals, sobs, and hugs that you should only have to endure once in your lifetime. I stop by Abigail's room and let her know that people are starting to arrive.

"Okay, I'll be out in a little while," she says through the closed door. By the time I make it back to the front door, Phil has already parked their cars in the field next to the house. The next group of cars is a mixture of close friends and family, followed closely by the groom and his family. By this time Phil has rousted out the valet parkers, and they are getting into the swing of things. The next car up the drive is the minister. I show him into the great room, and one of the valets parks his car next to the string quartet's minivan so he too can make a quick getaway.

The next vehicles to arrive are the shuttle buses from the Hotel Jerome and the Hyatt Grand Aspen, where most of the out-of-town guests are staying. These people are part of the small group of guests who will attend the wedding. We have two of our best site managers at each hotel, trying to round up these guests and get them on the buses.

It will take a few trips for each of the three shuttles to get everybody here quickly. Abigail did not want anybody eating or drinking before the wedding ceremony, so the early arrivals had nothing to do but wait in the foyer and the living room. A few of the men wandered around out in the yard, but the amount of time they had to wait with nothing to entertain them made me cringe. I finally got the string quartet to play some background music, and that seemed to reduce the level of boredom.

It was at this time that Abigail made her grand entrance—a grand entrance made all the more interesting by the four-inch heels she was wearing and the decreased level of balance she seemed to display. There were a couple of murmurs and a gasp at the sight of her dress and the level of difficulty with which she descended the large staircase. I think you would have to look far and wide to find somebody who doesn't know that you don't wear white to a wedding. I think you would have to search even harder to find somebody who wouldn't think it was tacky to wear a white dress to your own daughter's wedding. The dress wasn't completely white. There was just enough color in the tiny flowers that dotted the dress to make it the ultimate in passive-aggressive couture.

Minutes later the father of the bride made his way down the stairs, looking rather dashing in a well-tailored tuxedo with a teal paisley vest and bowtie. More hugs, kisses, and handshakes while the mothers and fathers of the bride and groom greet their guests. As the last shuttles pull in from the hotels, the one girl we had in position to check the arrivals against the guest list for the ceremony gives me a nod and a thumbs up, indicating that everybody who is supposed to be here is, in fact, here. It's show time!

ONE SHORT NOTE about the ethics of the event planning industry. It is completely unacceptable for a meeting planner to mingle with guests in hopes of drumming up business. It is not, however, unethical to be seen by as many people as possible with a clipboard and a radio and a headset. I call this being visibly invisible. I've found that it becomes blatantly obvious, even to the casual observer, that I am the conductor of our crew. Sam, Phil, and Nelson each have a small stack of my cards as well.

By the end of the evening, we will be asked for a card by, at least, twenty-five percent of the people in attendance. In most cases, the client is all too happy to introduce me or Phil to guests. I don't think that's going to happen in this case.

THE WEDDING CEREMONY is a thing of beauty and manages to go off without a hitch. The ushers get the families seated in the front rows, and Phil, looking mighty dapper in his tuxedo, gets the groom and his groomsmen in position at the front of the room. The five-year-old flower girl and the six-year-old ring bearer do their jobs with some coaxing from the crowd.

At this point I see Phil rush out of the back of the room and out the front door. Miracle of miracles—he had noticed our van with the marooned keyboard player turning into the front gate of the grounds. To get to the backyard, where the tent is located, the van would have had to pass right in front of the windows in the great room. You can imagine how disastrous that would have been with the video cameras rolling on this lovely wedding scene.

Caught on tape forever and ever, Phil leaves our driver with strict instructions not to let any vehicles pass until he gets the all-clear sign that the ceremony is over. This makes the keyboard player none too happy. He has to lug a few very large cases around the other end of the house in order to get set up with the rest of his band mates. Oh well. Maybe he'll rethink trying to drive a thirty-five-year-old van with a leaky transmission over one of the gnarliest passes in Colorado next time he has a gig up here.

WE GET TO take a breather while the ceremony takes place. We have little or nothing to do with it. Kris and Chris have the photos and video covered. I love to watch weddings, and normally I'll admit I get a little weepy when I see one. I know way too much about this family, however, to feel anything but empathy for the groom. Had he seen any of the shenanigans we've witnessed over the past couple of weeks, I'm sure we'd have found him curled up in the fetal position, humming the tune to The Beatles' "Yesterday." I take the opportunity to run through our checklists one last time before the next wave of guests arrives.

I take a quick tour of the catering tent and find Nelson and his army of minions preparing tray after tray of hors d'oeuvres, including shrimp cocktails, for as far as the eye can see. A peek into the main tent finds Phil helping the keyboard player set up his equipment and Chuck and Bob inspecting each and every table. They are being followed by a throng of wait staff trying to keep up with the orders they are barking. The only person unaccounted for is Sam. After her duties were done with our bride, I'm quite sure she took a break and is somewhere in the house having a good cry. I hesitated at first before I ever asked her if she wanted to help me with weddings. I knew they would bring back some bittersweet memories for her. She always tries to make it look like it doesn't bother her, and for the most part, it doesn't. Just when the wedding march begins, she can't be within earshot without melting into a puddle of tears.

THE NEXT TRICKY bit of choreography we have to make sure goes as smooth as silk is the transition between ceremony and reception. We have to escort most of the guests who are there for the ceremony out to the tent while herding the wedding party, parents of the bride and groom, the minister, and anybody else Anne Marie has designated as photo-worthy to the front of the house so Chris can snap all the "arranged" shots. Hopefully, if we've calculated correctly, the first large bus of reception guests will be arriving about the same time all of this is happening. Meanwhile, the food crew is sneaking a few appetizers into the kitchen through the back door, the idea being that the wedding party, parents, and close friends will hang out in the den while the rest of the guests make their way to the tent. We thought it would be a nice touch to have a little something to nosh on while they are waiting and maybe sneak in a glass of champagne to get things started. I make my way into the kitchen just as the first trays of drinks are being delivered.

The scene in the foyer is one of joyous celebration with hugs and slaps on the back for all involved. What had gone unnoticed by most of my crew was that Mom had hit the bottle pretty hard before the ceremony and was also the first to grab a champagne flute off the first tray that passed her way. Her husband and daughter are clearly annoyed at her boisterousness already, and the party is just getting started. The groom is doing his best to distract his new bride. While Dad is trying to contain his wife, the first trays of appetizers enter the room. Luckily, Kris is doing an excellent job of recording the goings on.

I've watched the tape over and over, and I'm still not sure we could have planned for what happened next. I'm sure the United States Geological Survey recorded a seismic event on their Richter scales. The first trays to appear in the room are laden with Mom's special shrimp with several different sauces. I look on with pride as the group oohs and ahhs at the presentation. Meanwhile, I catch a glance at our bride, and she is turning a shade of red not normally seen in nature. Anne Marie shouts, "Mother!" and the place is suddenly uncomfortably quiet. Mom wobbles around to see her daughter with her hands on her hips and stomping her way across the room toward her. Her newly acquired husband is unable to do anything to stop her.

"You ordered this shrimp, didn't you?"

"Well, of course, I did, Sweetie," her mom responds, doing her best to annunciate her words. "Everybody loves shrimp!"

By this time several of the people in the crowd have found a convenient excuse to find somewhere else to be.

"Hello, Mom, is there anybody in there?" Anne Marie is mere feet from her mom, and her bridesmaids are doing their best to keep this from becoming a professional wrestling match. "I'm allergic to shrimp!" Anne Marie screams at the top of her lungs.

"I'm sure there are plenty of people who are allergic to shrimp, Sweetie. That doesn't mean the rest of us can't enjoy them, does it?" spews her mom right back at her.

I hadn't noticed that Dad had left the gathering, but he came flying back into the room when he heard the commotion. I'll give Anne Marie credit for one thing: She sure knows how to clear a room. I nod to Kris and Chris, and they follow the crowd out the front door. Sam is right on their heels. I am confident she will help Chris start with all the different group photos while Kris will head over to the tent to start shooting the reception. Meanwhile, Dad is doing his best to calm his daughter and glaring at his wife.

Dad gently places his hands on his daughter's shoulders and says, "Sweetheart, this is your wedding day, the happiest day of your life. Don't let something like this ruin it for you."

By now the crowd has thinned to just the newlyweds, both sets of parents, and the maid of honor. I'm stuck in the den, and my only way out is through the foyer, right through the middle of the melodrama.

Meanwhile, Mom teeters over to where Dad and Anne Marie are standing and, doing her best not to slur her words, says, "Something like this? What do you mean something like this?"

Dad turns to his wife as Anne Marie slumps into the arms of her new husband and sobs.

"Ordering shrimp for our daughter's wedding! Wearing a white dress for our daughter's wedding! Getting so trashed you can hardly stand up at our daughter's wedding! That's what *something like this* means!" Dad says in a voice much calmer than the situation called for. "I know it's hard for you not to be the center of attention, Dear, but it's not your day. Can't you let her have one day without having to pile on all your self-centered bullshit?" This said in a voice not quite as calm as before.

Mom wheels and stomps toward the stairs and with a dramatic pause turns to her family and says with just the right amount of snippiness, "Well, maybe you wouldn't care so much about it if you knew she wasn't *our* daughter!"

With that, she literally pulls herself up the stairs with the aid of the railing.

"What?!" Anne Marie screams. She has clearly lost her equilibrium and is desperately looking at her father for answers. "Daddy, what does she mean by that?"

"I don't know, Sweetheart, I just don't know," says her crestfallen father.

The wreckage Abigail leaves behind is devastating. Everyone's mouths are agape as the implications of what Abigail said sink in. The groom's parents are trying to figure out what they are supposed to do since there is no set protocol for wedding day meltdowns. You can almost feel everybody thinking, "No, she didn't *really* say that!"

The silence goes on for an eternity. I slump down into a chair as I inspect the outer walls of the den to see if there is any possible way I can break out of here. There are windows, but I'm not sure I want to be seen crawling out of one of them. My chance to escape comes in short order when Dad says, "I'll take care of this" and bolts up the stairs. The newlyweds head into the great room, and the groom's parents and the maid of honor make their way out the front door. I take a peek out of the door of the den and see that the coast is clear. I take off my shoes, tiptoe into the kitchen, and escape out the back door. I put my shoes back on and race over to the tent to gather my crew and give them a briefing on the situation.

"What is going on in there?" queries Nelson.

"Well, it wasn't pretty," I answer, looking around to make sure nobody else is within earshot. "What's going on in the tent?"

"There is a definite buzz going on in there. I think a few of them know something happened, but they aren't sure what," says Phil.

"Okay, are the hors d'oeuvres being served?"

"Yes," interjects Sam.

"And the champagne?"

"Yep."

"All right, get the band to play some background music and tell the wait staff to push the champagne," I add. "What the hell are we going to do for dinner now?" I ask, just realizing what a mess that has become. The familial earthquake has thrown a serious wrench into the gears.

"How the hell are we going to have a head table when it's half empty?" I ask nobody in particular. "Sam, you and I are going to have to go talk to Anne Marie and Bart," I say, not relishing the thought of the task ahead of us. I was expecting some protest from Sam, but she was already walking toward the house by the time I finished the sentence. As I run to catch up with her, I turn and walk backward as I say to the rest of the crew,

"Do whatever you can to get them back into the party mood." They see a bit of humor in that request that I didn't intend. Then, twisting and turning to walk forward again, I manage to trip on the largest clump of grass in the whole yard, adding a bit of physical comedy to an otherwise dismal situation. I have to give Sam a lot of credit for catching me before I fall flat on my face. That would have been the pièce de résistance. The last thing I need right now is a nice grass stain on my suit. I'm sure the meadow muffins I was about to land on would have added an appropriate air to our present situation.

It takes us a little while to find them, but when we enter the kitchen, we come upon the newlyweds sitting at the center island in the kitchen and talking in very low tones. Bart has done a miraculous job of calming his bride down. They turn to look at us as we enter the room.

Sam puts an arm on Anne Marie's shoulder and says, "I am so sorry, Sweetie. Is there anything we can do for you?"

"No," she answers and pauses before saying, "She won. She managed to make this day all about her."

Bart reaches across and holds her hand.

"I know, I know," adds Sam.

Bart cracks a wry grin and says, "See? Eloping wasn't such a bad idea, was it?"

"What?" Anne Marie snaps back. "And miss out on all of this? No way!" and finishes with a smile I never thought possible.

"Anne Marie," I start, "Sweetie, we really need to talk about how you want to proceed with the rest of the evening. You have about five hundred people out in the tent now, and it's getting close to the time that we need to start serving dinner. You also have a photographer out on the front steps waiting patiently to take all of your photos."

"Yeah, I know," she responds, "but I'm not going out there without my dad." With that, she slides off her stool and heads off to find him.

I look back at Bart as Anne Marie exits the room. "Is she going to be okay?" I ask him.

"I'm sure she will. She's been putting up with her mom's crap her whole life. This takes the cake, but I'm sure she'll get over it."

THE REST OF the evening is a surreal mixture of laughter and tears. Anne Marie, Bart, and Anne Marie's father enter the tent to a thunderous ovation from the crowd. I can't watch the father-daughter dance. There aren't enough tissues in the whole city of Aspen that would have gotten Sam and me through that. We did have a head table, and Mom is the only person missing. Most of the crowd buys into the idea that the bride's mother has suddenly taken ill and is in bed for the evening. Those who do know the truth pass it off as a case of alcohol and prescription drugs producing a nasty side effect. I am so proud of my crew and the way they handle things, which is to say they go about their business as if nothing out of the ordinary has taken place.

AFTER SLEEPING LATE in the morning, we all make our way back to the scene of the crime to supervise the load out of all the equipment. A now-familiar voice says, "Another gorgeous morning, isn't it?"

I turn to see the father of the bride walking toward me. "Yes, sir, it certainly is," I say, matching his enthusiasm. "And soon enough all of this will be gone, and you will have your yard back to normal."

"Well, you and I both know it will take a lot longer for this place to get back to normal after last night." He sighs. I have no earthly idea how to respond to that, so I take this opportunity to say nothing.

He turns to me and says, "I appreciate how you and your company handled yourselves last night. That didn't go unnoticed."

"I appreciate that, sir; we do our best."

He hands me a rather large envelope and says, "Here's a little something for the effort. I'd appreciate it if you distributed this to all the people you had working on this wedding. I value their discretion." Without giving me a chance to respond, he turns and walks back to the house. As I stand there and watch the crew disassemble everything and load it onto the trucks, I try to think to whom I can refer the next bride who dials our number 'cuz I'm not going through this again.

CHAPTER 4

Everything's Bigger in Texas

"I brought donuts," Nelson announces with a big grin as he searches for a place to set the box down. Sam is laid back in one of the chairs in Phil's office. Her arms are crossed, and she throws one skinny leg over the other and starts bouncing her foot up and down. Steam is actually shooting out of her ears. I thought that only happened in cartoons.

"Great, I hope you enjoy your little fat bombs while you listen to my stomach growl," she snaps. Nelson's smile, now covered in frosting, only grows bigger.

"Ooh, breakfast of champions!" Phil says as he digs through the box looking for a maple-glazed donut.

"I just restocked the fridge with yogurt, and there's a big basket of fruit on the front counter that just got delivered from Aspen," I say to Sam as I lean against the doorway to Phil's office. It takes a second for that to sink in, but once it does, everybody stops and looks at me, eyes wide with amazement.

"No…friggin'…way!" exclaims Chuck, drawing it out to emphasize each word.

"Yes, way. He wrote a nice note that came along with it. He was rather embarrassed and apologized for what happened, but he was more than pleased with our part of the wedding," I say with a smug grin.

Everyone breathes a collective sigh of relief and relaxes just a little more. We've all been a little tense since Anne Marie's wedding. We know we did everything we could to make it a success, but we couldn't feel satisfied until the guy who signed the checks gave us a thumbs up.

"Okay, so let's get this over with," Phil says, surveying the assembled group. We do a postmortem on every event we do, just so we can learn from any mistakes we, or any of our vendors, have made. It's the only way we get better.

"Donna," he asks, "would you like to start?"

"Sure," I respond, and all eyes turn toward me. "Let me first say that I'm proud of each of you for weathering the storm we had to endure, and, second, that's probably the last wedding this company will ever do." I'm not sure there is anything else I could have said that would make this group any happier. Chuck and Bob launch themselves off of the couch to give me a group hug. Sam shoots her arms over her head and does a little happy dance right there in her chair. Nelson starts to sing a little KC and the Sunshine Band, "That's the way I like it."

The dance that accompanied it was not a pretty sight. Phil just leaned back in his chair, clasped his hands behind his head, and flashed a ginormous grin.

"That doesn't mean I won't go out and find one if you guys don't keep me happy," I say, doing my best to be threatening. "Let's go through this one, though, and see where the kinks were."

The next two hours are spent going over every last detail of the wedding in Aspen to see what or how we could do better. Mostly the conversation somehow ends up returning to the mother of the bride, at which point Phil steers it back to our critique.

"Donna, that phone call you were waiting for is on the line," Zoe, our receptionist, whispers into my ear.

"I have to take this call," I say as I gather up my things. "You guys keep going if you need to, but I think that just about covers it."

As I make my way down the hallway to my office, I hear the conversation turn back to my decision not to do any more weddings.

I knew this call was coming. I had seen this client at a charity fundraiser we planned a couple of weeks prior, and she told me she needed to talk to me about a party she wanted to throw. She said she'd call after she and her husband got back from a short trip they were going to take.

"Hi, Clara, how was your trip?"

"Oh, Donna, it was just fine, but I can only take so much of New York City." Clara's Southern accent is as thick as syrup, and there has to be a special spelling for the way she says "I." I think it lies somewhere between "I" and "ah." We've done a few parties for Clara, each one of them bigger and quirkier than the last.

"I know what you mean," I say in my most sympathetic voice. "How can I be of service?" trying to get to the point. I had learned long ago that if you don't keep Clara Bell on point you could be on the phone for a very long time. Her penchant for lengthy stories and her inability to talk any faster than half speed can make for some painfully long conversations.

"Well, I want to throw another party, a big old Southern barbeque but with a theme. I want to get a band too," she drawls. I think to myself that they live in a townhome not too far from our office. Now, this isn't just any old townhome. It's big, but I don't see how we'll pull off a party as big as she's talking about in a gated community of luxury townhomes and condos. "Can you come over and maybe you and I can talk this through?" she asks.

"Absolutely, Miss Clara. I have some time this afternoon. Does that fit with your schedule?"

"Oh, Darlin', you'll need a little more time to get here. I'm in Dallas."

WHEN I WAS a little girl, riding on airplanes was something special. People actually got dressed up for the occasion. The stewardesses were tall (at least from my perspective), lovely young ladies who were pleasant, and the food, even though we made fun of it back then, was actually pretty good. You and I both know it's not like that anymore. Flying nowadays is nothing more than a glorified bus service. And!!! Getting a seat at the last minute is both expensive and risky. You know that if you can even get a seat you'll be wedged between two sumo wrestlers at the very back of the plane. The worst part is if you've ever flown on a private jet, it spoils you forever from riding in steerage class again. I've been both cursed and lucky enough to have had the privilege. It's really the only way to fly, but unfortunately, I didn't marry into money, and the event business hasn't gotten me to where I can afford that luxury. Yet. When Clara asked me to fly into Dallas Love Field rather than Dallas-Fort Worth because it was closer to her home, I agreed, doing my best to be accommodating. What I didn't know was that, instead of being a nice, short two-hour flight to DFW, the only seat I could get for the next morning to Dallas Love Field involved a seven-hour odyssey with connections in Atlanta and Memphis! To top it all off, that flight leaves at 6 A.M.! Luckily, I was able to upgrade to first class for the flight, but I had to spend an insane amount of frequent flyer miles.

Now, the plan was for Miss Clara to be at the cell phone lot when my flight landed. I only had my purse and a small carry-on. I was to call her while I was walking from my gate to the arrival's door. She would come pick me up, and we could make a quick getaway. That was the plan.

I get off the plane, turn my phone on, and call her. No answer. Hmmm. It's then that I remember that Miss Clara hasn't been on time for anything in her life. She is going to be late for her own funeral. I find a nice place to perch, and I call her again—no answer. And again. Still no answer. Then I call her house, and her husband, Chief answers the phone.

"I'm not sure what to tell you, Donna." His accent is only slightly less syrupy, but at least he talks faster than she does. "Her cell phone is sittin' here on the kitchen counter." How do they manage to make "cell" a two syllable word? *Say-ell.*

"Um, hmmm. Well, what kind of car is she driving?" I ask.

"I'm not sure, lemme look." I hear footfalls on what I imagine to be hardwood floors and a door opening. "Looks like she took the Cadillac. It's a big white SUV thing."

"Okay, well, I guess the best thing to do is wait outside and see if she shows up," I say, trying to hide my frustration.

"She left a good long time ago, so she should be there. She allowed plenty of time for her to get lost a couple of times. I'd say if she doesn't find you in the next hour or so, just take a cab, and she'll just give up and come home. That's what normally happens."

Normally happens? So this isn't the first time she's pulled this? Grrrr...

So I grab my bags and stomp out to the passenger pick-up zone just in time to see a big white Cadillac go zooming by in the far lane. I wave frantically to no avail. So, let's see if she does another lap. A few minutes go by and, sure enough, here she comes again. I start waving at her well in advance, but, no, she's not looking for me. I think she's just having a good time driving around the airport. I see her rouged cheeks, perfectly coifed silver hair, and a look of pure determination go whizzing by me for the second time.

Okay, next time around I'm going to throw myself in front of her three-ton behemoth and see if that works. It's probably the only way I'm going to get her attention. A few minutes pass, and here she comes again. I've positioned myself on the curb by the outside lane of the passenger pick-up zone. There's one car a little bit ahead of her, so I have to wait for the right moment to start my maniacal waving so I don't confuse the wrong driver. Wait for it, wait for it. Okay, so the car passes, and I wave my arms like a castaway on a deserted island trying to flag down a passing airplane. I see her steely look of determination turn to one of utter surprise, and she slams on the brakes. The cacophony of screeching brakes and the blaring of horns from the cars following her is *trés* impressive. I run to the passenger side, fling my bags in the backseat, jump into the front seat, and we sit there. In my mind I saw this whole thing ending with her speeding off like we had just robbed a bank. But no. She sits there.

"Hi, Donna!" she says with a bit of high squeal excitement added to her Southern drawl.

"Hi, Clara," I say as I steal a glance out the back window to make sure a mob with torches and pitchforks isn't descending upon us. "I think we'd better get out of here before the people behind you start a riot." By now a police officer is angrily motioning for us to get going, and I see he is saying something too. I wish I could read lips. I'm sure the conversation he is having with us is quite interesting. And colorful. Miss Clara looks at the cop, looks at me, and then glances in the rearview mirror. She relaxes a little in her seat and hits the accelerator.

Clara is the epitome of a proper Southern woman.

She's pampered, perfectly coifed, and not too many days go by without her getting a mani-pedi.

"I just didn't know how I was ever going to find you! I stopped at that cell phone lot, and I couldn't find my phone! I don't know where it is. I just can't imagine where it got off to. I know I had it when I left the house. I just know it," she says melodiously while dividing her attention between me and the road ahead of us. I look out the window at the passing scenery and pray that the drive to her house is short, but, alas, it's not. The forty-five-minute trek includes a running commentary on how glad she is that *she* found *me* and how she'll have to get another phone since her current phone mysteriously lost itself somewhere between her home and the airport. I debate whether or not to tell her that her phone is on her kitchen counter but, ultimately, decide not to. The look on her face when she finds it will be comical, and I'm sure that will be enough for me.

CLARA AND CHIEF's mansion is on a big lake east of Dallas. We turn off the main road onto a long dirt driveway lined with huge old moss-covered oak trees, giving it the look of a long, cool tunnel. It is almost a perfect replica of Tara from *Gone with the Wind*, and it sits on a sizable chunk of land. The expansive estate is covered in perfectly manicured grass and lots of shade trees, with a generous amount of shoreline and a stunning view of the lake. As we pile out of the Cadillac, Chief comes out to greet us.

"Chief, honey, I'm gonna need to get a new phone," she states matter-of-factly. "I don't know where mine got off to, but I just can't find it anywhere!" Clara says while half-sliding, half-falling out of the SUV. Chief winks at me while he waves hello. Chief is an old-time oilman. He started as a kid wildcatting in the oil fields in East Texas, worked his way up the corporate ladder, then made the big jump and opened his own company. He got his nickname a long time ago when he was the head of a drilling crew, and it's been with him ever since. I grin and return his wave. Clara is not a small woman, but she always tiptoes. If she is particularly excited about something, she does what can only be described as prancing. Having missed the opportunity to give me a proper hug at the airport, she literally bounces around the front of the Cadillac and draws me into a big embrace without allowing me time enough to put my bags down. It's like being hugged by the Marshmallow Man.

"I am so glad you are here!" she exclaims. I just smile while thinking, I've just spent three-quarters of the day flying here with two layovers and a drive that took entirely too long. I'm just glad to be anywhere. "Let's get you settled in, and then I'll show you around," she says while leading me into the house.

"How was your flight?" Chief asks.

"Oh, fine," I say, feigning a pleasant demeanor. *Flight? Flight? Do you mean my three flights? Oh, they were just dandy. Thanks sooo much for asking… There's nine hours of my life I'll never get back!*

I barely get my bags set down on my bed when Clara grabs my hand and drags me down the grand staircase to give me a tour of the home and the grounds. The house, open and airy, is opulently appointed with elegant antique furniture and family heirlooms. After a quick trip through the house and a walk around the grounds, we flop into a couple of chairs on the screened-in back porch that faces the lake.

"It is certainly a beautiful place you have here, Miss Clara," I say, truly impressed with the size of both the mansion and the grounds.

"Well, thank you, Sweetie!" she says even slower than usual. "I always dreamt of having a house just like this." I wonder if she spent an equal amount of time dreaming of marrying a man who could afford a place like this.

"What kind of party were you thinking about?" I ask, hoping to get to the reason why I'm here. Now, Clara has thrown some interesting parties, and they are legendary for their guest lists. They are all costume parties, and it seems like most people who attend them accept her little eccentricities and have a good time. There was the Fourth of July party last year and the Halloween party the year before. The best one yet was her Chinese New Year party earlier in the year. Chief appears in the doorway to the house, just in time to hear what his wife's plans are; after all, he'll be the one paying for it. He's also carrying Clara's phone, and he slides it across the table to her as he settles his wiry frame into a chair next to his wife. It's a smartphone that has been covered in pink rhinestones, and it sparkles in the afternoon light. She looks at the phone, then at him, and then back at the phone. She sighs, smiles, and looks back at me.

"I don't want this to be any old party," she starts. "We'll probably have three hundred people, and I want this to be the most fun party anybody has ever been to." As she continues with her vision of the party, I open my notebook and start taking notes. "I want one of those big tents, a band, a barbeque, and lots and lots of décor." And then she gets to the theme. My hand stops writing as I look up from my pad and find her grinning like a kid on Christmas morning.

"She wants what?!?!?" screeches Bob with more than just a tad of incredulity. It's Tuesday morning, and I've gathered the crew together to give them the lowdown on Miss Clara's party. (I took Monday off to recover from my odyssey.)

"She wants the whole nine yards," I start. "I'll take care of the band. Sam, can you help me find face painters, balloon twisters, one of them rope trick cowboy guys, and whatever else you can think of. This is just outside of Dallas. There has to be some good talent down there. We've got contacts down there from the time we did that defense contractor conference."

"Yeah, I'll look them up," Sam responds while taking notes.

"Oh, this is going to be fun," Chuck says in a voice almost too creepy, even for him. Bob smacks him on the back of his head, and Chuck flinches and gives Bob a look that screams "What?!?" Phil's eyes glaze over, and he's already thinking of a thousand different details that will go into throwing a successful White Trash Party.

"Yep, a White Trash Party," I say. "And she's given us carte blanche on the décor. The trashier the better. I took a few photos of the grounds so you guys can see what we're working with."

"I realize that I'm not the most PC guy on the planet, but…" starts Phil.

"I know," I say, interrupting him, "but this is what she wants."

"What did Mr. Clara have to say about it?" asks Bob.

"Oh, you know Chief," I reply. "He chuckled, shook his head, and then disappeared until dinner time."

"When does she want to have this little shindig?" Phil asks.

"The fourth weekend in September, so we have lots of time to plan this," I reply. "She wanted it the weekend before, but Chief pointed out that the Cowboys were playing, and that would cut down on the attendance. I guess the Cowboys have a day off on the 24th," I explain like I had even the slightest clue what I was talking about. "We need to listen to a lot of Blue-Collar Comedy and watch some *Beverly Hillbillies* to get our creative juices flowing." My suggestion is not met with enthusiasm by either Chuck or Bob. "Oh, stop whining—I was only kidding."

"I know this isn't going to be a huge challenge for your culinary skills," I say, handing Clara's menu to Nelson, "but she's put a lot of thought into this, and she's real excited about it."

He peruses the menu and flinches.

"Beer butt chicken?" he says with just a soupçon of disbelief.

"Does this mean we actually *go* to Texas?" asks Chuck. "You know it's hot and humid there."

"And they have bugs," adds Bob. "Big bugs…"

"Yep. And here are your plane tickets," I say, passing one to each Chuck, Bob, and Phil. "You two go visit with Miss Clara about the décor, and Phil, you can go get the lay of the land and get the tent company out there so they can give us a quote for a tent big enough for a band and three hundred people."

EVERYBODY GETS READ in on the party, and the fun begins. Over the next few months, we set aside part of our weekly staff meetings just to develop more wild ideas for the décor. The decorations will be easy. The hard part is getting a band. Clara is bound and determined to have this one particular country band at the party. What I can't quite get through her head is that most national touring bands are already booked a year or two in advance. It's even worse if they've recently released a new CD, but she remains undeterred. She gave me the name of the band that she wanted.

I already know they aren't available since I pulled up their website while talking and saw they were in Atlanta that weekend. I can't make it look that easy, though, so I tell her I'll check it out and get back with her. I let a little time slip by and call her back to give her the bad news. Touring. She gives me the name of another band. Again, a phone call a few minutes later with the bad news. Booked.

"Why don't you give me a list of the bands you'd like to have at the party?" I suggest softly. Meanwhile, I call my contacts at the agencies in Nashville and Los Angeles and do it the easy way.

"Can you send me a list of who's available on Sunday, September 24th?" I asked politely several times to several different agencies. Soon, my inbox is full of lists, and not one of them includes any of the bands Miss Clara wants nor would any of them be a good fit for this party. So I call my ace in the hole, Bobby, at one of the smaller agencies in Nashville. He always manages to find the best new talent, and we've booked many acts through him right before they hit the big time.

"Hey, Lil' Red, how's things out in Colorado?" Bobby asks.

"Not too bad, Bobby. How're things with you?"

"If I was any better I'd have to be twins."

"Who do you have on the way up that can play a gig just outside of Dallas on September 24th?"

"Well, lemme look. Dallas, you say?"

"Yeah."

"I got these guys that are real good. They won a couple of awards at the CMAs last year. They're playing in Austin the night before."

"How far is that? Can they get to Dallas and play the next day without turning into zombies?"

"Sweetie, these guys are in their twenties. They aren't suffering the consequences of an ill-spent youth yet. Besides, they have a tour bus, and it's only four hours from Austin to Dallas."

"How much? Private party, flat rate, no admission, no advertising."

"A hundred and twenty-five k."

"That's not bad," I say, wondering how Chief will react to this price. "Okay, can you send me a demo?"

"You can get everything you need on their website."

"My client isn't computer savvy. I need a demo, or you can email some MP3s to me."

"How 'bout I do both?"

"You're the best."

"That's why I make the big bucks, babe."

"I've never heard of them," Clara says flatly.

"Well, they are getting a lot of airplay right now, and they're playing the Country Music Awards this December." I figured I'd drop that on her right away.

"Have I heard any of their songs on the radio?" she asks with a hint of dejection in her voice.

"I overnighted their demo to you. The third song on the CD is getting quite a lot of airplay, so you'll probably recognize that one," I say, being as positive as is humanly possible.

"How much do they cost?"

"They're pretty reasonable. One hundred and twenty-five thousand," I answer and then cringe as I wait for her reaction. "The demo will be there tomorrow morning. Give it a listen and let me know what you think," I say, again sounding as upbeat as possible.

"All right," she says, even slower than usual. "Oh, Chief has one small request."

"Okay?" I respond, knowing that this won't be a *small* request. We've pulled a rabbit out of the hat way too many times for Clara, and she is under the impression that we can do anything she can think of and make it look easy.

"Chief wants the General Lee car here for the party."

"Okay, I'll see what I can do," I say while I Google "General Lee" since I have no earthly idea what she's talking about. I know that General Lee, the person, won't be able to make it to the party, but I'm not sure what *the* General Lee is. I find it astonishing that the results for my search reveal the Wikipedia entry for the General Lee car from *The Dukes of Hazard* actually rank above the Wikipedia entry for the real Civil War general.

CHUCK AND BOB are seated in the chairs in front of my desk. They can barely conceal their excitement. They run through a long list of ideas they've come up with for the décor for the estate, the house, and the tent. The pièce de résistance is an antique car from a junk yard not too far away from Clara and Chief's place. It has no windows, and the paint has almost completely faded away. The owner of the junkyard sent photos to Chuck and Bob, and they knew they had hit the jackpot. The owner of the junkyard is also willing to let them use his pickup as a prop.

"He just couldn't get his head wrapped around the idea that we just wanted to rent them," Bob explained.

"Yeah," continued Chuck, using wild hand gestures like he does when he's had too much coffee or is overly excited about something. "He goes, 'Okay, let me get this straight—you want to pay me to deliver the car and the pickup and then come pick it up two days later,' and I'm like, yeah, exactly. They're going to be the centerpiece of my creation," he says with a little dramatic flair.

"He's got a bunch of antique washers and driers that we can put out on the lawn too," adds Bob. "I'm sure he thinks we're just a bunch of crazy city folk with nothing better to do with our money."

"That's exactly what we are, except we do it with other people's money," I point out. "Well, here's the next thing on your scavenger hunt. We need to find the car from *The Dukes of Hazzard* and see if we can get it to the party," I say while I'm passing them the photo, I printed off the Internet. "It's a special request from the guy who's signing the checks, so I know you'll come through for me," I say as I wrinkle up my nose and give them a bratty little smile.

FINALLY, SHE ANSWERS!

"Hi, Clara; it's Donna. How are you?"

"Oh, fine." Shit. "Oh, fine" in Clara speak means everything is not all sunshine and butterflies in her world.

"I listened to the CD you sent me. It doesn't sound much like country to me, but Chief heard it too, and he likes it. That's even before I told him how much they cost. I called two of my granddaughters, and I guess they love them. I asked one of them if they would be a good band to play at the party, and she screamed so loud I think I might suffer a little hearing loss in that one ear. I can't even tell you what the other one said. I'm just shocked at what comes out of the mouth of a twelve-year-old nowadays."

"So, would you like me to book them?" I ask cautiously.

"I suppose," she says with a hint of dejection. "It's three against one, and heaven help me if I disappoint any of my grandbabies."

THE LAST PIECE of this puzzle has yet to be put into place. A day and a half goes by, and Bob has been burning up the phone lines and the Internet to find the General Lee. I need this one last detail so I can put it in the contract and send it off to Chief. Finally, right before I am going to call off the search, I hear Bob singing the "Hallelujah Chorus" from Handel's *Messiah*.

"Oh, Donna..." he sings. "You owe me."

"Where is it, and how much does it cost?" I ask.

"I found one of the originals," he explains, "but it's in a museum in South Dakota, and they aren't letting it out of their sight no matter how much money we throw at them. But I found a replica in Birmingham, and he's willing to trailer it out here for twenty-five hundred dollars as long as he gets an invitation to the party."

"I think that can be arranged."

Great! Now everything is in place. The décor, the catering, the tents, tables, chairs, the band, and the car. I put the finishing touches on the contract, wrapped it up nice and neat as a PDF, and emailed it to Chief. The next morning I received a fax with Chief's signature on the contract and a phone call from our banker saying that a wire transfer had just landed in our account. I love it when a plan comes together.

Are we there yet?

As Bob wheels the rental car into the parking lot, the windshield wipers clear away the last of the rain shower we had to drive through to get to the hotel. We manage to find a parking spot up close, and I spy our vans parked side by side in front of the hotel. Phil and Nelson, along with my dear hubby, left early the day before to make the thirteen-hour drive from Colorado to Rockwall, Texas. Luckily for us, they brought all of our luggage down with them, so our flight to Dallas-Fort Worth was a breeze. We had politely turned down Clara and Chief's offer to stay at their house. We work very hard during the run-up to an event this big, and tensions can run a little high, so it's good to have the ability to get away and have some alone time. Besides, spending six days at Clara Bell's house would have sent me around the bend. I call Phil on his cell, and he meets us in the lobby with our room keys.

"Where are Nelson and Dave?" I ask.

"I haven't seen them since breakfast. I think they're out by the pool. All of your bags are already in your rooms," Phil informs us.

"Let's get settled in, and then we can go by Clara and Chief's so everybody can see the house and the grounds," I suggest.

"This looks nice," observes Bob, eyeing the hotel lobby.

"Yeah, Dave and Nelson were afraid it might be a little too nice for them. We had to go find a more comfortable bar last night."

Phil's grin lets me know that their search was successful. "All of our rooms are right down here," he says as he guides us down the first-floor hallway.

"Okay, let's meet in the lobby in fifteen minutes, and we'll head out to the house," I say, hoping against hope I won't hear a lot of protests.

To my surprise, everyone just shrugs and says, "Okay."

Luckily, our rental car has a GPS. I never paid attention when Clara was driving us to her place, and I have absolutely no recollection of how we got there.

"Destination, ahead, on left," announces the snotty female GPS voice.

"Yeah, turn here," I say, pointing at the tree-lined driveway.

Our motorcade pulls off the main road and drives through the leafy tunnel that leads up to "Shangri-la." Yep. That's what Clara calls it.

"This place is so pretty," says Bob from the back seat.

"Yeah," I concur. "I could get used to living here."

We pull up to the large outbuildings off to one side of the driveway and come to a stop with the two vans behind us. Sam and Nelson exit their van and join us.

"Where will the tent go?" asks Nelson, walking up to us while he looks around, getting a lay of the land.

"In the opening on the other side of these trees," I say as I point to the large field.

"And parking?" Dave asks.

"Right over there," I say, doing a one-eighty and making a wide sweeping motion toward the pasture beside the work shed. "And Clara says a lot of the people who will come to the party will park out on the road. Chief said we can use the barn as our headquarters."

"Cool," says Phil while he looks around.

"You're right," says David, "it is a replica of Tara!"

"I can't wait to trash it up," exclaims Chuck, wringing his hands with a glint in his eye.

"Yeah, this is going to be fun," adds Bob.

"Donnaaaaaaaaaaaa!" Clara screeches as she bounds out of the front door of the mansion. We all make our way over to her as she prances her bubbliness toward us.

"Hi, Miss Clara!" I respond, slightly amused at her enthusiasm. "You remember the gang, don't you?"

"Why, sure I do," she says while giving each of us a big marshmallowy hug. Her charm is certainly contagious. "Well, come on, ya'll. Let me show you around."

Dave, Sam, and Nelson follow her into the house. Chuck and Bob tag along as well, even though they've already seen the place. Phil and I hang back and run through the schedule for the next day.

"So, the tent goes up over the next two days?" I say, running my finger over the timeline.

"Yep. That takes care of Wednesday and Thursday. And then everything else gets delivered on Friday, and the food prep starts early Sunday morning. I left Saturday open just in case. We have a chance of thunderstorms for the next couple of afternoons that the tent goes up, but we should be okay," replies Phil.

"I asked Chuck and Bob to push the junk delivery on Friday back a few hours to give the rentals folks a little more time to get the tables, chairs, and stage set up before they start decorating," I say.

"Good call. You know it's going to be in the nineties the day of the party, don't you?" asks Phil.

"Yeah, I've been watching the forecast for the last few days."

"And they still don't want air conditioning," Phil states, shaking his head.

"No, they're used to this heat."

"Yeah, I guess. At least they have exhaust fans on the top of the tent for ventilation."

"Maybe we could request a nice breeze off the lake for that afternoon," I say hopefully. "Can you call the weatherman and see what he can do for us?"

"I'll get right on that…"

I'M ALWAYS IMPRESSED by the efficiency with which a good tent crew can erect one of these monstrous tents. After a leisurely breakfast, David and I drive out to the house and find Phil fully in charge of the operation. I marvel at how effortlessly he can establish himself as the lead dog and get things to run smoothly. Without any prompting by him, he has the entire crew calling him "Boss" and asking what else they can do to help. He's a natural-born leader and would have done well in the military.

The tractor-trailer that delivered the tent is off to one side, and two other, smaller box vans are parked alongside where the tent is going up. The whole scene looks like an army of ants silently going about their business.

"Were they on time?" I ask Phil.

"Actually, a little early," he says with a grin. "These guys are good."

"Did they bring everything we ordered?" I ask while spotting the stakes in the ground, marking all the buried utilities. It's always good to know where they are when you are driving four-foot stakes in the ground. Puncturing a gas line isn't on my list of things to do.

"Yeah. We had a little problem with the generators, but that's being taken care of."

"What?" I ask flatly, purely out of curiosity.

"They sent two huge diesels. We'd never have been able to hear the band."

"Ooof. So they're bringing the right ones out?"

"Yeah, they should be here anytime now."

With nothing else to do while the tent is being erected, Dave and I grab Nelson and go find the catering company that will be handling the barbeque to make sure everything is on track there.

THE FOLLOWING MORNING, the whole crew assembles at the site just in time to see the final touches being put on the tent. It took much less time to put up than we had scheduled, so we call in the other deliveries. The tables, chairs, and stage are delivered in short order and are in the process of being set in place when I notice an old landbarge of a car turning onto the driveway. The black mass creeps up the tunnel of oak trees and comes to an abrupt stop not far from where Phil and I are standing.

I was starting to get a little worried since the only thing I could see were two little bundles of knuckles hanging onto the steering wheel and two beady eyes peering out from over the dash. The old beast had to have the original shocks on it, judging from how long the car kept bouncing after the wheels had come to a stop.

"What on earth is that?" I ask.

"That there is your basic early seventies land yacht, I'd guess."

We slowly make our way over to the side of the car in time to see the proverbial little old lady struggling mightily to open the colossal driver's door.

Phil springs into action and provides the assistance necessary to accomplish the task. As the massive door creaks open, it's obvious that she isn't expecting any help since she's still clinging to the door handle. When Phil opens the door, he just about drags her out of the car. I get to her while she's flailing her arms around, trying to regain her balance.

"Watch it! Get your hands off of me!" she protests. She's dressed in old blue jeans and a well-worn, moth-eaten chambray shirt.

"Hi, are you here to see Clara and Chief?" I ask in my most sugary-sweet voice.

"You're damn right I am! Who the hell are you, and what are you doing here?" she croaks.

"Well, my name is Donna, and this is Phil, and we're..."

"Aaagh." She waves her hand to shut me up like I've already taken up too much of her time. She's a tiny little thing, but she literally pushes us out of the way and marches her little butt up to the front door, muttering to herself the whole way. She pushes the doorbell and doesn't let up until the front door opens.

"Well, hello, Mrs. Johnson," I hear Chief say. "Come on in." I can tell by the tone of his voice that he's none too thrilled to find her on his front porch. She disappears into the house, and I look at Phil.

He shrugs and says, "Well, *that* happened."

"Yeah, *that* can't be good," I say, pondering what *that* was all about.

We dive back into the task at hand and quickly forget about the cranky old crone. Chuck and Bob had practically bought out every thrift shop in Dallas. The lawn is now strung with clotheslines that display XXXL-size ladies' panties in every shade and bras ten sizes too big for Dolly Parton. Sam has rounded that out with an assortment of wild negligees (some trimmed in green-and-purple faux fur) and tiger-striped men's boxers. The boys have amassed a collection of shopping carts and filled them with as much junk as they could find from garage sales and flea markets. Colored lights hanging from drop cords line the entire property.

The junk man shows up with Chuck's prize piece of décor, a beat-up bucket of bolts. Most of the original light blue metallic paint has faded down to bare rusted metal, and the upholstery is in tatters. The junk crew positions it right smack in front of the house, jacks it up, pulls the wheels off, and settles it back down on cinder blocks. They park the pickup close to the barn. We leave a little room off to the side of the tent for the General Lee.

Chuck and Bob supervise the offloading of some hideous old couches, chairs, antique washers and dryers, some old tires to be stacked at various places around the estate, and a whole host of other things that add just that little *je ne sais quoi* to the whole décor package. Inside the tent, things are coming together nicely. I thought it would have been a whole lot harder to find camouflage table linens, but evidently, there is quite a demand for them. Having burlap table runners and ties for the cocktail rounds was a stroke of genius, and the toilet plungers on every table that held rolls of paper towels are absolute perfection. The cardboard tiers stuffed with Twinkies, Ho Hos, Sno-Balls, and Ding Dongs will finish everything off nicely.

As I survey the scene, I notice Chief out in front of the house in an apparent fit of apoplexy. I hustle over to him to make sure the guy who signs the checks isn't about to keel over on me. As I get closer, I realize he is laughing so hard he's crying. I'm bathed in relief when he catches his breath enough to tell me that we've transformed his estate to look exactly like his old Uncle Earl's place in Tennessee. I also realize our sourpuss has left without our noticing. I want so bad to know what that was all about, but I don't figure it is any of my business.

It's now Friday afternoon, and everything seems to be running like clockwork. You know what they say—if things are running smoothly, you're overlooking something. I gather the team together, and we pore over the contracts and checklists to make sure we aren't forgetting anything. Alas, nothing is missing, and we are on track to have a day off before the party.

LATER THAT AFTERNOON, I stroll through the lobby on my way to my room.

"Nelson's not happy with the catering crew," says Sam, who is lounging on a couch, looking like she's doing a photo shoot for *Vogue*. "He's fine with beer butt chicken, potato salad, and deviled eggs, but he's not too happy with the turkey leg booth, Cheez Whiz on crackers, or funnel cakes."

I wince as I recall his reaction to Clara's request for Ding Dongs and Twinkies for dessert.

"Why don't you go up and have a talk with him?" I suggest. "You seem to be the only person who can help him get things in perspective."

"Sorry," she says with a frown. "Not my thing."

"Oh, come on! You've been friends for years. You must know how he feels about you." I resist the urge to mention that she's had several flings with men not nearly as worthy as Nelson over the past few years.

"Because he wears Hawaiian shirts with fruit and pigs and flowers on them," she says, fiddling with her hoop earring.

"That's just because he has to wear those stiff chef coats all day," I reply. "Besides, underneath the pigs and fruit beats the heart of a really great guy."

"Why don't you go comfort him, then?" she snaps.

I know she doesn't mean it. I can only imagine how horrible it would be for me to lose David and face the trauma that Sam has been through. Still, she needs to move past her grief. I don't picture Sam spending the rest of her life alone.

"I'm sorry," she says, standing up to hug me. "I'm just tense. Putting together this Hillbilly Hoe Down is making me a little crazy." We hold the hug for a beat. "Besides, his name is Nelson, for God's sake," she says.

"What's in a name?" I say, waxing theatrical. "Beer Butt Chicken by any other name would taste just as good." That brings a little smile, but she is still resisting.

"He's barely half an inch taller than me," she says, offering her next lame excuse. "In heels, I'd tower over him."

"Sam," I say, "I'm not buying that. I recall at least two vertically challenged gentlemen you have dated. I know you feel the same way he does."

She suddenly has tears in her eyes, and I wonder what horrible thing I said to cause this.

"You're right," she says. "But what if we do take the next step and something happens to him? I can't go through that again."

Finally, I get it. I quickly steer her into the bar and buy her a margarita.

We talk about trivial things, the latest hot guy in baseball, why blondes shouldn't wear fuchsia, Jessica Simpson's latest escapade, etc. Nelson wanders into the lobby and invites us to go to this great little Mexican restaurant he has discovered. I am exhausted, so I beg off and retire to my room. As I look over my shoulder, I see them headed for the door, and I say a little prayer for them. Sam is her high-fashion self, and Nelson's shirt has monkeys playing trombones on it. Where does he get that stuff?

Ah, Saturday morning and nothing to do. David and Phil left early in one of the vans to go fishing. Nelson and Sam (!) took the other van and drove into Dallas for breakfast and some exploring. Chuck and Bob grabbed the keys to the rental car and just said, "See you later." David had asked if I wanted to go with him and Phil. They were going to go rent a boat and spend the day on the lake. He was just being polite. He knows the last thing in the world I'd want to do is bake in the sun all day, watching them drink beer and catch fish.

"Do you want me to get you another rental?" he asked with just the right amount of concern in his voice.

"Nope, I'm just going to stay here and relax. I might take a dip in the pool. You guys go and have fun. I'll be all right," I said reassuringly.

Okay, I admit, I'll be bored, but I can take a long walk and be perfectly happy. I'm just not used to doing nothing. I order some room service for breakfast, and I thumb through the complimentary newspaper that came with the food. After a long steamy shower, I curl up in bed and fall back asleep. I'm not sure how much time has passed before I'm jolted out of a dead sleep by the ringing of my cell phone. It takes me a moment to get the fog out of my head and find my phone.

"Hello?" I say, sounding exactly like a person who has just woken up.

"Donnaaaaaaaaa, where are you?" drones Clara with more than just a little impatience.

"I'm at the hotel, Miss Clara. What can I do for you?" I ask, hoping nothing is wrong.

"Where is everybody? I thought ya'll would be here getting ready."

"No, ma'am. Remember? We talked about this yesterday? Everything is set and ready to go. The only thing left to do is the food. Nelson will be there bright and early with the barbeque folks to get that going."

"Oh, okay. I was just worried when I didn't see anybody here this morning. What are you doing today?" she asks.

"Oh, not much. Just relaxing," I say, still half asleep.

"Well, that just won't do. I can't have you stuck in that hotel with nothin' to do. I'll be right there, and you can come spend the day with me."

Now, who didn't see *that* coming? Me, evidently. Seeing no way to get out of it, I reply, "Yes, ma'am, I'll be in the lobby waiting for you."

"R U UP?" I text to Nelson. I send the same thing to Phil.

It's 4:30 in the morning, and, typical of the night before a big gig, I can't sleep. A few seconds later I get a response from both.

"Yep." Since they are rooming together, I should have known they'd both be up early.

"coffee?" Phil asks.

"sure, I'll be right over," I respond. I grab the event book, my laptop, and my purse and quietly let myself out the door. David won't be awake for hours. I knock on the door, and it opens. The smell of fresh-brewed coffee hits me like a slap in the face. Phil and Nelson have been up for a little while too. They are showered, shaved, and ready to go. The problem is we will have to wait a couple of hours for the rest of the world to catch up with us.

"Get any sleep?" Nelson asks, already knowing the answer.

"Nope, you?" I reply.

"Yeah, I went to bed early and got up about a half hour ago," Nelson says while stifling a yawn.

"What about you?" I say, directing my attention to Phil.

"Yeah, I managed a few winks. I suppose you passed the night away reading the event book," he says, knowing full well that's exactly what I did.

"How was your dinner?" I ask, looking at Nelson.

"Uh, oh, yeah, it was good." I'd never seen him get so flustered over such a simple question. I smile, knowing that something good must have happened between Sam and him to evoke that kind of response.

"What are our options for breakfast?" I ask after I feel my stomach growl.

"Well, room service doesn't open for about an hour and a half. There are a couple of fast-food joints right up the road here. Other than that, not much," replies Phil.

Nelson slaps his hands on his knees as he rises from his chair, looks at Phil and me, and shakes his head.

"Do you really think I would let my fellow early birds go without a good breakfast?" he asks the two of us. Phil and I look at each other and shrug.

"Yeah, I guess we kinda did," we say in unison.

"Oh ye of little faith." With that he opens the mini-fridge and extracts three plates, unwraps one, and pops it in the microwave.

"What are those?" I ask.

"Just a little something I got yesterday at the catering company," he responds with the proper amount of smug satisfaction. "You shoulda seen the looks on their faces when I told them you were a vegan! It was like they'd never heard of anything so unnatural."

"I'm surprised they even let you in the state," adds Phil with a grin.

"Well, the carnivores will just have to get over it," I say defiantly.

The microwave dings and Nelson proudly presents me with a plate of roasted potatoes, veggies, and vegan sausage. (Yes, there really is such a thing, and it's pretty yummy!) He pops one of the other plates in the microwave, and in short order he presents Phil with a beautiful green chili-and-cheese omelet with a side of hash browns. A couple of minutes later he produces the same thing for himself. A few glasses of orange juice and a bowl of fresh fruit round out our wonderful breakfast.

"Thanks! I really wasn't relishing the idea of going out for breakfast," I say with a mixture of gratitude and relief.

"Yeah, thanks," adds Phil. "There really are some great perks that come with rooming with you. I think this makes up for your snoring."

"You're welcome. My pleasure," responds Nelson.

"Are we just going to take the vans when we head out?" asks Phil.

"We might as well. Sam, David, Chuck, and Bob don't need to be there until around noon. They can just all ride together in the rental car."

"Works for me," Phil says with a shrug.

***

We get to Clara and Chief's place before sun up. Except for one light over the doors of the outbuilding it is dark at their place, so we try to be as quiet as possible. We open the tall sliding doors to the barn and flip on the lights. The lights in the catering tent run off of extension cords running from the shed. Nelson heads that way to start getting things ready for the barbeque folks to show up. Phil takes a flashlight and walks over to the main tent to make sure nothing walked off during the night. Mere moments later, he pops his head into the shed, just as I'm getting my laptop set up.

"You might want to check this out," he says.

"What…" I say in anticipation of some really bad news.

"Can you smell that skunk?"

"Yeah, a little."

"You need to come inside the tent."

"Ohhhh nooooo!"

"Oh yeah."

"What are we going to do?" I ask frantically as we walk over to the tent.

"Well, we need to get the sides up on the tent and turn the exhaust fans on."

"Can we do that with without firing up the generators?"

"Nope. We only need one of them, but I can't wire the fans to the house power."

"I guess that can't be helped. We need to get the smell out of there."

"Okay, I'll fire up the generator, and I'll get Nelson to help me raise the sides."

"I can help you with that too. Why do we even have sides on this tent?" I ask.

"Well, they said it was to keep critters and thieves out. They did say that we might need them in case of rain, too," he replies as he walks over to the generator. He fires it up, and it is loud. They're not so loud in the middle of the day, but first thing in the morning when the birds aren't even chirping yet, it sounds like a jet engine, and once he turns the fans on it's even worse. Even with half the lights on, the place is lit up like Christmas. I cringe at the thought of waking our clients up. Luckily, Clara and Chief's bedroom is on the other side of the house. I scurry around to the lake side of the house and hold my breath. I stand there for a few minutes, waiting for any signs of life, and am relieved to see none. I walk back to the other side of the house and help Phil and Nelson raise the sides of the tent. The exhaust fans at the top of the tent are amazing. Just standing there, you can feel the breeze created by them.

"I'm not so sure that the skunk actually went off in here," says Phil, having to raise his voice just a little to overcome the noise of the fans and the generator. "I walked all over in here, and there isn't one place that's really strong, and I can tell it's clearing out fairly well."

"Well, it is a white trash party. Maybe having a little *eau de mouffette* will be a nice touch. If anyone says anything about it, just tell them it was part of the décor and ambiance plan," I say.

"Yeah, I wonder if we can charge extra for the polecat package," he says with a grin. "Hopefully, we get a little bit of a breeze once the sun comes up to help us clear it out."

"Yeah, that'd be nice. Did Nelson get any of this in his tent?" I ask.

"Nope, not a bit."

"Huh, that's odd."

Not too much time passes before I see lights come on in the house. At least it's 5:30 now, and I'm pretty sure Clara and Chief are early risers, so I'm not too concerned. It's probably their normal time to get up. About that time a pair of headlights sweep their way onto the long driveway.

"I hope you enjoyed your peace and quiet," says Nelson with a sigh.

"Yep, I did. And I don't think we're going to get much of that until about twenty hours from now," I say, not relishing the thought of being on my feet that long.

It's light enough now that I can see it's a pickup truck towing a trailer with our General Lee on it.

"Hey, you Donna?" asks the grizzled old guy inside the pickup.

"I am. What's your name?"

"Stump," he replies. "Where do you want it?"

"Right over there with the front of it toward the tent," I say, pointing real casual like.

"Where can I put the trailer?" asks the grizzled guy.

"Right behind that barn," I say, again pointing in the general direction.

"Okey doke."

He wheels the pickup around and hops out to slide the ramps out of the underside of the trailer. I now know why his name is Stump. He is no taller than I am, but his stocky frame makes him look just like an old stump. His greasy cap and coveralls complete the look of someone who hasn't spent too much time indoors. By this time Phil and Nelson have joined me to watch the proceedings. Stump hops up onto the trailer and fires up the General Lee. It's blatantly obvious, even to the casual observer, that this car has no mufflers. He revs it up and gives us a toothless grin.

"Sounds good, don't she?" Stump proclaims proudly. The three of us look at each other and back at him, nodding in agreement. Stump throws the car in reverse and backs it off the trailer. Phil guides him to the spot we've designated for the car. Stump turns the car off, and the low rumble of the exhaust goes silent.

"That's quite a machine you've got there," says Phil admiringly.

"What's that?" Stump asks, louder than I thought necessary.

"I say, that's quite a machine you've got there," Phil repeats, matching Stump's volume decibel for decibel.

"Yep, yep, built 'er from the ground up," replies Stump. Loudly. I think Stump has been around too many loud cars for way too long. "What time does this party get started?"

"About three," I yell

"This is a barbeque, right? I ain't gotta dress up er nothin', do I?"

"Nope," I shake my head to emphasize my answer, "just come as you are."

"He's going to fit right in," Nelson says under his breath.

"You got that right," says Phil through a grin without moving his lips.

Stump climbs into his truck, and the three of us wave goodbye as he heads down the driveway. The commotion has stirred Chief from the house. It pains me to watch him walk. It's quite obvious that he hasn't got all the joints limbered up.

"Now, that's what I'm talking about!" says Chief with heavy emphasis on the "I'm." "The owner's comin' to the party, right?"

"Oh yeah," I say, "he'll be here."

"Good, I can't wait to meet him," he says while caressing the front fender of the orange beauty.

We get a few moments of respite before the next couple of arrivals. What comes through the gate next is more than a little puzzling for me. Four pickup trucks are towing four more, older pickup trucks. They reach the end of the driveway, and Nelson is there to direct them to their appointed spots. A fifth truck, a flatbed, follows behind them. Each of the trucks positions its towed pickup, end to end, in an arc on the far side of the tent. Phil and I stay out of the way and just watch as Nelson and the drivers confer and then set about jacking up each of the old pickups, removing their tires and lowering them on cinderblocks, very much in the same way as our beat-up relic is set up. We then watch in amazement as they raise the covers on the beds of the pickups to reveal a barbeque pit.

"Wow, now *that's* cool!" exclaims Phil.

"I have to agree with you there," I respond.

Nelson gives us a tour around the pickup/grills and points out the grocery carts that have been offloaded from the flatbed. They had taken the wheels off of the carts and put a pan on the bottom rack where the coals go.

"They use these to grill corn and cook the beans. They have to take the tires off the pickups so they don't burn up when they light the grill, but I think putting them on cinder blocks fits right in with our theme."

"These are so cool!" I say, not wanting to sound too enthusiastic. I mean it's all pickup trucks and barbeque stuff. Total guy toys, but it was pretty cool. Phil crosses his arms and inspects the construction of the mobile grills.

"A lot of work went into making these," he says authoritatively.

About this time the truck with the band's equipment shows up, and Phil directs the crew to the stage inside the tent. Phil has been a musician all his life and always gets involved in helping a band get set up. The whirlwind of activity that goes into setting up all the equipment for a band has always amazed me. It's a mystery how a whole spaghetti ball of wires and cables gets hooked up to all the right things, but it does, and over the years I've managed to purge that from the list of things I worry about. The next few hours pass awfully quickly, with the whole crew showing up, the barbeque guys getting their grills ready to go, and the décor team putting the final touches on the tent and the yard. I see Clara and Chief walking around in the yard, pointing and laughing at things.

"Donna, you've outdone yourself this time," says Clara as she hugs me.

"Thank you, Miss Clara, I appreciate it. The crew has had a great time putting this together for you," I say, making sure she knows this has been a team effort.

"Well, the first guests oughta be showing up about anytime now," says Chief. "We'd better get upstairs and get ready."

"Okay," says Clara, not really paying any attention to him. "What time did you tell the boys to be here?" she asks Chief, referring to their three sons.

"Well, I told them to be here about an hour ago, but, you know, with their wives and kids we'll be lucky to see any of them by sundown," he responds with just a hint of impatience.

"Oh, now," she says and smacks him on the arm, "remember, this is a party and we're going to have a good time."

"Yeah, okay," he says, sounding properly scolded. He takes her hand, and they stroll back to the house.

Sure enough, not fifteen minutes later, the guests start to arrive. The invitation said the party was to start at three o'clock, and, by golly, at three a whole caravan of cars starts to arrive. ("By golly"?!?! I just said "by golly"! It might take months of therapy to purge all this *Southern* out of me!)

It was obvious from the very start that these people needed some adult supervision when it came to parking in an open field. Phil jumped on that, and with a little guidance, the arrivals finally got the idea that parking in neat rows might be a good idea. Not long after the first guests appear, Clara and Chief emerge from the house decked out in their best white trash getups. She's wearing a ratty old house dress, and her hair is up in curlers. He's wearing an old pair of blue jeans and a western plaid shirt with the sleeves torn off. They position themselves between the General Lee and the tent so they have the best chance of greeting all the people who show up.

The procession of oilmen, politicians, Dallas Cowboys players (I was corrected when I said they had the day off; I guess it's called a "bye week." Sounds an awful lot like a day off to me!), and celebrities that followed was impressive, to say the least. Unbeknownst to me, Chief had arranged for a few sedans to shuttle people from the local airport to the party for those who had flown in on their private jets. Judging by how many times the sedans made the trip to the airport, I'd have to guess that there were about a dozen private planes now sitting at the Rockwall Municipal Airport.

Almost everybody who arrived was "dressed" for the occasion. Seeing the crème de la crème of Dallas society and beyond dressed down as the great unwashed was truly a spectacle. One very pregnant young lady showed up in a lacy, white crop top with her baby bump on full display and wearing a wedding veil. Another gentleman had the names of about eight ladies "tattooed" on his arm, with each one of them crossed out, save for the very last one. Stump was one of the first to show up, and he did, indeed, fit right in. Most of the guys had at least some of their teeth blacked out, and a few of the ladies showed up in cut-off shorts and way too much makeup. Seeing these women, I bet it costs a lot of money to look this cheap. I wondered how long it took some of the ladies to get their hair to look so bad. It was a real mind bender to hear the greetings of "Hello, Senator" or "Nice to see you, Governor," or "Great to see you, Sheriff" and hearing the guests comment that Miss Clara was the only person in the world who could get all these people to dress like this.

The three sons did finally show up, though one of them clearly refused to play along with the theme of the party. Two of the sons were now running Chief's oil company, but it was the third and youngest who did not lower himself to the level of the party and was clearly not happy about the theme. He was a conservationist living in Houston and showed up sans family, much to the disappointment of Miss Clara. Hmmm, the son of a Texas oilman choosing to become a tree hugger! Do ya think there might be some issues there?

From what I could tell, the most common topics of discussion were the décor and the creativity people put into their outfits. People were pointing and laughing at each other and all the junk scattered throughout the yard. The General Lee and the relic up on blocks were a real hit as were the clotheslines with the oversized bras and panties waving in the breeze. Stump stood by proudly and talked with anybody who stopped by to admire his car. The face painters and the bounce houses were a hit with the kids. The magician was supposed to be for the kids, too, but he found himself surrounded by adults most of the day. We had set up three horseshoe pits and probably could have done with about ten more. The redneck horseshoe pit was by far the most popular of the games. The stakes were a little taller, and they weren't as far apart, but the "horseshoes" were actually U-shaped toilet seats. There was some big money won and lost on that game. The line of cars coming up the drive was an endless procession of Mercedes, Jaguars, and a few Bentleys and Rolls-Royces thrown in for good measure.

After a while the whole place was a sea of people having a great time. It was a wonderful afternoon, and the weatherman couldn't have done a better job. There was a slight cloud cover and just enough of a breeze to keep it comfortable.

I was standing over by the barn with Sam and Chuck when I noticed a lady scurry by us with her husband in tow. She gets in their car, slams the door, and off they go. The three of us look at each other and shrug. Chuck and Sam couldn't bring themselves to dress down for the party, but I managed an old pair of blue jeans and a tight white T-shirt that says "I (heart) Bubba." I guess it was my clipboard and walkie-talkie that made it obvious we were the working folk. A rather large lady walked up to us and said: "Are you part of the help?"

"Yes, ma'am. How can I help you?" I ask, forcing a smile.

"Look at my arm!" she demanded.

Emblazoned big as day on her arm was a fake tattoo that stated "Big,

Dumb and Ugly."

"Is this somebody's idea of a joke?" she sputtered.

"No, ma'am. Where did you get that?" I asked sympathetically.

"From your tattoo artist on the other side of the tent."

"Chuck, would you be so kind as to show this lady to the kitchen and help her get her tattoo off?" I ask as soothingly as I can.

"It doesn't come off. I've already tried," barks the offended woman.

"Sure it does," I reassure her. "A little rubbing alcohol, and it'll wipe right off."

Just then another woman stomps by with her husband in tow—in the car, with a slam of the door, and off they go.

"She was in line right behind me," says the lady. "She must have gotten something just as awful."

"Okay, what I can tell you is this, we didn't hire a tattoo artist, but I will go find her and see if I can stop her," I say while taking her hands in mine, trying my best to calm her down.

"Well, you better do it fast. There's a whole group of women who are lookin' to kick her skinny little butt."

I make my way toward the far side of the tent when Phil intercepts me and guides me back to the General Lee.

"You better come with me," he says while he redirects me back toward the front of the house.

"What's up?" I ask, struggling to keep up with him.

"It's Stump. Somebody told me he's arguing with the mayor of Austin."

As we close in on the situation, I can hear the mayor yelling at Stump about his apparent lack of football knowledge. (I'm paraphrasing, of course.) Stump is yelling something completely unintelligible in return. The only thing I can make out is "Crimson Tide." I haven't the foggiest idea what he's talking about, other than maybe his face, which is now a lovely shade of red. Turns out, what started as a friendly discussion about who has the better football team quickly devolved into a shouting match about which state, Texas or Alabama, has the lower average IQ. Just then, the crowd that had gathered to witness the quarrel turns its attention to the driveway. I notice this at about the same time I hear the quick siren blasts from one of the three police cars coming up the drive.

Whoop, whoop… Holy crap, they got here awfully quick if someone called about this fight. Even the mayor and Stump have turned their attention to the police cars. I see Clara and Chief make their way over to the cruisers. The driver's door of the first police car opens, and a tall cop gets out, puffs his chest out, and puts his hands on his hips.

"I'm shocked, shocked to find that gambling is going in here," he announces, stealing the line from *Casablanca*. He relaxes and sticks his hand out to shake Chief's and hugs Clara.

"Good to see you, Chief."

"Good to see you too, Bob. I don't suppose our neighbor has anything to do with you being here, does she?"

"Have you had a party here in the last ten years when she *didn't* call me?" he queries.

"Nope. She was even kind enough to come by and warn me that she was going to call you. I see you brought reinforcements." *So that's what the mystery lady in the big black car was all about.* The eyes of everyone at the party are now on Chief, Clara, and the police.

"Yeah, you never can tell when one of these will get out of hand. Looks like you've got some real bad hombres here."

"Oh, now stop. You boys get over there and get yourselves something to eat," Clara says while smacking him on the arm. I get the idea she likes to do that.

Bob, as it turns out, is the chief of police here in Rockwall and grew up with Clara and Chief's oldest son. As the police make their way through the crowd, you can hear them greeting the local politicians and businessmen.

"I'd rather they not scare the shit out of me like that," I whisper to Phil.

"Yeah, I was about to make a run for it," he says with a modicum of mock terror in his voice.

"Let's go check on Stump."

"Eh, no need. When the police cars showed up, he disappeared. I don't think they ever finished their argument, though. I think Stump was a little outnumbered."

"Well, good, I'm glad that's over. Do you know anything about a tattoo artist?"

"No, why?"

"We've had some complaints about unflattering tattoos."

"We didn't hire one, did we?"

"Nope, but I'd like to find her."

"Do you know where she is or what she looks like?"

"Nope," I respond, "I guess we'll just have to look for where all the pissed-off women are."

"Now *that* sounds like fun," Phil says, the dread dripping from his voice.

As we wend our way through the crowd, we spot a few women showing off their tattoos. Some are laughing about them; others are not so amused. I have to admit, some were pretty funny, but others were pretty distasteful. We finally managed to find the last woman the artist had worked on. The lady only had half a tattoo and told us when the tattoo artist heard the sirens, she turned an ashen shade of gray, gathered up her things, and left her mid-tattoo.

"What did she look like?" asks Phil.

"Well, she was about my height, long brown hair, and just kinda plain lookin'," answers our witness.

"Which way did she go?" I ask.

"She took off over towards where all the cars are parked," she says, pointing in the direction of the parking field.

"Okay, thanks. That will come off with rubbing alcohol," I tell her.

"It better. I'm a bridesmaid next weekend, and I have to wear this gawd-awful sleeveless gown."

Not knowing what else to say, Phil and I turn and walk away in the direction of the parking lot. When we get far enough away from the noise of the crowd, the music, and the generators, we can hear a car that just won't start. We can also hear a few voices coming from a gaggle of women who have congregated around the car that just won't start. I can almost hear the panic in the starter, which is getting slower and slower the closer we get to it. We get to the car as it whirrs one last time and then just gives up.

"Please get out of the car. We'd really like to talk to you."

"Yes, please do. I really would like to know why you put this tattoo on my arm."

"It's okay, you can unlock the door. We would like to get to know you a little better."

Okay, okay, so that's not what the ladies huddled around the driver's door were really saying, but I think you get the idea.

My sidekick and I gather up the angry mob and assure them that we will take care of this. Phil knocks on the window, and the girl inside ignores us as she twists the key just a little harder in the ignition, hoping against hope that it will somehow magically transport her out of here. Phil knocks on the window again, this time a little harder.

"Come on out, Sweetie; we just want to talk to you," I say as soothingly as I can. She looks up at us with a pitiful look and slowly opens the car door. She slumps back in her seat and starts to cry.

"Why are you crying?" asks Phil.

"I don't know," she answers, her voice muffled by her hands covering her face.

"Why did you run when the police got here?" I ask.

"I don't know," she says again between sobs.

"Who hired you to do this?" Phil tries and looks at me and mouths the words in unison with her.

"I don't know." With that, her sobbing becomes almost uncontrollable.

"I think you need to come up with a different answer for us," I say, trying my best badass cop-show interrogation voice.

"I don't wanna go to jail," she wails

"Whoa, whoa, whoa!" I say, snapping out of my bad ass cop-show voice. "Nobody said anything about you going to jail. We just want to know who put you up to this."

"I really don't know," she says, now alternating sniffles and sobs between words. "This guy I work with said a friend of his girlfriend would pay me to come out and do this. I didn't want to be mean to these people, but I really needed the money." Again, with the sobs. Phil gives his head a quick shake, trying to unscramble what he just heard.

"So, let me get this straight, a friend of a friend of a friend paid you to do this," he states flatly.

"Yeah."

"Gimme your driver's license," demands Phil.

"I don't have it. I was late getting out here, and I left my purse at home."

"Wow, you're in a bad way. No purse, no license, no money, and a car that won't start," Phil says, pointing out the obvious, which just starts the waterworks all over again.

I give Phil my "Why'd you have to go and do that for?" look. He shrugs and rolls his eyes.

"Sweetheart, we're willing to help you out here, but you have to help us in return, okay?" I say, trying out my sweet old aunt voice. One of these has to work.

"Okay," she says as the tears slow to a trickle.

"If we help you start your car, you have to promise that you'll give me a call with the name of the woman who put you up to this," I say, handing her one of my cards.

"Okay," she says, looking at the card, then at me, then back at the card. We close her door, and I turn to Phil.

"You wanna give her a jump?" I ask.

"Nah, she's too young and skinny for my taste."

I give him my best "Why did you have to go *there*?" look, and he flinches and says, "Okay, okay, I will help her start her car," enunciating each word clearly so there is no misunderstanding.

I tap on the window and tell her that Phil will be right back with the jumper cables, and she mouths the words *thank you* back at me as her face contorts and she resumes crying. Later, Phil catches up with me back at the barn, and I ask him if she got out of here okay.

"Yeah, it took a while, but it finally started. I wrote down her license plate," he says as he hands me a slip of paper. "They were Colorado plates."

My stomach churns a little, and I realize that I won't be hearing from her anytime soon.

THE REST OF the party went as planned. The food was great, and the drinks flowed. The band went on as scheduled, and people danced the night away. I convinced Chief that he should use the sedans he had hired to shuttle people to the airport for those folks who'd had a little too much to drink. I told him the last thing he needed was to have a bunch of his guests get DUIs on their way home. Once the band finished at nine, the crowd started to thin out, and by ten the last guest had left. There were still about two dozen cars scattered in the field and one or two out on the road. I was glad and relieved so many people had taken advantage of the free ride home.

I was actually surprised by how early the party had ended, but I guess it being a Sunday, most people had to get up and go to work the next day. The real perk was that we got almost everything packed up by about midnight, and we were in bed a few hours earlier than I had anticipated. The band and the barbeque folks were out of there in no time flat. Stump put the General Lee on his trailer and took off without a word. I hadn't seen him since his debate with the mayor, and it looked like he had been sleeping for a good long while by the time he left. All we had to do was show up the next day to make sure the tent, generators, and the rest of the rental stuff, junk and all, got packed out.

We all chuckle as one of the cars out in the field starts up and drives off. The rather young, rumpled couple in the front seat waves and smiles as they drive by.

"Hmmm," is all I can think to say.

"Yeah, hmmmm indeed," Bob adds.

"What happened with the tattoo girl?" asks Nelson.

"I'd like to know that very same thing," I respond.

"Why would anybody do that?" asks Chuck.

"I have no idea," I respond.

"Remember that little problem we had with the salads last month at the charity fundraiser?" asks Nelson.

"Yeah," a few of us respond in unison.

"I've had this sneaking suspicion that that wasn't just an innocent mistake."

"What are you saying?" I ask.

"I think somebody did that on purpose. No concrete proof, just a hunch."

"Well, it was a good thing you caught that in time," notes Sam.

"Yeah, jalapeños instead of green peppers would have been a disaster," Nelson adds.

"Oh great!" I say. "That's all we need is somebody trying to sabotage our events."

We walked around the grounds of the mansion the next day, making sure everything was cleaned up. About mid-afternoon we had the vans packed up and ready to go. David and Phil took off in one van, and Nelson and Sam took off in the other. Because of their late start, I extracted a solemn promise from all of them that they would not drive straight through. They all reassured me that they would stop in Amarillo, which is really close to being halfway home. Nelson had already scouted out a good restaurant for them to eat at when they got there. We never did see Chief or Clara that day. Even with all the noise and commotion of the teardown and load out, we never saw any movement inside the house.

Later that afternoon, while Chuck, Bob, and I were waiting for our boarding call at DFW, I hear my phone ring.

"Hello?"

"Donna, this is Clara."

"Hi, Miss Clara, how are you today?"

"Oh, I'm just fine, thanks. I have to tell you, we had the very best time yesterday. You all did the best job ever on our party, and Chief and I wanted to thank you for that. I'm sorry we didn't see you today. I so wanted to give everybody a big old hug before ya'll left."

"I sure appreciate that, ma'am. It's always fun working with you on your events."

"Well, I think we make a pretty good team, you and I. I'm sure we'll be doing a Halloween party up in Colorado, so I'll be calling you for that one."

"Thanks, I'll mark it on my calendar."

"Oh, and by the way, Donna, how do I get this silly tattoo off?"

CHAPTER 5
Ho, Ho, Ho

Well, I hope all of you had a wonderful Thanksgiving and are very well rested," I say to the mob gathered in our conference room. "As you can see," I say while pointing to the two big dry-erase boards on the wall, "we have more parties over the next three weeks than we know what to do with."

I guess in any other industry the prospect of working long, grueling hours late into the night might elicit some groans, but event planners are different. This is what we live for. This bunch is rarin' to go. Each board is a grid of dates, clients, times, and all the other gory details we need to know about an event. The boards are full. There will be stretches of days over the next few weeks when I will not see daylight in my condo. I'll get home in the wee hours of the morning, sleep a few hours, and leave before sun up. I usually have to reintroduce myself to David after the last party of the season.

"Hi, my name is Donna, and I'll be sleeping with you tonight," is my traditional post-party-season greeting to him.

Assembled in the conference room is a group of event managers we use on an as-needed basis. They all started out as worker bees and then apprenticed as assistant event managers before we let them out on their own.

"Phil is passing out a list of events and who will be the site manager for each of them," I say in my serious taskmaster voice. "You'll notice that a few of you have multiple events on the same night. That means we have more than one event going on at the same venue. Please make sure the event information sheets you have match up with the events you'll be handling. It's very important that we get this right. You are split into three groups. Your team leader will be Sam, Phil, or me. Also, at the very top of your event sheets, you will see our cell phone numbers. If you have any issues, that's the person you are to call to get them resolved. Right below that you'll see the main office number. If you can't get your team leader, you can always call here. Zoe will be on duty on Friday and Saturday nights and a couple of the busier nights in between. She'll have access to all the client files and should be able to answer your questions as well. Your team leader will be the same person for all of the events you'll be managing. The three of us will be stopping in at every one of the events we are in charge of, so it's not like you'll be out there all by your lonesome. Mondays are pretty light, as usual. Fridays and Saturdays, however, are out of control, so please make sure you get all of your questions answered today. Now, those of you who have Sam's name at the top of your sheets, please go meet with her in her office. Everybody on my team can go ahead and move into my office. Everybody on Phil's team can stay put. You'll be meeting with him right here." I did that so nobody would have to be subjected to the chaos that is Phil's office.

Zoe had only been with us for a few months before the holiday crush. She was fresh out of college and had a preternatural ability to organize. Within the first three weeks she worked with us she had completely reorganized the filing system so it made sense and we could find things. She looked at the way we did things and was able to come up with either tweaks or wholesale changes that made the office run so much smoother. She also just happens to be David's niece. Nobody knew it at the time, and we planned to keep it that way. She had worked a minor miracle in getting everybody's event information sheet ready for the meeting. These sheets included all the vital information an event manager would need to know. They included the date, time, and location of a party, including the name of the client, the name of the VIP from the company, and the contact person from that company. They also included all the other information every event planner would need to run an event. The contact's name at the venue, what time the décor team was to arrive, the time the entertainment was to arrive, when they were supposed to perform, and on and on, ad nauseum. But we still needed to make sure everybody knew everything they needed to know, and that's why we were having this pow-wow. Sam, Phil, and I were going to go through each and every client file with each of the site managers, just to make sure we had everything covered because no matter how well you think you are prepared, there will always be questions.

Chuck, Bob, and Nelson are excused from these duties since they will be working harder than anyone else throughout the holiday season. Practically every one of the parties has some sort of décor package included, and about half of them need catering. Every time I think I'm about to fall over from exhaustion, I just think about the job those three are doing. It doesn't really make me feel any better; it's just nice knowing that there are people out there more tired than I am.

Chuck pops his head in the door of my office. "I hear you're doing the dentist's party this Saturday."

"I am!" I respond with some enthusiasm. The dentist in question is one of our better clients. "Tiffany and I will be working that one."

"Cool! If I dress up as an elf, can I come too?" he asks.

"You don't have to dress up as an elf to come by, but if you want to..." I don't really want to see him in tights. "It's not going to be much of a party if I can't find a replacement Santa. The one we had booked for that party has managed to get the flu. And why on earth do you want to be there? You're decorating it as the Playboy Mansion for cryin' out loud!"

"Well, he's my dentist, and I want to be there to receive all the kudos when he sees what we do to his house. Bummer about Santa," he adds as an afterthought.

"Yeah, bummer," I say while scrounging through the papers on my desk.

He tosses his head with a bit of panache and glides away.

The grin he has plastered on his face should be cause for alarm, but I'm too busy even to think about it.

"Ho Ho, Inc. just called. They have a Santa for you," reports Zoe and quickly rushes back to her desk to catch another phone call. I'm bathed in relief. I have a Santa. Yes! I do a little happy dance right there in my chair.

"Did you get his name?" I shout after her. Too late, she's already answering the phone. A few seconds later somebody's phone rings in an office down the hall. Just then a dark blur flashes past my door. I'm too busy rummaging through the papers on my desk to notice who it was. A dark cloud is forming above my head. I can't find a file I just had in my hands no more than a minute ago. Do I have to tear the whole office apart to find it? Will I be dumpster diving in search of it? Why would anybody take my file?

The dark blur appears in my doorway again and stops. It's Sam. She leans on the doorframe, has one hand on her hip, and the other is twirling a necklace. She's wearing a black turtleneck, a dark gray wool miniskirt, black tights, and black boots. Nobody deserves to be that tall, thin, and pretty. I could forgive her if she was a ditz, but she's not. Aargh.

"You'd better have a damned good reason for looking that good in the middle of the day," I say with as much growl as I can muster.

"Don't hate me because I'm beautiful," she mews, sounding like something out of a seventies aftershave commercial.

"Oh, no...I've got plenty of other reasons to hate you, but that still ranks right up there. Is there a reason you're tormenting me at the moment? Can't you see I'm busy?"

"No, no reason. I just wanted to stop by and see your smiling face. It makes me feel so much taller when I'm around you."

"Zoe!" I shout. "I can't find the file for that construction company!" Zoe scampers in and takes the missing file off the top of my In Box, hands it to me, and just as quickly scampers out. I really hate it when she does that. "Zoe!" I shout again. She scampers back in. "Kill her," I say, pointing to Sam.

"I don't remember that being part of my job description, ma'am," she says while looking up at her new assignment.

"It was in the fine print," I say while grinning all evil-like at my best friend. "You should have read your contract a little better. Now, please, get it done, and don't ruin the carpet."

"Yes, ma'am," she says and scampers back to her desk.

"The force is strong with that one. You've trained her well, I see," says Sam in a villainous voice.

"Yes, and you know how hard it is to find good minions these day," I say while flipping through the newly-found file. Nelson appears in the doorway behind Sam. He puts both hands on Sam's hips and moves her out of the way so he can get through the door. She doesn't seem to mind that his hands linger a little after he repositions her. Hmmm…

"You have to call whoever is writing the checks for this one," he says as he hands me a file.

"Pourquoi?" I ask, trying to sound all sophisticated.

"The head of the party committee just called and wants to change the menu. That wouldn't be so bad except that it almost doubles the price of the entrée."

"Well, that's not good. Don't change anything. They have a very limited budget, so I know he's not going to agree to anything like that," I say, laying the file in the middle of my desk so it won't get lost or stolen. I notice Phil and Eugene, the intern, walking down the hall, carrying a ladder and a toolbox. That can't be good.

"What are you doing?" says a voice down the hall.

"Hold still—this won't hurt." I recognize that voice as Chuck's.

"What's going on out there?" I ask Sam.

She leans back and peers down the hall. "You really don't want to know," she says, looking back at me. Nelson squeezes through the door without repositioning Sam. She gives him a hip check once he gets past her and sends him into the wall across from my door.

"Hey, hey, hey," I scold them. "No roughhousing indoors. If you want to play like that, go outside." Sam sighs heavily and rolls her eyes.

Zoe's head appears in the doorway. "There's somebody on line three for you. He said to tell you it's Mr. Procrastination." Ah, one more party to throw together at the last minute. We charge extra for miracles.

"Thank you," I say, and the disembodied head vanishes. "Oh, Zoe?" Her head reappears.

I point at Sam and ask, "Why is she still alive?"

"Another Saturday night and I ain't got nobody…" Eduardo sings as he sets out the trays of hors d'oeuvres. The mansion is a beehive of activity. The catering team is busy setting out the food, the bartenders are stocking their posts, and Chuck is putting the final touches on the décor. The place is awash in red and white with lots of nineteen-sixties props. The male staff is dressed in tuxedos, and the models we hired as female servers are clad as a cross between a Santa's elf and Playboy Bunny. Not your typical holiday season theme, but it reflects the personality of the client to a "T." The jazz trio arrives and starts to set up in the far corner of the library. "Hef," as our client wishes to be addressed for the evening, appears at the top of the grand staircase clad in black silk pajama bottoms, a deep burgundy smoking jacket, and a royal blue ascot. A children's pipe that blows bubbles finishes off the ensemble.

"Donna, would you pin these to the tree for me?" he asks and hands me a stack of envelopes. "I want Santa to hand these out while he's here."

"Okay, I'll put them all over to the side so they don't take too much away from the other ornaments."

"Okay, good idea," he says while inspecting the bar setup.

Chuck snatches the envelopes out of my hand and announces, "I'll take care of that."

Oh, dear God, he *did* dress up as an elf. I would have been perfectly happy to have lived my whole life without seeing that.

"Charles, so good to see you," says the dentist. "Nice outfit."

"Thanks, Doc. Ho, ho, ho, and a merry Christmas to you," responds Chuck. I always forget that we are the only ones who call him "Chuck." Phil called him Chucky once, and I thought his head was going to pop off.

I feel my phone vibrating in my pocket, so I excuse myself and slip into the kitchen to take the call. I look at the caller ID and see that it's one of our site managers.

"Hello, this is Donna."

"Hey, Donna, it's Karen."

"Hey, Karen, how's everything going?" *Beep.*

"Great." *Beep.* "I just wanted to…" *Beep.*

"Karen, hang on, I've got another call coming in." *Beep.* I look at the caller ID and push the call waiting button and say, "Hello, this is Donna."

"Hi, Donna, Svetlana from Ho, Ho, Inc. How are you doing tonight?"

I know if I'm getting a call from a vendor on the evening of an event it can't be good, so I lie and say, "Oh, fine."

"I just wanted to let you know that your Santa might be a few minutes late, but it'll just be five or ten minutes."

"That's fine, just as long as he's not too late. Is he one of our regular Santas?"

"No, he's one of our newer guys, but we've been getting rave reviews from the parties we've sent him out on."

"Okay, great. Thanks for letting me know. I've got a call on the other line that I have to take, but I appreciate you letting me know." I take the phone from my ear, and right before I push the call waiting button, I hear a faint, "Okay, but…"

"Sorry, Karen, what's up?"

"Do you remember if this client had said anything about the band being dressed in Santa and elves costumes?"

"No, they're a tropical band—they always dress in shorts, Hawaiian shirts, and flip flops. Why?"

"Well, the client thought they were going to be dressed in Santa stuff, and I don't think he's too happy with the beach look."

"There's a whole box of red felt Santa hats with the white fur at the office. See if the band will wear those and ask the client if that will work. If that makes everybody happy, you can run over to the office and grab them."

"Okay, I'll try that," she says and hangs up.

As I step out of the kitchen into the dining room, I see that some of the guests have started to arrive. The guests at this event are the other dentists in the practice, dental hygienists, the office staff, and a few friends and family members. Chuck and Bob have done an amazing job of turning this house into the Playboy Mansion, and the guests are all dressed in nineteen sixties fashion. In the back of my mind I questioned the PCness of having a Playboy-themed holiday party for a company made up primarily of female dental hygienists and office staff. But they all got into it and went to great lengths to dress for the occasion. I don't know where they found all the vintage outfits, but they were great. I forgot how short the mini-dresses were back then. I know that fashion is cyclical, but I'm awfully glad the hairstyles from that era have not made a comeback.

I thought I would start out at this party since Tiffany is one of our younger site managers, but with Chuck hanging around I feel confident that, between the two of them, they can handle this party just fine. Once this one gets started, I can make my rounds to the other events we have going that evening. The catering, bar, jazz trio and décor are already set, so there isn't anything else to check on except Santa.

The dentist is notorious for being very finicky about his guests being punctual, so within a few minutes of the appointed hour everybody has arrived. I guess when you're the one writing the bonus checks and handing out the presents, you can do that. Once everybody has been equipped with a drink and gathered in the expansive living room, our host signals the music to stop and commences to make his speech. I thought he was going to wait until Santa arrives since part of his spiel is to hand out bonuses and presents, but being the prompt person he is, he has decided the time has come to start the festivities. I hustle over to him and whisper that Santa is going to be a few minutes late.

"That's fine," he responds, "I'm just getting things started. We can wait to do the Santa thing."

Not too long into his monologue, the doorbell rings. All eyes turn toward the front door. I raise my hand and give an "I'll get this" nod to our host. I know all the guests have arrived, so this must be our Santa. He had explicit instructions to enter through the side door, but he must have missed that little nugget of information. Chuck gets to the foyer about the same time I do, and I twist the handle and open the door—and what to our wondering eyes should appear but a medium-sized person with dark, sunken eyes and skin as pale as any I've ever seen on a human being who still is among the living.

OMG, how the hell am I going to make this work? His outfit is a little worse for wear, but in its glory days it must've been quite a sight. It is a red, floor-length coat made of plush velvet that is worn in spots. The collar, cuffs, and hem are trimmed in white fur that has turned a dingy gray. The stag horn buttons are impressive, even if a few of them are missing. His large red mittens are embroidered with a large snowflake on each of them, with a few stitches that had been snagged along the way. His fake mustache is thick and white, and his beard is wavy and hangs down to his knees. The roundish hat atop all of this is made of the same plush velvet as his coat with white fur trim that completes the whole well-worn ensemble. In his right hand, he holds an ornately carved white staff accented with gold paint that is about a foot taller than he is. In his left hand, he carries a crumpled-up brown paper bag. Unless there is a new vodka-scented cologne out there that I don't know about, this guy had been drinking for a while before he got here. I turn to see if anybody in the living room is watching us. Seeing no one, I grab Chuck and drag him outside with me and quietly shut the door behind us.

"Um, hi," I say, still stunned by the sight of him. "I suppose you're our Santa?"

"I am Ded Moroz!" he announces proudly in a thick Russian accent. I thought he said "dead morose," but I wasn't sure.

"Hi, Dead. Nice to meet you."

"Ded Moroz," says a female voice out of nowhere. "Dedushka Moroz is the Russian version of Santa Claus. It means 'Grandfather Frost.'" Out from behind Mr. Frost steps a pretty, thin wisp of a girl dressed in a baby blue floor-length coat made of a shiny satin material. It, too, is trimmed in white fur, and her headdress is an ornate lace snowflake. The white braids cascading down from her headdress extend down past her waist. Her hands are buried in a furry white hand muff.

"Who are you?" I ask.

"I am Snegurochka, the Snow Maiden," she says with just a hint of the same Russian accent that Granddaddy Frost has. "Snegurochka is Ded Moroz's granddaughter."

"Are you two...?" I ask, pointing back and forth at the two of them.

"No!" she answers, like only a teenager can. It was as if I had just asked the dumbest question ever. "He's my mother's boyfriend."

"Ah, okay. Well, let's go around to the side door." We traipse through the six inches of fresh snow to the kitchen door. It's then that I remember the faint "Okay, but…" earlier as I was switching calls from Karen to Svetlana at Ho, Ho, Inc.. I think I know what the "Okay, but…" was all about now. My stomach knots up a little.

"All right, so, I'm Donna. I'm the event planner for this party," I say, sticking out my hand to shake both of theirs.

"Hi, I'm Anastasia. You can call me Ana."

"I am Anatoly Sergeievich Zhalobovskaia. Friends call me Pete."

"So, Pete, do you speak English?" I ask.

"Yes, little," he announces while Ana gives me a subtle shake of her head, nullifying his answer. Great, now my stomach is doing a full gymnastics routine. These guests haven't had nearly enough to drink to mistake this guy for a real Santa. "After the client is done giving his speech, he wants Santa to hand out gifts," I say, looking at Pete. Not getting any reaction, I direct my gaze at Ana. "Do you think we can do this?"

"Sure," she responds with a shrug. "I'll help him."

"Okay, just hang out here, and I'll come in and get you when it's time to hand out the gifts." Ana is explaining the plans to Mr. Moroz as I slip out of the kitchen and back into the party. Hef has concluded his speech and is mingling with a few of his guests as I sidle up beside him. He excuses himself from the people he is talking to and turns his attention to me.

"Santa is here, so we can go ahead with the presentation when you are ready," I say, just loud enough so only he can hear me.

"Okay, let's wait a little bit. How long is he here for?"

"We have him for an hour, but I can see if he can stay a little longer if need be," I respond, hoping against hope that we'll have enough time for everyone to get looped before Santa does his thing.

"See if they can wait an hour. I'd like to wait as long as possible. The crowd has a way of thinning out as soon as the gifts and bonuses are handed out," he says with a wry smile.

"Okay, I'm sure they'll be fine with that."

He gives me a quizzical look, and I immediately realize that Santa is not normally referred to as "they."

"The client wants to wait for about an hour before he brings you out. Are you two okay with that?" I ask.

"Da."

"Sure."

"Okay, just hang out here. Try to stay out of the way of the catering staff. Are you hungry?" I ask, alternating my gaze between the two of them.

"Da."

"Sure."

"I'll get the catering guys to put a plate together for you," I say in hopes that a little food and some coffee will bring our Santa back to life. Now I find myself in the precarious position of trying to get a crowd buzzed enough and a Santa sober enough so they can, somehow, meet in the middle. "Charles, my little elfin friend, I need you to go be a distraction," I say under my breath as I push him out the kitchen door." I follow him out the door and quietly blend in with the background, trying to assess our chances of getting out of here with our reputation intact. The crowd is loud and boisterous. The two bars we have set up in different rooms both have lines of people waiting for more drinks. Chuck, clad in his elf costume, and the models we hired as wait staff dressed in their bunny-Santa's helpers outfits are wonderful diversions. Just as I start to think this might work out, I pop back into the kitchen to find Ded/Anatoly/Pete asleep at the kitchen table. Ana is seated beside him, deeply engrossed in texting somebody. He's as relaxed as a wet rag, with his head tilted all the way back and his mouth wide open. Every once in a while he snorts as his body twitches in a minor spasm. It's not a pretty sight. I look around the kitchen, trying to find something to hit him over the head with when I spy an espresso machine.

"Do you know how to use that thing?" I ask one of the catering staff.

"Sure! If you find me something to brew, I'll whip you up a batch," replies the overly enthusiastic foodie.

"Okay," I say as I rummage through cabinets and the fridge. I hit the jackpot at the bottom shelf of the massive refrigerator and hand the bag to my new best friend. "Make it as strong as possible."

"You got it."

Within minutes he hands me a demitasse filled to the brim with the strongest espresso I've ever smelled. "Thank you—and keep 'em coming. I don't care if he doesn't sleep for a week; I need him awake in the next ten minutes," I say while sliding the cup across the table to Pete.

"Pete? Pete? Wake up. Come on, buddy, wake up," I say as I grab a handful of red velvet coat and shake him as violently as I can without actually shoving him out of his chair.

"Ana, a little help would be good."

She finishes her text, puts her phone in her pocket, and proceeds to pat Pete on the cheek. Pete snorts one last time, and his eyes pop open like they are spring-loaded. He looks around the room to get his bearings, looks at me, and recoils—and is finally comforted by the sight of Ana. She says something to him in Russian and hands him the espresso. He takes a sip, scrunches up his face, and shakes his head. He says something to her in Russian, and she looks at me and asks, "Can he get some sugar?"

Oh, this will be great: caffeine buzz and a sugar high. Well, at least he'll be awake. I look around the room and find the five-pound bag of sugar the catering crew is using for the coffee service. I grab a small bowl out of a cupboard and fill it up. I put the bowl of sugar and a spoon in front of Pete, and he pours a generous amount into his espresso and stirs. He takes another sip and nods in approval.

"Make sure he keeps drinking those," I say, pointing at Ana.

"Does that thing only make one cup at a time?" I ask my supplier.

"Yep."

"Well, do your best. Just keep him well supplied."

"Yes, ma'am."

While I leave Pete doing caffeine shooters, I push my way through the kitchen door, nearly knocking my client into the next week.

"Oh, Hef, I am so sorry. Are you okay?" I ask, thanking my lucky stars that I had prevented him from witnessing the dastardly deeds occurring in his kitchen. I slip my arm through his once he regains his balance and steer him back out to the party.

"I'm fine," he says, a bit startled. "I just wanted to see how things were going in there. How's our Santa?"

"Couldn't be better," I say while patting his hand. "Who is that lady over there in the green dress?" I ask, trying to direct his attention away from the kitchen. "I know I've seen her before, but I can't remember where."

"Oh, you know her. She's the wife of one my partners at the office," he says with a bit of impatience coating his words. Damn! I think he sees through my tactics. "I'm going to get everyone's attention in a few minutes. Once I announce that we have a special guest, have Santa come out, and we can hand out the gifts."

"Absolutely: special guest, Santa, gifts. Got it." I hustle him over to a group of people, and he's immediately swallowed up into their conversation. I spin a quick one-eighty and rush back to the kitchen. As I barge through the swinging door to the kitchen, one of Santa's bunny-elves does a pirouette in an astonishing feat of balance and acrobatics, trying to avoid me and spilling a tray full of pâté de foie gras. One more spin around and she is out the door with her tray. I don't even mind the dirty look she gives me. I notice, almost immediately, that Pete is on his feet and Ana is helping him straighten out his outfit. I also notice five empty cups on the table and a half-empty sugar bowl. On further inspection I notice a slight tremor in Pete's hands and that his eyes are as big as sewer lids. He's speed-talking in Russian to Ana, and he sounds like one of those TV announcers who do the disclaimers at the end of used car adverts, only with a lot more consonants. I'm quite sure if he doesn't slow down he's going to hurt himself. I put my hand on his shoulder and pat him on the chest.

"Are we ready to go?" I ask, looking at Ana.

"Uh, yeah," she says, a little amazed at Pete's miraculous return from the dead.

"Come over here and stand with me at the door. I'll let you know when to go out. Ded, you go out first, and you can follow him, Ana. There are envelopes on the Christmas tree. You need to take each one of those off the tree, call out the name written on it, and then hand it to that person when they come forward. It's pretty simple. Do you both understand that?" I ask, looking for some sign of comprehension from Pete. To my amazement, they both nod. "There are presents under the tree as well. Do the same thing with those after you give out the envelopes, okay?" Again, they both nod. Mere moments later we get the sign, and out the door they go.

"...and I'd like everybody to give our special guest a warm welcome," says Hef from the third step on the staircase in the foyer. All eyes turn toward the swinging door as Pete and Ana make their entrance. A polite round of applause is accompanied by a few snickers from the crowd. People are turning to the person next to them and making comments. Pete makes his way over to the tree and waves to everyone and gives a mighty thrust with his white staff. Ana, following close behind, takes on the personality of the shy snow maiden. Hef's brow furrows as he looks at Pete and then at me. *I watch as my career goes up in smoke. My fledgling company flushed down a whirlpool before my very eyes!*

"I am Dedushaka Moroz," Pete announces in a booming voice. "I am Grandfather Frost, and this is granddaughter, Snegurochka. She is Snow Maiden." I am relieved that everybody applauds, this time with fewer giggles. Maybe, just maybe, Santa's alcohol consumption and caffeine intake have reached some magical equilibrium. "I come to give gifts," he continues, "unless you have been bad. Then I freeze you," he says with another thrust of his white shaft, sending a wave of nervous denial through the crowd.

"What about the Snow Maiden? Can she party with us?" a male voice asks from the crowd. The rest of the males applaud with their approval.

"No!" says Pete, again with an angry, thunderous voice, quieting the raucous mob. "Snegurochka must not fall in love. If she falls in love, she melts."

All the males groan in disappointment, and the women let out a sarcastic "awww" in mock sympathy. I survey Hef's face for some sign that he's not going to throw us all out. His brow is still furrowed, but it looks to me like he's more curious now. At least that's what I'm hoping, and I'll cling to that for a little while.

Ana coyly hands her hand muff to one of the younger good-looking guys and asks him to hold it for her, whereupon Ded promptly freezes him with his shaft to the applause of the women and the groans of the men. Hoping to get more than just a hand muff out of the deal, the young man stays frozen.

"I tell you again. Be bad, I freeze you," says Ded.

Ana and Pete had started to warm the crowd up with their act. Pete hopelessly mispronounces every name he calls out, and Ana flirts with every one of the guys, only to have them flash frozen. Ded rewards the women, who have obviously been much better than the guys, with tiny bottles of vodka he retrieves from his coat pocket.

"Ver-o-nika," he calls out. A tall, curvaceous lady with a dangerously low neck line appears from the crowd. "Ohhhh," groans Ded. "*Lubov moya,*" he says, admiring the sight before him. "*Milaya moya,* you come live with me in Russia! Be *babushka* with me. I keep you warm at night." The crowd is hysterical, and the lady plays along perfectly. She puts a finger under Ded's chin and directs his gaze upward from her décolletage to her face.

"What will you give me if I agree to come with you?" she asks.

"I give you...this envelope!" he exclaims, holding it up, remembering he actually did have something to give her. "And all my wodka," he stammers.

"Don't do it, Ded—she's evil," says a voice from the crowd.

"Oh, don't listen to him, Ded," she whispers, "that's just my husband."

Pete peers around her at the crowd makes an angry face, and vigorously shakes his shaft. "Quiet, or I freeze all of you!" By this time the crowd is doubled over in laughter.

"I'd be happy to be *babushka* with you, Ded, but you'll have to do better than that to get me to move to frosty ol' Russia," she says while running her fingers up his intricately carved scepter.

At that she sashays off stage, leaving a quivering Ded behind. His face has turned a shade of red not unlike that of his coat.

Ana quickly saves the moment by stuffing another envelope in his hand and says, "Ah, Dedulya, remember what they say about old dogs who chase cars..."

One lady spews a sip of chardonnay across the room. Ded sits down on the steps as dejected as any man I've ever seen. By this time the guests are laughing so hard they're crying. After they compose themselves, Ded and Snegurochka finish handing out the bonuses and gifts. Evidently, most of the men had misbehaved badly during the year and are admonished by Ded to be better or he'd be back to freeze them again next year. It doesn't take long until all the women are huddled around Pete and most of the men have been frozen. The guys happily go along with it because they know a kiss from Ana will free them from their immobility.

I notice that the elf bunnies are not at all happy that the attention has been taken away from them, so I gather them in the kitchen and tell them not to worry—Ded and Sneg will be out of there in short order. They take the news rather well and are soon out serving up more drinks and food. Ded intercepts a dirty martini off a passing tray and makes a toast.

"I vant for to make toast," he says with a dramatic flair. "Over the lips and troo da gums to grandmother's house we go," bringing peals of laughter from the crowd, and they respond in unison with "Nastrovya!"

"No, no, my friends. We no say *Na zdorovje*! Say *budem zdorovy*!" The guests manage to mangle that and down whatever they had in their glasses.

"What's that mean?" someone shouts.

"'Let's stay healthy,'" says Snegurochka.

"How do you say 'Let's get hammered'?"

"*Davaĭte napivat'sya*," replies Ded.

"Donna," Hef says as he walks up beside me, "I have to tell you I was more than a little worried about these two when I first saw them." I didn't have the heart to tell him that I almost wet myself when I saw the look on his face when they first entered the room. "This was hilarious. I never thought about getting a prank Santa for this. Where did you find these two?" he asks with a little chuckle.

Prank? This was no prank! This was proof that there is a parallel universe where the laws of nature are absurdly altered, and we, somehow, ended up there tonight. This reminds me that I now have to recall all the things I said I'd give up in my prayer of desperation to whichever deity was listening. I hope I didn't say anything about drinking. I'm going to need some liquid therapy after this.

"Oh," I say, trying to think up a plausible answer, "you know us. We're always trying to go for that 'wow' factor."

"Well, you managed that, at least. Make sure we get them again next year."

Whew, that was a huge relief. Sadly, though, there won't be a next year for Ded and Sneg. A couple of days later I read in the newspaper that Ho, Ho, Inc. was busted as a front for a Russian prostitution ring. Pete was the ring leader, and Ana was one of the girls. They went out on a few gigs just to make it look legit. It was a real shame, too; I could have made a lot of money off of them…but I guess it doesn't pay to be on Santa's *naughty* list.

CHAPTER 6

Someone Borrowed, Someone Blue

March is not a big month for weddings, but the bride and groom were determined. In this case the groom was to graduate from the ROTC program at Colorado State University. The bride was to graduate at the same time from the University of Northern Colorado with a degree in physics. They wanted to spend as much time as possible with each other before he went off to his advanced training and she started on her master's degree.

When Sam, Phil, and I first met with Amy and Chad, we didn't have to explain how iffy the weather can be in March in Colorado. They knew it could be seventy and clear or snowing so hard you couldn't see across the street. They were young, in love, and very determined. They were the cutest couple ever. He looked like a little toy soldier, and she was a petite little thing with the straightest, shiniest blond hair I've ever seen. They had that optimism that somehow is replaced with cautiousness as one grows older. It was refreshing and exciting just to be around them.
It made me optimistic, too.

They had chosen a nice hotel in Loveland, Colorado, for the wedding and reception. Everyone would stay there, and relatives and friends from all corners of the country had been invited. Loveland held a special place in their hearts since it is equidistant from their respective alma maters, and they had gone there on several dates. Besides, how could you pass up a chance to be married in a town called "Loveland"? That was infinitely better than the couple I knew who spent their honeymoon on Battle Lake!

"I haven't met many on Chad's side, and he hasn't met any of my crazy crew," Amy says, beaming with enthusiasm. "This will be a wedding and family reunion all in one!" she continues. "A large group of people who are seeing each other for the first time will become family with just a couple of 'I dos.' Isn't that amazing?" Her mood was infectious.

Sam, Phil, and I drove up three days before the wedding and checked into our rooms. So far, everything was going like clockwork. Phil checked with the band, and they were locked in. They were to arrive three hours before the reception and set up. The photographer was confirmed. Everything from limos to linens should be there on time.

"If all weddings were this easy, I wouldn't mind doing them," I say to Sam while we are unpacking.

"Well, I hate to be the voice of reality, but you know this is a rarity, right?" she says while hanging her clothes in the closet.

"Yeah, I know. A girl can dream though," I say wistfully.

"Dream on girl, dream on."

The hotel has the food and drinks covered, but Nelson is personally delivering the cake the day before the wedding. His SUV is equipped with a frame that can take a Faberge Egg through a rollover without a scratch. He has arranged for a master pastry chef to decorate his masterpiece with edible flowers.

I'm puzzled by Phil's mood when we meet in the hotel bar for a drink. This will be the smoothest wedding we've ever planned. The bride is the opposite of TBOF (The Bride of Frankenstein), and everyone involved is smitten with her. The couple is looking forward to a perfect day for themselves plus all their family and they are thrilled to death with the disco band we got for them and couldn't be happier with everything else we've done. These are the kind of people you don't mind going above and beyond the call of duty for. Yet, Phil's mood is unusually grim.

"What could go wrong?" I ask.

"Um, have you checked the forecast since we got here?" he asks with a bit of concern in his voice.

"Um, nooooo," I answer. "Why, what's up?"

"We're going to get dumped on! The whole Front Range is getting ten to twelve inches," he fires back.

"Oh, they get the forecast wrong all the time. We've got three days until the wedding. That forecast can change a million times by then," I say. "Besides, when was the last time they closed the airport in March? I'm sure DIA can handle a little snow."

Phil polishes off his beer and says, "I'm sorry, Donna. It's just these long trips are starting to wear on me. Saturday is my twentieth wedding anniversary, and I won't be there. Kathy and the twins are down with flu, and I just feel guilty. Regardless, I have a bad feeling about this one."

It suddenly dawns on me that we have been working some long, hard hours for the last six months, and it has taken its toll.

"If you need a break, all you have to do is let me know," I say. "Chuck and Bob have been itching to run an event. This would be perfect for them."

Suddenly, Phil's on the defensive. He orders another beer and says, "Those guys are great, but they could never handle all these details. I've seen them spend two hours spacing tables just right. They'd be rearranging the flowers till the last minute and totally forget about something else!" His professionalism has taken over. He took this job on, and, by golly, he's going to see it through.

Before I can respond, I see Chad and Amy's hometown pastor walking toward our table. He is as kind and soft-spoken as they come. We talk about how Amy's father died when she was young and how she is relying on her favorite uncle to walk her down the aisle. He is coming from Vermont. Her mother is coming from Miami.

"I understand we might have a problem with the weather," says the pastor as calmly as he possibly can.

"Yeah," I say sympathetically. "We're watching it and hoping for the best."

"If it gets bad, is there a possibility of postponing it a day or two?"

"That all depends on whether the hotel already has its rooms booked. It might not work with most people's travel schedule, but, yeah, I was going to talk to the banquets manager about that," adds Phil.

The next day (two days before the wedding) it has turned gray, and the wind has started to howl. We start monitoring the weather on an hourly basis. It looks like the weatherman got it right this time. Damn! Nelson arrives a day early.

"Better a stale cake than none at all," he says. "I got my pastry chef to make the flowers a day early. The crew is storing everything in the walk-in."

HOTELS BOOK BALLROOMS months in advance of an event, sometimes years! You can't very well cancel because of the weather. We cross our fingers that the storm, which the weather service was predicting to reach biblical proportions, would let up. Fortunately, the band thought like Nelson and arrived a day early. I keep repeating my Event Mantra to myself and the crew: "There are things you can control, and things you can't. Take care of what you can, and play the rest by ear."

THE NEXT DAY, after strategizing with my crew, I reach for the phone and punch the zero.

"Hotel operator, how may I direct your call?" says the voice on the other end of the line.

"Um, yeah, I need to speak with Ron, the banquets manager, please."

"My pleasure to connect you."

"Banquets, this is Ron."

"Hi, Ron, it's Donna. How are you?"

"Not too bad. How are you?"

"I'd be a lot better if we didn't have a blizzard threatening to blow away my wedding," I say dejectedly.

"Yeah, this is supposed to be a biggy."

"If the storm shuts everything down, do you have a ballroom available where we could do it if we have to delay things a day or two?"

"Lemme look," he says, followed by a few seconds of silence. "Well, Sunday is completely open, but it will be tight if we go to Monday.

We have a pretty large conference starting, and they have everything booked up except one of the smaller rooms. I'm not sure you'd fit everybody in there. We'd have to get the general manager's okay to switch it, though, and he's out of town, so that leaves us with our assistant GM—and good luck with that."

"What do you mean?" I ask.

"Well, let's just say he's young and rather intransigent," he says, while being more diplomatic than he'd like. I'm quite sure there are other words he'd rather use to describe him.

"Can you transfer me to his office?" I ask.

"Sure, hang on."

"Assistant General Manager's office, Mr. Buchanan speaking," says the very young voice, trying its best to sound a lot older. Nice try, Sonny, but I ain't calling you *Mr. Buchanan!*

"Yes, hi, this is Donna Vessey. I'm the event manager for the wedding that's supposed to happen tomorrow."

"Ah, yes, Mrs. Vessey, how are you?" *Mrs. Vessey?!* I can't even recall the last time anybody called me that.

"Well, I'd be a lot better if you could cancel the blizzard," I say, trying to lighten things up a little.

"Well, I wish I could, but you know, there isn't a thing I can do about that," he says so seriously that it's blatantly obvious he has no idea I was kidding.

"Okay, so, here's my question," I say, getting to the point. "If this storm shuts down the airport and messes up everybody's travel plans, we might have to delay the wedding a day or two. I talked with Ron in banquets, and he says it's not a problem on Sunday and Monday will be tight, but there is one room we could use. What do we have to do to make sure that can happen?"

"Well, I'd have to look at your file first, but we would have to rewrite the contract, and we'd have to charge you extra for the room rental."

"But wait, if it's delayed and we don't use the room on Saturday, can't you use what we've paid already and just move it to Sunday or Monday?" I ask, sensing that this isn't going to end well.

"No, ma'am. If you don't use the ballroom on Saturday, you'll end up forfeiting that money, and we'll have to charge you for any additional room rental. Additionally, Ron may have spoken out of turn regarding the rental of a ballroom for Sunday or Monday. I'd have to approve any rentals for Sunday, and we typically hold an extra room for a conference of the size that will be starting here Monday."

"So what you're saying," you little shit (I say with my inside voice), "is that if it doesn't happen as scheduled on Saturday, we're out of luck."

"Yes, ma'am, that appears to be the case."

There are very few times in my life when I've actually been able to feel my blood pressure rise. I feel it increase to the point that I'm afraid my head is going to burst like a balloon. My head is swimming, and I sit down on my bed and allow myself to flop backward. I stare at the ceiling for a few minutes until Sam comes into the room.

"Whoa, missy, what happened?" she asks. "You look like…well, never mind what you look like. What's up?"

I allow a low groan to emanate from somewhere deep in my body. Sam stands by the edge of the bed and looks down on me.

"That bad, huh?" she says with her hands on her hips. "You wanna go with that?"

"I just had a little chat with the assistant general manager," I say, closing my eyes.

"Oh, you mean Mr. Buchanan? I met him in the lobby. He's très impressed with himself. I thought he was a college intern. What did he have to say?"

"Basically, if we don't have the wedding tomorrow, as planned, Chad and Amy are pretty much screwed."

"What do you mean?" she asks turning a bright shade of red. "They have to have ballrooms available for Sunday, and they can't be completely sold out on Monday!"

"Well, they do have rooms Sunday, but they would forfeit the money they paid for the rooms on Saturday, and they have a big conference that's taking up most of the ballrooms on Monday. So, if the guests can't arrive today as planned, the whole thing is flushed down the toilet."

"Well, then, I guess we're going to have a cozy little wedding. They just closed DIA. None of the family would be able to make it here by then anyway."

Again, I let out a low groan and try to sit up. I call Amy's room and ask her and Chad to meet me in the bar. I need to give them the bad news, and I figure we can all use a drink. When she comes off the elevator, I hug her, and she breaks down in tears. She knows their families won't make it. A few of them got to Denver before the storm hit, but unless Avis has started renting snowmobiles, they aren't going to make it to Loveland.

The lobby is full of angry, panicked travelers, and we try to find a quiet corner to sit and visit. You can catch snippets of the cell phone conversations.

"I love you, too. I'm sure they'll open the airport tomorrow."

"I know, Sweetie—we'll just have to celebrate your birthday a little late."

"I know they wanted the presentation in the morning!"

"Hey, it's springtime in the Rockies. What can you expect?"

"Well, when *is* the next flight!"

Everyone is stressed and unhappy. It's the worst blizzard in years.

I call Phil's room, and he comes down to meet us. Even stressed out, his mind is working overtime on a solution, and we are both trying to comfort Amy and Chad.

"This is one of those moments when you find out what you're really made of," Phil says, trying to be philosophical.

"It's like untangling Christmas tree lights," I add. "With a lot of patience and the right mindset, you can do it."

Phil is listing the pros and cons. "The pros are we have a bride and groom, a minister, the cake, and the band. We have a ballroom and enough food for a couple hundred people." There's really only one con, but it's a biggie: We don't have the guests!"

Amy looks around her and says, "Look at all these people. They're stuck here just like us. They're away from their families, too. They're all angry and upset."

I begin to relate my conversation with the assistant general manager to Phil, Chad, and Amy. I'm a few minutes into the story when I notice that Amy is no longer at the table. How did I miss her leaving? I look around the lobby bar, and, to my amazement, Amy has climbed up on one of the chairs at the concierge desk; then, one foot after the other, she summits the desk.

"Oh, my God, what on earth is she doing?" I ask incredulously.

"I don't know, but this ought to be good," replies Phil with a huge grin. Chad looks at us for direction, and Phil puts his hand on Chad's shoulder and smiles.

Amy is small, only five foot two, but up on that desk she towers above the crowd.

"Excuse me, ladies and gentlemen," she starts out. Only one or two people notice her timid little voice. It's then that I notice she's wearing a sweater that's much too big for her, a pair of flannel pajama bottoms, and a pair of big pink fluffy slippers. Her hair is pulled back in a ponytail, and she doesn't have a speck of makeup on. She looks absolutely darling. She musters up the courage, folds her hands in front of her, and tries again.

"Excuse me, ladies and gentlemen," she belts out with more gusto than I thought possible. "I'm sorry to interrupt, but, please, bear with me for a few minutes." This time even the front desk clerks look up from their computers and listen. "My fiancé and I are to be married here tomorrow at one o'clock. Our families and friends are obviously not going to make it." There's a catch in her voice, and she pauses to regain her composure. She has everybody's rapt attention now. "They're stranded all over the country. Probably feeling like a lot of you folks," she continues, "frustrated and anxious." The crowd draws nearer. "Chad and I have looked forward to this day for a long time," she says.

"Oh, my God," I say under my breath.

"Yep, this is going to be good," whispers Phil. Chad looks at us like he still doesn't get it.

"We would be honored if each and every one of you would be our guests at our wedding and reception tomorrow at 1 P.M."

The entire lobby erupts in applause. Phil claps his hands together and lets out a loud "*Yes!*" Chad rushes over to the concierge desk to help his blushing bride down from her perch. Our little bride managed to, in one fell swoop, change the mood of everybody in that hotel. It's as if all the anxiety, ire, and disappointment had vanished in the blink of an eye.

That night, the hotel staff hand drew an invitation, made copies of it, and slipped it underneath the doors of all the occupied rooms. The next day, everyone stuck at that hotel shows up for the wedding. The dinner has been changed from a plated dinner to a buffet since none of the hotel staff can make it through the snow. The staff members unlucky enough to be working the day before have spent the night at the hotel and are working their third shift in a row. Nelson guides the skeleton crew in the kitchen, and everything works perfectly. Amy looks beautiful in her long white dress, and Phil gives her away. The minister asks everyone to offer up thanks to all their new friends in the room. There isn't a dry eye in the house.

It's quite a scene—strangers dancing with each other and having a wonderful time. The band plays two hours past their time for no charge. I've put on dozens of weddings, but this one reminds me of what it's really all about. It's not the size of the cake or the diamond ring. It's about people sharing a special moment they will never forget.

The little gift shop at the hotel was sold out of everything that could be remotely considered a wedding gift. Most of the gifts have been wrapped in newspaper, with toilet paper serving as ribbons. The cheesy little gifts they've gotten from that crowd will probably mean more to them than any toaster they'd have gotten otherwise. The amazing thing is Amy and Chad collected over $5,000 in cash and checks that evening. They have a unique story to tell their children and grandchildren. They'll have a reception in a couple of weeks with all the people who couldn't make it, and while they're catching up, they'll share an album full of pictures of strangers who made their wedding day very special. I wonder how many lives have been changed that afternoon. How many of them have come to realize the big picture? When life hands you some big, fat, snow-covered lemons, you make the best lemonade ever!

CHAPTER 7

There's No Business Like Ho Business

"No one can know of this," Nelson yells through my office door while I'm changing. "Not even your cat."

"I get it," I yell back as I pull the world's tightest miniskirt over fishnet stockings. I top this off with a sequined sleeveless blouse that barely makes it over a padded bra that magically changes a 34B to a 36D. Who needs surgery? "You can come in now; I'm...uh...indecent." Sometimes I just can't resist a bad joke.

While I love all the details of planning an event, the theatrical side of me also loves being part of the entertainment. Every now and again a gig comes to us that allows me to do just that. This particular one came through Nelson, oddly enough. He has a friend who is a senior partner in one of the bigger law firms in Denver. The occasion is the closing dinner marking the end of a three-day conference on international intellectual property law. Joe Smith (the names have been changed to protect the guilty) wants to prank a buddy of his, another partner in his firm who is celebrating a monumental birthday that very night.

Nelson barely notices my very curly blond wig. My mascara is almost too much for my eyelids to support. Sam is about to arrive, probably looking even trashier than I am.

"Now, listen," I say, grabbing Nelson by the shirt collar with both hands. "Everyone knows how you feel about Sam. So, when she gets here, don't criticize her costume because that's all it is! A costume! Got it?"

Nelson has no room to criticize anybody's outfit anyway. He's clad in flip flops, khaki shorts, and a Hawaiian shirt with kittens in grass skirts and hula hoops all over it.

"Why would I do that?" he says with a shrug. "She never comments on my clothing."

I add a second coat of bright red lipstick and face him. He is quite a picture with that shirt, his big goofy glasses, and a fanny pack. I am about to launch into a lecture about how it wouldn't hurt to wear a suit and tie every once in a while, as Sam walks in.

Nelson does a double take, let's his jaw drop, and goes into a state of shock. She is wearing four-inch stiletto heels, and her heavily padded butt is offsetting her heavily padded chest. She is wearing a Spandex skirt that barely covers her naughty bits and a gold lamé top that plunges deeply in the front *and* the back. I'm similarly attired, and yet Sam gets the big reaction. What am I? Chopped liver?

"You're not going anywhere in that outfit!" he almost growls at her.

"This is a gig, and a rather lucrative one, Buddy," Sam snaps back. "And, I might add, *you're* the one who booked it. I *will* promise not to bend over, but only because, if I did, I wouldn't be able to straighten back up. Besides, I have a pair of spandex shorts on," she says as she hikes her skirt up. "Nobody's gonna see anything they wouldn't see if they saw me at the gym."

"Yeah, but…" Nelson stammers.

They try to out glare each other for a couple of minutes as I stand by, the invisible, forgotten member of this triad.

"Okay, you two," I say, trying to break the tension. "It's time for us tramps to hit the road."

"I'm going with you," Nelson declares. "You two need protection." By "you two" he means Sam. I could have been abducted by aliens at that very moment, and he wouldn't have noticed.

"Not tonight, Big Guy. We're going deep, deep undercover on this op. We can't afford to have our cover blown by somebody wearing a shirt with kittens on it," I declare as I grab Sam and determinedly attempt to walk out of the room. Somehow, my wobbling on high heels, about to fall on my butt, ruins the effect.

I WHEEL MY Acura SUV into the parking garage a block from the conference center. We arrive with plenty of time to spare since the directions our client gave us to the door, where we are to meet him, are anything but clear. We take the elevator down to street level and make our way out to the sidewalk. It's early evening, dark, and traffic on the streets is pretty heavy. It's also a Friday night. Sam and I are engrossed in looking at the map and the directions we'd been given, and we're busy trying to find street signs to get our bearings. It takes us a little while to figure out that the honks of the horns from the passing cars are actually for us.

Suddenly, out of nowhere, a voice says, "Ladies, I need to see some ID."

I look at Sam and she at me. The looks on our faces are pure puzzlement. I slowly turn and see two of Denver's finest on bicycles. The blood suddenly rushes from my face. *Oh, holy...*

"Hi, officers—this isn't what it looks like," I say, heaping on the charm.

"It never is," he replies. "ID please."

Sam doesn't have a purse, and I only brought a teeny, tiny little thing to carry my car keys.

"We don't have it with us," I say coyly. "But, I just parked in that parking garage, and we can get them for you." A visual flashes through my mind of Sam and me sitting in a grungy cell somewhere in downtown Denver, waiting for my husband to come bust us out. It's not a pretty picture. The thought of a strip search makes me weak at the knees.

"What are your names?" queries his partner.

"Okay, look, my name is Donna Vessey, and this is Samantha Stephens. I own an event planning company, and Sam works with me. We've been hired by a lawyer at the conference going on at the convention center," I say, pointing at the building behind us. "We're here to play a prank on one of his friends."

It dawns on me that I never go anywhere without business cards. I quickly reach for my purse, and one of the bicycle cops grabs my arm.

"Whoa, keep your hands where I can see them," he says, suddenly turning more harsh than I thought necessary for the situation.

"I have business cards in my purse. You can look in there and find them."

He takes the purse by the gold chain hanging from my shoulder and opens it up.

"Is there anything dangerous in here? Any needles or knives?"

"No, officer, there's nothing in there except my car keys and, hopefully, a few business cards." He takes out my car keys and looks at them. He pauses at the Acura key ring and studies the other keys. He then runs his fingers through the bag while visually inspecting the contents. He pulls out a business card and reads it very carefully.

"So, this is you?" he asks, flashing the front of the card at me. I see that it is, in fact, one of mine.

"Yes, sir, that's me," I reply.

He hands the card to his partner, who looks at it intently and turns away from us to speak into the microphone clipped to his collar. I'm frantic now. The extra time we allowed for finding our rendezvous point is rapidly evaporating.

"So, we see two ladies, dressed as you are, meeting somebody at the convention center. What are we supposed to think?" he asks, still looking through my little, bitty purse.

"I know what you are thinking. We really aren't in that line of business. We don't do it often, but occasionally people hire us to play practical jokes."

At that point, Starsky taps Hutch on the shoulder. He hands the business card back to his partner and shakes his head.

"She's got an unpaid parking ticket, that's all." Oops, forgot about that!

"Well, we might have to call the paddy wagon and have you ladies hauled away for the evening," he says, handing me back my purse.

"In the future, you might want to wait until you get to your party to change into costumes like this," adds his partner.

"Yeah, lesson learned," I say.

"So, are we free to go?" asks Sam.

"Yes ladies, you are free to go."

Just then a passing car full of guys honks, and the passengers yell some things I can't write in this book because my mother will probably read it. Starsky quickly writes down their license plate number and turns his attention back to us.

"Good night, ladies. Have fun."

With a quick thanks we take off.

WE HUSTLE TO the side of the convention center and see our client surveying the passing crowd. As we approach, his expression turns from one of concern to one of total and utter shock.

"Are you Joe?" I ask.

"Yes. Yes, I am. And I'm hoping like hell you are Donna and Sam."

"Yes, I'm Donna. This is Sam," I say with a chuckle.

"Oh, this is going to be good," he says with an evil grin. His gives us the "once over" a couple of times and, very furtively, slips a photo out of his suit coat of William, the birthday boy. "You'll be able to spot him right away. He's at the table that's right up front and to the right of the stage. He's wearing a gray sport coat. I think he's the only one in the room who isn't wearing a black or navy blue suit. And, remember, your cue is when I say, 'In closing, I'd like to thank…' That's when you can come in and do your thing."

"Got it," we say in unison.

WE HAD TO do a little research for this one. The week before our gig, I asked Phil to find a "gentlemen's club" close to the convention center. He found one called the Kit Kat Club. Despite the clichéd name, it was famous throughout the state and definitely *not* the sort of establishment William would frequent.

"Oddly, I've never heard anyone say they've been there," Phil said. "And, yet, when I peeked inside, the place was packed, despite the rather exorbitant cover charge."

While Sam and I are not quite as youthful and curvy as the girls at the Kit Kat Club, we are confident in our ability to pull this off (so to speak). We stand outside the door to the ballroom and wait for our cue. Once Joe starts into the end of his speech, Sam and I barge through the door, take a second to gain our balance and straighten out our outfits and march boldly through the crowd of well-dressed attorneys. We clomp, real lady-like, up the stairs of the stage and to the podium and push Joe out of the way. Sam wraps one of our red boas around his neck and sends him packing.

"Yeah, yeah, yeah, thank you so much. I'm sure we're all glad that's over with," I say into the microphone.

By now, the crowd is laughing and figuring the joke is on Joe, who leaves the stage looking convincingly puzzled and irritated. Kudos to Joe for playing his part well! Sam rolls her eyes melodramatically and leans into the mike and says, "We hear our friend Billy Boy is in the house, and we need to see him," she drawls.

From the nervous laughter, we can tell everyone heard her. I yawn, check my nails, and look around the room.

"Yeah, Billy," I say in my best kewpie doll voice. "We heard it's your birthday, and we thought we'd come over and liven things up for you on account of how generous you've been with your tips over at the Kit Kat all these years."

By now, everyone is looking at William, who is probably slouching as low in his seat as I've ever seen a person slouch.

"Ya know," drawls Sam, "ya'll can come over to the Kit Kat after this stuffed shirt convention and catch our act. We're the Kane sisters. I'm Kandi, and this here's Sugar, but it's pretty easy to tell that I'm sweeter… and younger."

I glare at Sam, but I am only half-acting. *That* wasn't in the script!

I SEE JOE over in the corner barely containing himself. The crowd goes silent as I scan the room while snapping my gum. "Come on, Billy," I say. "It'll be just like old times." We make a show of adjusting our skirts down and our bodices up as if suddenly realizing we are out of our element.

IT'S PRETTY EASY to spot William at this point. He's the one looking like you do when you are praying the teacher doesn't call on you.

"Oh! There you are!" I exclaim and rush offstage to give the guest of honor a big hug and a kiss on the cheek.

The crowd enthusiastically cheers and claps.

In my best baby doll voice, I ask the crowd if anyone can loan me a chair. Suddenly, a chair appears on stage as if by magic while I drag Billy back up with me. With a little firm coaxing, Kandi and Sugar put Billy in the hot seat.

"Seeing as how we're dancers and Billy here is our best customer," Sam says, "we think it's only appropriate that we give him a little performance on the house." The crowd goes wild.

We shimmy our hips to more applause. "We don't just dance. We sing, too," I say as I drape one of our red feather boas around "Billy's" neck. We both lean over him on either side and cover his cheeks with bright red kisses. Then, in our best Marilyn Monroe voices we sing "Happy Birthday" to him. All the lawyers join in as the hotel staff rolls in an enormous cake with way too many candles.

"You know how to do this, don't you, Billy?" I purr. "You just put your lips together and blow." With promises to see him later, we make sure everyone sees us give him a faux hotel room key card and make our exit, blowing kisses to everyone.

On our way out, a middle-aged, slightly intoxicated, and rather bloated barrister says to Sam, "Hey, babe! How 'bout I buy you a drink, and then we can go up to my room for a little 'private dancing'?"

Before I can react, Sam has the guy by the necktie and whispers something in his ear. The poor guy turns chili pepper red and beats a hasty retreat away from us.

As we make our grand exit to the applause of the crowd, I lean over and ask Sam what that was all about.

"Oh, he was an acquaintance of my dearly departed husband. I just asked if he would like to invite his wife, Isabelle, along for the ride."

"Poor guy, looked like he was going to have a heart attack."

"I'm pretty sure Isabelle would've sent me a thank you note…"

CHAPTER 8

Dances with Donkeys

If someone had told me six months ago that one of my most memorable gigs would involve maneuvering my way around donkey "pies," I would have thought, "Someone's from Crazy Town!" It turns out, at least for this gig, that I was apparently the *mayor* of Crazy Town.

This gig was yet another referral. Once you've built a rep in this business, it's like *Field of Dreams*. "If you do it, they will come." We had been hired to do a dog show a while back, and the client was so pleased that she recommended us every chance she got. Designing a dog show was easy. It was just a theatrical production with mutts. A donkey show was just scaled up a little, right? How different could it be?

When I describe this gig to Chuck and Bob, their hands flutter in the air like a pair of deranged hummingbirds.

"Well, I hope we don't make asses of ourselves," Chuck says, who immediately receives a sharp poke in the ribs from Bob.

Phil and Nelson, though, take it all in stride. Phil starts by pulling the file on the dog show and writing down detailed notes on the logistics of doing a donkey auction. How does he know all these things? I doubt he's been within one hundred yards of a donkey in his life! Nelson is already dreaming up everything he can do for a real "down-home" southwestern feast.

Even Sam is jumping on the bandwagon (or should I say hay wagon?). She's already got outfitting our crew and clients under control.

David and I go to meet our clients, Lucille and Kenny, a month or so before the event. When Lucille picks us up at the airport, she looks like she just came off the set of *Gunsmoke*. She is every bit of six feet tall, even without her cowboy (girl?) hat. Her boots have definitely kicked some… well, you know. The term "distressed leather" barely does them justice. The ride from the airport is a bone-jarring ordeal in her old pickup truck. The well-maintained roads in town quickly turn to pothole-riddled county roads and then to teeth-rattling dirt roads on the long drive out to their home. I am worried about kidney failure by the time we get to the ranch. On our way from the truck to the house we pass by a corral occupied by a few horses

"I WAS BORN and raised on this ranch," she says as she pulls a carrot from her back pocket. Who keeps carrots in their back pockets? Holding one end of the carrot between her teeth, she leans into the nearest horse stall. The head of a magnificent stallion appears and gently takes the carrot from her mouth.

We are joined by her husband, Kenny. "Now, that's what I call a kiss!" she says with a broad grin that makes her deeply tanned and weathered face crinkle all over. The sun gets pretty intense here. I make a mental note to bring a vat of SPF one thousand sunblock and an extra wide sombrero to this event.

"Yep, we're the fifth generation on this spread," she says proudly, draping her arm around Kenny's shoulders. Her voice has that sort of roughness that comes from eating a lot of dust and washing it down with the occasional bourbon. Kenny looks as much like the Marlboro Man as anyone I've ever seen.

So it is that David and I wound up standing next to a barn on a warm New Mexico day in April. The whole place is quite picturesque, but the odor makes my cat's litter box smell like a bouquet of fresh flowers.

We have been invited up to discuss the set design, logistics, and so on for the upcoming donkey auction. David doesn't normally get too excited about photographing my events, but this is well outside of the ordinary, and it definitely gets his creative juices flowing.

After scoping out the stables and the open space, we hop in the couple's pickup and take a quick tour around their ranch, ending up at the most impressive ranch-style log home I have ever seen. The house is approximately ten thousand square feet, created from logs harvested from their land. They point out the sections that have been added since its initial construction. I can't wait to have my whole crew here. They will love this place.

Once we are in our room, I start to rummage through my suitcase for a pair of jeans that say, "I'm at home here at the O.K. Corral." Then my dietary concerns kick in.

"I'm sure they are serious carnivores," I say with some resignation.

"Just be honest, and tell them we're vegans," David says. That makes sense, but I still consider feigning a migraine to get out of dinner. In the end, David explains that while we aren't on a crusade or trying to convert anybody, we are vegans, and the massive roast Lucille just hauled out of the oven isn't part of our diet. They couldn't have been more gracious.

"Well, if you don't mind salad, potatoes, and my secret-recipe cowboy beans, I think you'll do just fine," our hostess says.

Over dinner, Kenny explains that, while cattle are their main business, they do raise other farm animals along with the donkeys.

"I've paid a pretty penny for those little critters," says Lucille as she loads our plates up. "Up to fifteen grand for some of them."

"What's their job around the ranch?" I ask, still trying to figure out why anybody would have any donkeys, much less expensive ones, lounging about. Kenny and Lucille burst out laughing and look at us like we don't get out much.

"Nothin' darlin'," says Lucille, adding, "but they sure are cute."

I think really, really hard, and I'm pretty sure I've never heard the words "cute" and "donkey" in the same sentence. I'm having my horizons broadened in ways I never imagined.

"They're more like pets than anything else," she explains.

"Yeah, it's not normal, but they are fun to have around," adds Kenny. "We buy them as an investment and hire them out for stud. A lot of people show them, but we never got into that. Every now and then we hold an auction to help get rid of some of them if we start to get overcrowded. We have other breeders come so they can sell theirs at the same time.

We figure, why not make it a big ol' party? It's the only time we get to see some of our old friends." They can see that we are still not getting it, and Lucille and Kenny exchange a knowing grin.

"After dinner, we'll go out and introduce you to them," says Lucille.

Okay, I think to myself. These two are having way too much fun with us. I sense something sneaky is going on, and hopefully, this will solve the mystery.

Over dinner we discuss a wide range of subjects, but we finally get around to talking about the auction. Turns out they've been doing this for years, but they always have tried to put it all together by themselves. That is, until two years ago. The event had grown into something more than just the sale of the donkeys and ended up being more of a party than anything else. It had become overwhelming, and they had decided to hire an event planning company to help out. Well, as much as I hate to say it, not all event planners are reputable, law-abiding citizens. They had found somebody on the Internet, met with him, and contracted with him to handle the event. They gave him a deposit and never saw him again.

"There ain't a magician alive who could have made him disappear any faster," Kenny says with a chuckle.

"That didn't do much for our opinion of event planners—I'll tell you that right up front," says Lucille, her voice laced with a little venom. "We went back to doing it ourselves last year, but our friends that you did the dog show for said we owed it to ourselves to call you."

I make a mental note to write a "Thank You" note.

"We were actually thinking about scrapping the whole thing and shipping our donkeys off somewhere else to get them sold, but as long as you don't disappear with our money, I think we'll be back to having a great time," says Kenny, leaning back in his chair.

"I can completely underst…" I begin to defend my profession.

"No, no, don't worry about it, Miss Donna," interrupts Kenny. "We checked you out seven ways from Sunday. Everybody we talked to sang your praises so much we were going to take you out to the pond and see if you could actually walk on water."

"Well, thank you, sir," I say while blushing a bright, crimson red.

"I appreciate your trust and confidence. I know it's hard to recover from an episode like that."

After we clear the table, we walk out to one of the barns on the property. Lucille undoes the chain on the gate to the corral and secures it behind us once we are all in.

"Watch your step in here—I haven't had a chance to clean out this place today," she says while looking around for any donkey droppings.

I look around in the fading sunlight and think, "Okay, maybe wearing my favorite loafers was probably not the best idea I've had lately." Evidently the sound of the gate opening and closing is enough to get the attention of the animals, and we hear the hoof beats from inside the barn. David and I watch the large barn door attentively, awaiting the prized possessions of our hosts. As the first donkey emerges from the barn, Lucille and Kenny turn to us to watch our reactions.

"Oh…My…God…" I say in total disbelief. David just starts laughing. We've been set up, and this is the punch line. These are miniature donkeys! Mini-mules! And yes, they are cute. Kenny and Lucille are beaming. They know this was the last thing we were expecting, and you can tell this isn't the first time they've sprung this on unsuspecting guests. Some of them are actually quite friendly, though some keep their distance from the strangers in their stall.

"We can't tell the others about this," I say as one of the more friendly ones sidles up to me for some attention.

"Yeah, I think we can have some fun with this," adds David, still chuckling at the sight of these diminutive donkeys.

"I keep expecting one of them to start talking and sound like Eddie Murphy from the *Shrek* movies," I say. They are about the size of a Great Dane, only wider, and they get the "leans" just like any big, friendly dog. One of them cozies up to David and just about knocks him over.

We are still in a mild state of shock as we walk back toward the house. We head for our comfy bed, worn out from our first day of traveling and touring.

"I can't wait to see Sam and Chuck's reaction to these little guys," I exclaim.

"This is going to be a hoot and a half," I say as I slip into my pajamas.

"Yeah," David adds, "this is going to be fun."

The next morning we spend mapping out the place and trying to decide where everything will go. Once we've gotten all the info we'll need to plan the event, Lucille drops us back at the airport, and we're back in time to stop by the office before everyone has gone home. We give them a brief overview of what is entailed and tell them we might need to adjust some of the ideas they came up with when we first started talking about this event.

"Sam, why don't you and I call the clients and talk to them about costumes and attire? Chuck, Bob, get with Phil and see what kind of stage we're going to have and figure out how to decorate it. Oh, and, we're going to need to figure out how to make bowties for the male donkeys and pearl necklaces for the girl donkeys," I say while trying to maintain a straight face. Chuck looks at me like I had just insulted Barbra Streisand, whom he idolizes.

Six weeks later David and I are back in New Mexico. We've come a couple of days early to make sure all of the local contractors are doing everything they are supposed to do before our crew arrives on site. It's a flurry of activity, with tents being erected and bleachers, stage, and sound system getting unloaded and set up.

The next day the gang arrives, and I'm like a kid on Christmas morning. It's very rare that I get to spring something on these guys, and the anticipation is just about more than I can stand. Phil is already in his "event manager zone," and everybody else is inventorying all the gear and supplies they ordered for their part of the event. We gather everybody together to give them the lay of the land. Lucille and Kenny join us, and we make their introductions. They take over the duties of tour guides and lead our gang over to the barn housing their special little critters. I can tell that Phil and Nelson are just along for the ride. Sam, Chuck, and Bob are not at all thrilled with the prospect of meeting the donkeys. I guess I should have warned Sam not to wear her good boots, but I figure she deserves the same treatment I got. I hear a big squish and can feel her glare burn right through me.

"You know, I bought these Mark Nason boots just for this. I didn't expect them to get so dirty the first time I wore them," whines Chuck.

"Now you know why they call them shit kickers," says Phil with a certain amount of glee. Bob laughs, and Chuck sneers at both of them.

"They look real good with those Diesel jeans, though," says Nelson with a certain amount of sincere admiration. "How much did you pay for those?"

Chuck ignores the compliment, and Bob mouths the words *two seventy-five*.

Just like with us, Kenny and Lucille open and close the gate once we're all through, and, sure enough, we start to hear the small stampede headed our way. When the first little guy makes his way out of the barn, Sam and Chuck go nuts. Chuck is jumping up and down like a housewife who just won a washer and dryer on *The Price Is Right*. Sam is doubled over in laughter. I quickly lose track of how many times she says, "No friggin' way!"

Nelson and Bob are equally amused, but I'm not sure if it's the donkeys or their coworkers that is the source of their mirth.

Phil, in his inimitable manner, grins and looks down at his clipboard. "I guess this means we can scale things down a bit?" he says, grinning with a certain amount of incredulity. Lucille, Kenny, David, and I exchange satisfied smiles.

Over four hundred people are expected to come to show and buy donkeys. Phil is so focused I'd have to set his hair on fire to get his attention, and I'm not quite sure that would do it.

"The main tent will be open on all sides, and the bleachers will be positioned so the animals will be visible to the crowd," Phil says, pointing to a diagram.

"Chuck and Bob are not happy about resizing all the bowties and necklaces for the male and female donkeys," I tell Phil.

"We may need to narrow the seating area," he says, pointing at his floor plan. He's in his own little world and continues, "We need to move some of these vendors so we have a place for the table where the phones are supposed to go." Phil doesn't even register my comment about Chuck and Bob. It doesn't fit into his reality at this moment. He points out a potential blind spot in the bleachers to me.

"Really, they are not amused," I continue.

"Who's not amused?" he asks.

"Never mind," I say. I give up. Wait a minute… "Phones?" I ask.

"Oh yeah," responds Phil matter-of-factly. "There will be bidders from Germany, England, Canada, and Japan during the auction." He says this without a trace of mockery or sarcasm. "This is a big deal," he adds and continues to study the floor plan.

"There's Nelson," I say, pointing him out to Phil. He is cracking the whip over his team of twenty.

"Good, good," Phil says. "Catering is far enough away from the main action." He squints at Nelson in the distance, who is preparing a southwestern feast of fajitas, burritos, and so on. The smell is mouthwatering, and it makes me realize it's been a while since I've had anything to eat.

"Are those rabbits on his shirt?" he asks.

"They're pink bunnies playing saxophones," I say. Phil shakes his head and wanders off, muttering something about the auctioneer's sound system.

Chuck and Bob come around the corner.

"I stepped in something nasty right over there," Bob says, pointing to the area between the third donkey tent and the vendors' tent. "Aren't these creatures housebroken?"

"This is the Wild West, you old sissy," says Chuck. "Nobody's housebroken!"

I try to appease Bob by noticing he has lost weight.

"Nice try, Honey," he says. "But these are Ferragamo's. And what's with all the miniature donkey calendars, statues, and key chains? I think I even saw license plate covers," Bob says, continuing his rant. "What are they, talismans to protect people from good taste?"

I am desperately looking for Sam to help get these two off my back. Finally, I see her giving final instructions to her crew of donkey escorts. Her first idea was to hire models and have them all dressed like Daisy Duke, complete with tiny cut-off jeans and plaid shirts, but Lucille nixed that. This came as a brutal disappointment to some of the guys. Lucille put us in touch with the local Four-H Club, and we hired our handlers out of their membership. Their outfits consisted of blue jeans, blue chambray shirts, cowboy boots, and hats. I'm sure this outfit is worn by these girls on a regular basis. The change, she explained, was mostly due to safety considerations. We wouldn't find out until later just how right she was.

The girls are all very bright and obviously have a great deal of experience around ranch animals. As I approach the gathering, I realize the conversation is directed the other way, with the girls telling Sam how this will go. It's obvious that Sam is way out of her element and quite happy that these young ladies know exactly what to do.

Sam, however, is dividing her attention between the girls and the catering tent. She is staring daggers at a tall redhead "conferring" with Nelson.

"Who the hell is that!?" says Sam in a less than genteel tone. I give my "I have no idea." shrug. "If she were any closer to him, she'd be behind him!" she mutters. For a woman who claims to be "just friends" with Nelson, she is suddenly quite interested in his social life.

With everything in place, all the guests start to arrive. They avail themselves of the troughs of beer and sodas strategically placed around the main tent. Once the appointed hour arrives, the auctioneers take the stage and welcome everyone. I'm backstage, trying my best to stay out of the way while watching Lucille and Kenny make sure the mini-donks are in the right order and ready to take the stage. I think it was Chuck and Bob attempting to put the pearl necklaces and bowties on the donkeys that caused the rebellion.

"Hello and welcome to the seventh annual miniature donkey auction," says Kenny into the microphone.

"We're so glad to see all of our old friends and to make some new ones," adds Lucille.

"I'm sure you all have had the opportunity to inspect all the donkeys up for auction today, so let's get the ball rolling," says Kenny with just the right amount of enthusiasm. He hands the microphone to a gentleman clad in black, formal western wear.

"Good afternoon, ladies and gentlemen. My name is Bob Williams, and I'll be your auctioneer for the day. My associates around the room are Dan, Mike, and Steve," he says, pointing out his assistants. "Now, remember, they are old and pretty hard of hearing, so you'll really have to work hard to get their attention if you have a bid." With that, each one of his assistants does his best "deaf as a post" act and asks a member of the audience what was just said. These guys are very animated, enthusiastic, and funny. It's their job to keep the energy in the tent at a high level.

"All right, folks, let's bring out our first donkey, number zero, zero, one in your catalog, and her name is Lulu Belle. She is the daughter of …" continues Bob the auctioneer. He reads the lineage of this fine animal while glancing back occasionally at the curtain, through which is supposed to appear said donkey. At that time Bob nods at the assistant closest to that curtain. I also notice Kenny and Lucille making their way backstage. I'm not sure what I can do to help the situation, but I make my way over there myself.

The scene backstage is as comical as anything I've ever seen in my life. Lulu Belle is about six feet away from the curtain and bound and determined not to move. In fact, all of the little darlings have decided, almost simultaneously, not to cooperate. It's as if the heretofore docile animals have suddenly remembered they are donkeys and, being donkeys, that they have a duty and responsibility to be stubborn.

The unfortunate handler is pulling with all her might, but that donkey isn't about to budge. Seeing this, Lucille jumps into action and, planting both hands on the donkey's hindquarters, gives a mighty shove. At this point, the poor animal still isn't moving of his own volition but is rather sliding on the wooden stage floor. These guys might be small in stature, but they have a full-sized bray. The visual that runs through my mind at that moment is of having roller skates fitted to the hooves of the donkeys which would make this job a lot easier.

Meanwhile, backstage, Chuck and Bob have enlisted the help of some of the other 4-H girls and are covering the stars of the show with glitter. One of the other donkey owners had seen it at another auction and claimed that the spotlights on stage made them sparkle when they were the center of attention.

"I had dreams," says Chuck wistfully. "When I was going to the Art Institute in San Francisco, I had dreams of being creative and designing interiors for buildings designed by famous architects. Look at what's become of me! I'm sprinkling glitter on little bitty donkeys."

"Yes, it certainly seems like a waste of a perfectly good degree," says Sam, heaping on the sarcasm. "I bet your parents are so proud."

"Yes, yes, I can hardly wait to tell my parents that we were selling a little ass this weekend," says Bob with a wry grin.

We had covered the entire stage with hay so it would seem more natural to the donkeys, but they weren't buying it. After the first donkey has been dragged off stage, the second handler is doing her best to convince her charge to be a good girl and come with her. I can see by the look in the stubborn animal's eyes that she isn't going on without a fight. So, this time Lucille and another girl give a little assistance from behind. This turns out to be too much. If you add irresistible force, an immovable object, and a slick, hay-covered stage together, you get what's commonly known as chaos. As I watch the events unfold, I hear "The Blue Danube" in my head as everything goes into slow motion. I watch helplessly as the three irresistible forces and the one immovable object go sliding off stage. The first and second row of audience members do their best to scramble out of the way. It's like the parting of the Red Sea. As the pandemonium subsides, some of the spectators help the girls and the donkey up from the floor. One of the Four-H girls pops up with her hands in the air like she has just nailed the landing after a dismount from the uneven bars. The other one takes her hat off and gives a deep, dramatic bow while Lucille waves to the crowd. Normally, I would think this is a disaster, but judging by the hysterical laughter and applause, I gather that this type of incident is not uncommon.

I catch Lucille backstage, and she's still brushing hay off her backside. She's laughing as she looks me straight in the eye and says, "That there is exactly why we don't have cute models in tiny shorts handling these little rascals."

THE WHOLE EVENT turns out to be a whopping success for all concerned, proving what I always say, "You can dress a donkey up, but you just can't drag him anywhere." Yup, that's what I always say, pardner.

As David and I wander back to the ranch house, holding hands, we pass Sam and Nelson having a rather heated discussion.

"What's that about?" David says.

"I'm sure I'll find out soon enough whether I want to or not," I say, giving him a squeeze. "Ain't love grand?"

God, I'm lucky.

CHAPTER 9

Livin' La Diva Loca

"This place must've been something in its day," Phil says as we walk into the old ironworks building.

"This is so cool," I add as we gawk at the cavernous interior of the converted factory.

"Why can't we have anything like this where we live?" asks Chuck, adding a little bitterness to drive his point home.

"Because they tore down all the cool old buildings back in the seventies to make way for ugly strip malls and boring office buildings," replies Bob dryly. The building has been transformed from an industrial-age relic into a magnificent event center.

Most event centers we work at are pretty generic-looking, and we have to work pretty hard to make them represent the theme of our client's event. Not this one. This one already has an overabundance of character, and it will be fun to see what Chuck and Bob come up with to make it sparkle.

This event is for the International Center for Foreign Relations, which conducts conferences worldwide. We handled one for them the previous year. The delegates loved us and told us they'd call us the next time they did a conference in our country. I love repeat customers and was thrilled to get another call from them. This event will be the culmination of a five-day conference on how to increase female entrepreneurship in developing countries. The host for this soiree is the Spanish delegation.

"Is one of you Donna?" asks the impeccably dressed, silver-haired lady as she emerges from the office doors.

Almost in unison, my crew points to me and says, "She is."

I smile and introduce myself to Penny, the building's manager.

"Come on, I'll give you the grand tour," she says after introducing her to everybody. She must give this tour a couple of hundred times a year because she leads us through the history of the building and its rescue from nearly being torn down and then follows that with everything we need to know about the facility. She obviously prides herself on covering everything so thoroughly that there are rarely any questions for her at the end of the tour. I follow her to her office to review the paperwork, and the rest of my gaggle goes on their merry way to begin preparing tomorrow's dinner.

I find Nelson inspecting the kitchen to make sure it lives up to his expectations. It passes. I note that today's shirt has cats dressed as bullfighters and little mice playing the part of the bulls. I sidle up to him and ask, "So, who was that woman you hired for the donkey event?"

"Which one?" he asks, knowing exactly to whom I am referring.

"The tall redhead—you know very well who I'm talking about," I chide him gently. Suddenly, he has developed an intense interest in the Jensen industrial oven.

"Oh, her," he says, looking over the oven instead of facing me. "That's Cara. She's a good kid. She has a lot of catering experience. I've got her working this event, too." He tries to put a degree of casualness in his voice meant to pass her off as just another employee. I've worked with too many bad actors to fall for it.

"Did you check her references?" I ask, adding, "Sam's worried that she's taking advantage of you."

"Yes, I did check. And why should she care?" he snaps, knowing the answer.

Why won't he look me in the eye? Sam and Nelson haven't spoken to each other since we got back from New Mexico. This not only makes everyone uncomfortable but it diminishes the strength of my team. I can't be worried about personal conflicts and keeping track of who's mad at whom. I have always felt fortunate that my team likes and respects each other. I constantly work to ensure we have fun at what we do while maintaining the highest level of professionalism. Of course, there will always be minor skirmishes or squabbles, but for the most part, we all treasure our tranquil working relationships. I leave Nelson in his kitchen kingdom and check on the rest of the team.

I walk into the ballroom to find that Chuck and Bob have again come through with flying colors. I see them from across the room, directing an army of worker bees, smoothing out tablecloths, arranging centerpieces, and setting out spectacular floral arrangements. As I approach them, I hear more and more of their discussion. They are having a grand time fantasizing about all the things they could do with the interior of this place. About the same time I get to them, Penny emerges from her office and compliments the guys on the great theme they've come up with.

"Thanks," says Bob, "we really appreciate it."

"But that's not going to stop us from kidnapping your staff," adds Chuck with a grin.

"I have to agree," says Bob with some amazement. "Where did you find an event services staff like this? Every single one of them is so eager to please."

Penny explains, "We make sure they know how important they all are to the success of each and every event we have here, and we pay them a pretty good wage."

"Well, Miss Donna, that seems like a formula we could incorporate into our little company, don't you think?" Chuck says as he throws an arm over my shoulder.

"Forget it," I say, matching him grin for grin. "I already pay you too much. Now go fluff a bouquet or something."

Penny smiles and winks at me as Chuck scurries off in a huff.

THE RUSTLING OF plastic stops me in front of one of the back rooms near the loading dock. I find Sam buried under a mountain of costumes and plastic garment bags.

"Doin' all right in here?" I ask gingerly.

"Oh yeah" she responds. "I'm just trying to separate these by size and by gender. I hope we don't have too many extra-large male servers," she mutters, and I'm not entirely sure she was talking to me.

"Need some help?" I offer.

"Huh? Oh, no, that's okay. I think I've got it under control," she says while diving into another pile of brightly colored costumes. She had found a great costume rental place in Chicago so we could have the servers match the flock of flamenco dancers we hired for the evening's entertainment.

Nelson has also had his shoulder to the wheel. He and his team, including Cara, have created a wonderful traditional Spanish menu. The main course will be veal cutlets sautéed in wine, bacon, brandy, roasted peppers, and fresh asparagus. Dessert will be Crema Catalana, which is, I gather, Spain's equivalent of crème brulee. The kitchen is a flurry of activity, with everyone prepping the food to make their lives easier tomorrow afternoon.

NOTHING LASTS FOREVER. The tranquil tour of the preparations is broken by Sam marching straight up to Nelson and growling, "Is *that* what you'll be wearing for the party?!?"

"Hey, the event's twenty-four hours away!" Nelson says defensively. "I'll be wearing chef's whites, and does it really matter what I wear in the kitchen?"

"Okay, break!" I say, stepping in between them like a good referee. "Wow, look at those flower arrangements. Aren't they awesome?" I ask, trying to distract them before this escalates.

Phil walks up with a clipboard, interrupting the action. Chuck and Bob are looking uncomfortable and disappointed. My crew isn't the tight little unit we usually are. We aren't the A-Team at the moment. Phil is in his event manager zone and seems oblivious to the clash. I think he's fully aware of what's going on and this is his way of defusing the situation without calling attention to it. Never looking up from his clipboard, he starts through the checklist for the event. The tension quickly subsides as we confirm everything is ready for tomorrow night. He compliments Chuck and Bob on the faux ivy on the walls and Sam on organizing the wardrobe room. Phil has ensured we have plenty of wait staff fluent in languages other than English. It appears that we are fully prepared for what lies ahead, and I'm comforted by the fact that I have a great team, even if we have some grumbling at the present time.

Our hosts from Spain have requested that we hire a well-known guitarist and flamenco dancer/singer duo. I found their website and saw that she is a mocha-skinned beauty with huge brown eyes and silky black hair, and he is an extremely handsome and distinguished-looking gentleman. Arranging for these two turns out to be a lot easier than I ever thought it would be. They are available, and their agent bends over backward to make the contracting process as easy as possible. I wish every agent I ever dealt with was as accommodating!

Phil has arranged a green room for the entertainers to hang out in before and after the show. Our guitarist, Miguel, arrives at 10 A.M. He is very professional and wants to ensure that the sound system and equipment we have rented for them are up to par before the guests arrive at five. I do, however, notice that he is a lot thinner than he is in his portrait on their website. This has the effect of making him look considerably older than the man I was expecting to see. I forget all about that when he starts his sound check. He plays the guitar with passion and poise, and it sounds heavenly. Everybody in the room stops what they are doing for the few short minutes he plays, and in short order, he seems satisfied with the setup. The gorgeous singer is supposed to arrive at noon. At 1 P.M., she is still not on site. Miguel claims no knowledge of her whereabouts, and Phil and I set out to track her down.

"I know Maria is in her room, but she won't answer the phone. She needs to be here, getting ready like everyone else," I say under my breath to Phil. "I know she's one of Spain's national treasures, but that doesn't excuse her. I know the room number. Let's go roust her out!" So off we go; while Chuck and Bob put the final touches on their décor, Sam attends to her dancers. "Events seem magical sometimes," I tell Phil. "But, as everyone knows, magic is just an illusion."

Meanwhile, Nelson is pacing around the kitchen among the scurrying minions preparing meals for five hundred people, including his new protégé, who is chopping scallions while gazing adoringly at him.

Occasionally, Sam directs a scowl in that direction, probably hoping that Cara loses a finger in the process.

Arriving at Maria's hotel room, we rap lightly on the door and wait. The door opens, and a thin little wisp of a girl invites us in. Ada, our performer's assistant, motions to a closed door.

"Maria is in bathroom. She is…" Ada motions with her hands, trying to find the right word. "*Señora, como se dice enojada?*" she asks the closed door.

"Upset!" comes the sharp reply from the other side.

Ada turns to us and repeats, "Upset."

"Maria, can you come out here to discuss this?" I ask, trying to remain calm. I hear her shuffle to the door and open it.

Okay, so I have to tell you, in the photo on her website, she looks like Selma Hayek. She is pictured in the traditional flamenco dancer pose. Her back is arched, and her head is tilted back slightly, and she is searing holes in the camera with a look that could only be described as smoldering. With one arm over her head and the other delicately arched in front of her, she looks every bit like a national treasure. I'm anxious to see her, but I'm slightly concerned about why she has barricaded herself in the toilet.

The door opens, and I'm stunned. That's the only way to describe it. The photo on the website is black and white. I thought they did that for an artistic affectation. I'm beginning to think they didn't have color film when they took it. The person I see before me is in her late fifties, and I'm being generous. She's forty pounds overweight, and her hair is no longer silky. She's wearing nothing but a ratty bathrobe, fuzzy slippers, and a scowl.

"My God!" I think. "We've hired a Spanish version of Norma Desmond!" I am holding a copy of her contract, ready to confront her with it. Her timid little assistant, Ada, hands Maria a tissue as her prima donna eyes well up with tears and ten pounds of mascara runs down her cheeks. I have dealt with many prima donnas before, but this one takes the sopapilla. I silently count to ten and remind Señora Maria that she is late for a very important event—an event hosted by her native country.

"Señora is upset," says Ada. "She has heard that there will be *other* performers."

I clutch the contract and get up close and personal with Ada.

"Is she also mute?!?" I ask, not even trying to hide my impatience. "As well as not looking a thing like her..." Phil grabs my upper arm at this point and tells Ada and Maria that we need to have a conference in the hall. He ushers me out of the room and closes the door behind him, leaving the hefty diva and her assistant alone for a moment. Phil has booked many rock bands and has regaled me with many stories of egomaniacal guitar players and drunk or stoned drummers and catatonic singers.

"Ooooh, please let me smack her! Just once!" I seethe.

"Whoa there, Little Lady. I know you've dealt with difficult actors before," he says, "but this is a different kind of animal. Now, please quietly blend into the background while I handle this." I grudgingly agree, and we gently knock on the door of her $400–a–night suite, for which the client is footing the bill.

Phil enters, all smiles, while I simmer at a low boil in the corner.

"It is such a privilege and an honor to meet you," Phil says to Maria, who is now sprawled on the couch while her assistant fawns over her. I wonder what horrible sin Ada is paying penance for with this job.

"I am a world-famous artist," Maria whines to Phil, who is nodding with an expression of total understanding. "I take the stage alone, yet I am told you have other dancers!" She pauses to mop her face with a hand towel, and I notice half a bottle of grappa on the coffee table. I now know why it was so easy to hire them. I'm quite sure this isn't the first time she's pulled this little stunt, and nobody in Spain will hire her now. Phil promises that the Spanish chargé d'affaires will escort her to the stage and tells her those other performers are there merely to mingle with the guests during cocktail hour.

"They're just background noise," he says. "You, Señora, are the sole reason all these people have come to this event. Why else would they be here?"

I need to pay Phil more. He had his powers of persuasion working in overdrive. He tells her she will have her own private green room, which she will not have to share with any of the other performers.

Right, I'm thinking, the performers I'll have to pay overtime to stall the audience until Miss Thing is ready. I call Sam and tell her to have an operating room on standby and to be ready for an extreme makeover when we arrive. Is it too late to call a cosmetic surgeon?

As we make our way to the limo, Phil ducks into the florist in the hotel lobby to buy a long-stemmed rose and to call Chuck and Bob to tell them to find a room, any room, and to turn it into a private green room.

He returns, presents her with the rose, and escorts her to the waiting limo. When we arrive, we hustle our rumpled diva off to our makeshift body shop. Sam performs a minor miracle, and the diva looks ten years younger in no time.

THE ROOM HAS been transformed into a Spanish villa, complete with fountains and statues. The black tablecloths are overlaid with red lace, and the candles in the sangria bottle centerpieces make everything sparkle. The guitar player has warmed up the crowd with a performance accompanied by the other flamenco dancers. We manage to get them out of sight before our diva readies herself to make her grand entrance. I see Phil on stage during the break talking to Miguel while the troupe dances its way out of the room. If I hear another castanet after tonight, I'm going to snap.

"This is Heather Goodbody, Channel 11 News. We interrupt your regularly scheduled program to cover this breaking story. It seems as though another deranged event planner has snapped. She is up in the clock tower you see in the distance, wearing nothing but a sombrero. The police have cordoned off the entire area and are trying to negotiate with her. They fear she is armed and unstable. I spoke with Police Captain O'Mahoney, who tells me she keeps screaming 'Stop the clicking, stop the clicking.' We don't know what that means, but we'll stay with this story until the end."

I SNAP BACK to reality and head to the kitchen to check on Nelson. I find him overseeing a production line of main course dinner plates.

"I thought all the meals were already served," I say while marveling at the speed at which Nelson and his crew can assemble a meal.

"Me too," he replies, "but somebody got confused and mixed bacon into the vegetarian meals. Luckily, there weren't that many, and only one person complained before our great wait staff was all over it."

That same great staff was patiently waiting to rush the repaired veggie meals out to the main room. Who confuses bacon with vegetables? I have a sneaking suspicion about that, and I fear that this will provide even more ammunition to an already well-armed Sam when she hears about this.

THE HEAD OF the Spanish diplomatic delegation escorts our diva to the stage and hands her off to her partner. Miguel takes her by the hand, kisses her cheek, and whispers something in her ear. All eyes are riveted to the stage as Phil, sounding a whole lot like the "Let's get ready to rumble" guy, introduces our star.

"Ladies and gentlemen, please welcome the most beautiful and talented woman in all of Spain," he pauses for a dramatic effect, "Maria Delgado!" The applause is deafening.

I SAY A silent prayer as she takes the stage. The lights come up, and she beams. Amazingly, she now looks twenty years younger, thirty pounds lighter, and a few inches taller. She dances and sings like an angel.
I literally have never seen anything quite like it. She receives a standing ovation, and the stage is strewn with bouquets of flowers.

"What were you saying to Miguel during the break?" I ask Phil, who is looking way too smug.

"I asked him very nicely to tell her that she has always been his muse and is dazzled by her beauty and talent," he replies. "I also slipped him two hundred and fifty dollars for his efforts."

Good grief, I feel nauseous. PHIL AND I can laugh about it now, but it's a memory we will never forget, no matter how hard we try.

CHAPTER 10

Minor Problems

With "Love Me Tender" running through my head, I squint through bloodshot eyes at the man I gladly agreed to spend the rest of my life with and who, as I contemplate what has happened to his compassion and sense of decency, I'm now sure is an alien being from another galaxy. I momentarily think to myself, "Does he have a tumor? Is the house on fire?"

It's 6 A.M., and David has thrown open the bedroom curtains. I am bathed in a flood of sunshine.

"Have you slipped and hit your head on something? Do you know what time I got in last night?" I croak with my raspy morning voice. I am trying to recover from last night's exhaustive party, a fifties-themed anniversary party for which Phil managed to come up with a dozen Elvis impersonators of various shapes and sizes.

Dodging the daggers, I am staring at him.

David hands me my cell phone, saying, "This is the fifth message in an hour, so I think it may be important."

That wakes me up. I start to panic. What could it be? Has Dad had a heart attack? Is Mom in the ER after being hit by a bus, waiting for her daughters to arrive before she…?

I clear my head of all negative thoughts and grab my phone. Jessica! I count backward from ten so my heart can return to its normal beating rate before calling her back.

"I could really use an extra-large martini and a couple of ibuprofen," I say to David before dialing the phone. He returns with a strong cup of coffee and a couple of Advil. Not quite what I had in mind, but he feels it's his job to protect me from myself.

Jessica is the original Last-Minute Gal. We once put on a cocktail party at her place in Hawaii with three days' notice. She appeared shocked and appalled that twenty people on her guest list were unable to drop everything and show up at her event. She lives up to her nickname.

Much as I try, it is impossible to dislike her. She's like the absent-minded professor. Her husband, Chester, is an investor (I know, Chester the Investor, you just can't make this stuff up) who has done quite well for himself. They have homes in California, Arizona, and Hawaii, plus the "Big House" in Aspen. Jessica loves a party, and nearly all of them are charity fundraisers. She has a heart of gold and a mind like a sieve.

"Thank God, Donna. I was wondering if you were ever going to call me back," says Jessica in a full-blown panic. "Connor is graduating in two days, and we have to throw him a party!" It's 6 A.M., and the fact that her son is graduating in a couple of days has kind of just snuck up on her all of a sudden. One would have thought she would have known this fact for, oh, I don't know, seventeen or eighteen years now.

"Congratulations, Jessica. This is an important occasion," I manage to say between swallowing the Advil and sucking down the strong coffee. The industrial-strength dose of caffeine clears the fog in my brain enough for me to grill her for more details while I scramble to get some paper and a pencil. I learned long ago that writing utensils and Post-it notes are as necessary on my nightstand as any face cream, although it does cause a certain amount of consternation with David to see my side of the headboard covered in sticky notes. We have put together more than a dozen parties for her over the past few years in each of her four homes and have never had more than a week to do so. Nevertheless, I have to kick it into high gear at this point.

"I would like to have the party at our Aspen home on Saturday."

What? Two days to plan a high school graduation party in Aspen. Normally, a high school graduation party would be a simple event. However, Jessica has never done anything the easy way.

"I've invited approximately one hundred adults and fifty teens, and, of course, we will need the works."

"Of course," I affirm, "high school graduation is a huge deal. It's like a rite of passage."

All I can think about is how self-centered you have to be to call an event planner at 6 A.M. to plan a party with two days' notice.

One thing that does make me a little crazy about Jessica is that she expects a full-blown spectacle for all of her parties when clearly, she has known for some time that a particular event was going to take place and require a professional. Jessica is also the type of woman who hasn't a clue how to find a caterer or decorator or whatever, and that's why she calls me. Many times, I have wanted to say to her that we couldn't possibly put together a party of that caliber on such short notice, but I am reminded that, as much as she seems to like me, Jessica would find another event planner who *would* put the party together for her in less than forty-eight hours. Her response to everything is—just throw money at it, and it will happen.

Armed with the information I need to get started; I wait until 9 A.M. before calling an emergency meeting at Phil's office. Every time we meet there, it seems like the clutter has grown. While Sam and Nelson glare at each other from opposite corners, I go over the facts.

"He's crazy for the band Silent Rust," I say.

"Not likely," Phil grumbles. "They're really hot now, and they're out promoting their new CD."

Phil calls the band's agent anyway; on the off chance they might have that night free. No chance. So, we scratch Silent Rust off the list.

"Let's go with a DJ," he says as he leaves the room to start calling his contacts.

He returns with the news that a white-hot DJ in Vegas; DJ Hub Snap is available Saturday night. His agent has some reservations about the travel plans and stipulates that all travel arrangements be made by us but approved by him. It seems that Hub Snap has a penchant for missing flights, so we have to make it as easy as possible to get him from Vegas to Aspen.

I call Jessica to break the news that Silent Rust is not available and listen to her complain for at least five minutes.

"How can that be," she whined. "It's Connor's favorite band, and you only graduate high school once in life."

I had to bite my tongue hard to keep from saying, "Because they are not sitting around waiting for the freakin' phone to ring, and had we been given more than forty-eight hours to book them, we might have had a chance." Instead, I confess my disappointment as well and offer her the next best thing.

"Why not a DJ?" I coaxed. "There is one who is super-hot right now out of Las Vegas who we could get here in time for the party."

"Well," she sniffed into the phone, "what other choice do I have? Isn't there someone else you can call to get them here? I really want Silent Rust for Connor's party."

I am sure she is stomping her perfectly manicured feet and pouting at this point. Isn't it against the law to act like this once you reach a certain age? Again, as we are currently under a very serious time constraint, I explain, "Silent Rust already has a concert they are playing that evening, so, no, sadly, there is no one else we can call. You must understand if they were booked already for Connor's party and someone else was inquiring about them, it would be the same thing. It's virtually impossible for them to take a break from a tour to do a private party," I explain. Good heavens, what planet has this woman been on all her life?

After much discussion I convince her to let us book the famous DJ Hub Snap and regale her with all his famous radio and television appearances.

"Really, television shows?" she asks with some disbelief. "Is he that famous?" she queries. I assure her that he is and confirm that she is willing to pay for this very pricy DJ. I am in the process of telling her that his fee is fifteen thousand dollars for the evening when Phil interrupts me to tell me about the airline issues and that he is doubtful he can get Hub Snap in on time. The DJ's agent isn't making this party any easier on us either. He was insisting on special turntable equipment, digital boxes, and special microphones, all of which would need to be rented out of Denver.

I am sure her head is gonna explode when she reluctantly agrees to have him perform at the party. Jessica is very impressed with fame, and this DJ is someone she could brag about to the ladies in her competitive social circle.

"Well, if he's that good, then he's probably worth the price. Go ahead, book him."

Now that I've convinced her, I lower the next boom. "We may have some trouble getting him here and switching planes in Denver and then to Aspen on such short notice."

"Call Chester's pilot and make arrangements to just pick him up—it'll be faster," she says, obviously very pleased with herself.

"Right! Why didn't I think of that? That's a brilliant idea and very generous of you." I commend her with about as much humility as I can muster. Whew, airline reservation crises over. Problem solved!

Phil calls Hub Snap's agent and starts to work on the details of booking this DJ extraordinaire while I call my friend Pat and beg her to let us borrow her condo in Aspen as a base of operations. Jessica has offered her home, but with Sam and Nelson at each other's throats, I do not want to risk having our reputation tarnished by one of their spats.

David has reluctantly agreed to be the photographer for this event. Recognizing my sense of urgency (read *panic*), he immediately sets out to rent a van that will accommodate Phil, Nelson, Chuck, Bob, Sam, and the two of us. It's a four-hour drive to Aspen, and we spend almost the whole trip discussing the logistics of the event. Chuck and Bob will start checking out the house as soon as we get there. They agree on lots of balloons, but Chuck wants to put up fairy lights.

"Sweetie, this is not *your* graduation party," says Bob. We'll do a couple of disco balls and some straight-colored lights and some programmable LEDs."

Nelson has reluctantly agreed to use the catering company we used the year before for Anne Marie's wedding. He has been reassured by the owner that his staff has been educated on the difference between a green pepper and a jalapeño. Nevertheless, Nelson is flying in four of his top people to supervise the catering crew.

"I hope that tramp isn't one of them!" sneers Sam.

"Lay off of Cara!" says Nelson. "She's had a rough year, with a messy divorce and an injury to her foot."

"She didn't seem heartbroken or crippled when she was sashaying around on the last gig," Sam shoots back.

"Oh, look, a moose!" David interjects, distracting them from their little love fest.

"Oh, cool," I say. "By the way, what are we going to do with the pool in the backyard?"

"We'll either have to have the party inside or somehow block it off," says Phil. Fifty teens, a bunch of drunken socialites, and a pool equal disaster. Someone is bound to fall or jump in."

"Not to worry, we've already figured out what do to with the pool," offers Chuck.

"We are working on a plan," Bob adds.

After some white-knuckle backseat driving over Independence Pass, we finally arrive, and Jessica greets us at the door. She's a gorgeous redhead who spends many hours getting manicured, waxed, and massaged. It shows, too. She looks ten years younger than Chester, even though they are the same age.

"Connors at his girlfriend's house," she says as we enter her sumptuous home. That should give you enough time to look around."

Decorating cannot start yet, but Connor will be hiking with friends all day tomorrow, so Chuck and Bob set about examining every square inch of the place and taking photos and detailed notes. Nelson is already in the kitchen and pondering the catering.

Phil and I go outside to the pool area, and Phil immediately snaps into the professional zone. I can't quite explain it, but I know when it happens.

"The DJ will set up right here," Phil says, pointing to the middle of the pool.

"Well, I hope he can dog paddle really well and doesn't mind an occasional electrical zap," says David, scoping out the place's photographic possibilities. His words do not penetrate The Zone, as we have all come to call the aura that surrounds Phil when he really gets into the project at hand.

"Where are Chuck and Bob?" Phil asks. "The pool needs to be drained immediately, and we will need the Plexiglas delivered by midday tomorrow."

It's now almost 5 P.M. the night before the party, and Phil gets a call on his cell phone. I hear him answer and barely notice when he turns and walks away, listening intently to whoever it is on the other end of that call. I turn my attention to David, who has climbed up onto the brick wall that surrounds the pool area.

I notice Phil drop the arm, holding his phone from the side of his head dejectedly. He walks over to me and shakes his head.

"We have a problem," he says.

"What? What is it?" I ask with some alarm.

"Our DJ isn't going to make it for the party tomorrow night."

"Oh, no, this better be good," I say incredulously.

"Well, not necessarily *good*," he says looking down at the ground. "He's dead."

"No way! Are you serious?" I ask.

"Unfortunately, yeah, I am."

"Oh, great—what time is it?" I ask.

"Five thirty, why?" asks David.

"The plane is on its way to Las Vegas to pick him up," I explain.

APPARENTLY, HUB SNAP had a little alcohol and drug problem no one knew about, and his agent informs Phil that Hub Snap has just died from a fatal dose of alcohol and prescription sleeping pills. I go back inside to talk to Jessica. She is looking at me like I have three heads.

"I don't understand," she says innocently. "He is booked for the party tomorrow night; we have a contract."

"Right!" I say incredulously, resisting the urge to smack her upside the head. "But his agent just called and said he is *dead*, so he won't actually be spinning records for us tomorrow night." Clearly, she is confused, so I turn into Mother Theresa, using small words and speaking very softly. "We will get another DJ! One who is just as good! Phil is working on it as we speak."

I wear a path into the rug between the kitchen, where Jessica is having a meltdown, and the pool area, where Phil has set up a small communications center. He has a Bluetooth earpiece in one ear and a cell phone in one hand while his other hand is frantically banging away on the keyboard of his laptop. I make about twenty trips between them, trying to console Jessica and getting updates from Phil. I am in the process of consoling her when Phil calls me from the pool.

"Don't panic yet," he says. "Hub Snap's agent has lined up another DJ who is ready to go and who has worked with Hub Snap for years. He plays just like him and can meet the plane and be here in time for the party."

"Good news!" I gently tell Jessica. "We have our DJ. He will meet the plane; all is good."

Jessica, still reeling that Hub Snap had the nerve to die before her son's graduation party, says, "How do we know this next DJ isn't gonna die during the party?"

I am sure now that I have an ulcer and make a mental note to pick up some Pepto-Bismol and a bottle of Jack Daniels on the way back to our guest house.

"Well, Jessica, there are no guarantees in life, but the good part of this is that we found out ahead of time about Hub Snap. I know that being as responsible a person as you are, you would not want drugs and alcohol around teenagers," I say confidently, feeling my lips start to swell from having to kiss this much ass.

IT IS NOW seven o'clock the night before the party. My crew and I are exhausted and still have miles to go before we sleep. So, I bid Jessica farewell, reassuring her she made the right decision not to hire someone who was about to die anyway. Unbelievable!

We make it back to the guest house, all of us on our cell phones continuously working on event details through the evening. God bless Nelson, who has already thought ahead and has a catered dinner for all of us. Stuffed mushrooms, artichoke dip, and grilled Portobello hamburgers with guacamole. This works for me, and everyone on my team is now an accidental vegan.

Phil cracks open the Jack Daniels to pour everyone a drink. At midnight I crawl into bed, no longer able to form coherent sentences, and think about the nightmare we have possibly avoided and wonder what it must be like to be Jessica.

At 6 A.M. the next morning Chuck and Bob are already on site, having drained the pool the night before, and are in the process of installing multicolored oscillating lighting into the bottom of the pool and then covering it with heavy Plexiglas. There is a huge truck, with a driver we had to pay overtime to get everything in from Denver on such short notice. Again, I remember that when you throw money at something, it will happen.

"Did you two get any sleep?" I ask as I survey the process.

"As much as you did," Chuck replies.

"Nelson is bringing breakfast for all of us," Bob says. He should be here at any time."

The dynamic duo hang two strategically placed disco balls and strings of colored lights. Chuck had wanted a strobe light, too, but Bob put the kibosh on that.

"Stop channeling the seventies!" he says as they set the DJ station up in the center of the pool.

Phil, Chuck, and Bob supervise the crew setting up a multicolored tent that covers the entire pool area. Then, Sam, looking gorgeous despite her lack of sleep, heads to the Aspen Airport in a limo to pick up Hub Snap's replacement and fill him in on the party details.

Phil (a.k.a. Event Man) has begun setting up the massive sound system, which arrived on the truck from Denver. It's not yet 7 a.m., and the entire crew is steadily working. We have a crew of ten who came with the truck to help with the setup. None of us has had more than a few hours of sleep, but by Saturday afternoon, we have managed to transform the entire pool and surrounding area into a tropical disco.

Chuck and Bob have surrounded the pool with pots of tropical plants and palm trees. The effect of the oscillating lights on the disco balls is stunning.

Nelson (a.k.a. The Catering Drill Sergeant) has lectured his entire crew about asking anyone who looks under thirty years old for ID before serving them alcohol. Phil further emphasizes the importance of this by telling the bartenders that anyone who is caught serving an underage person will be sacked immediately.

THE VALET PARKING team arrives an hour early, and Phil instructs them where the cars will be parked and that at the end of the evening if anyone appears to have had too much to drink and probably shouldn't be behind the wheel, they are to call him.

The day flies by. Sam arrives with the DJ. He surveys the scene and starts to check out all the equipment with Phil. It's going to be a long night for the DJ as well, so Phil lets him know we will bring him whatever he wants for dinner and anything nonalcoholic to drink all night.

Finally, we literally roll out the red carpet, another item brought in from Denver. I am wishing I had time for a shower when Jessica, looking like ten million dollars, comes out to survey the work. She actually gets tears in her eyes at how beautiful everything looks.

"Thank you so much for pulling this together for me at the last minute, Donna," she sniffs and wipes a tear from her eye. "I could never have done this without you!"

The guests, who had been instructed to be there early, start arriving in droves and are keeping the valet hopping. Phil and I make one last round to survey everything. At this point, the bartenders are jumping to supply drinks to all the thirsty guests as the catering crew begins to pass hors d'oeuvres.

"Well, it looks like we're all set," Phil announces.

At this point, the party starts to take on a life of its own, and there isn't much else we can do except get out of the way.

The DJ is set to crank up the tunes when Jessica runs out of the house, flailing her arms and screaming, "Be quiet, everyone—they just drove up. Chester is going to bring him out to the pool. Get ready to yell *surprise!*"

I was really excited to see Connor's reaction. Would he really be surprised? Jessica's parties are legendary, and he has grown up with these parties. Chester leads Connor out to the pool, and Jessica, having placed herself next to the DJ, screams out "*Surprise!*" into one of the microphones. It is clear that Connor doesn't have a clue what's going on. All the guests shout "Happy Graduation!" as if the large banner above the dance floor isn't enough. Connor is clearly moved. He hugs his mom and shakes his dad's hand. I guess dudes don't hug. Nelson and two helpers roll out an enormous cake, which reads "Happy Graduation," with a hundred sparklers jutting out of the top as the DJ kicks off the music with Connor's favorite song. Before this poor graduate can even cut the cake, Jessica suggests he open his gift. His mom grabs him by the wrist and guides him to the front of the house. A whole gaggle of people follow them. Connor's dad hands him a garage door opener and tells him to "Point and click." As the garage door opens, I can't tell who's more excited, Jessica or Connor. A bright red sports car is revealed with the biggest bow I have ever seen on the roof.

"If you can pass a breath-o-lator test at the end of the party, you can take it for a test drive," his father says, giving him a manly clap on the back.

"Funny," I tell Phil, "I don't recall my father giving me that option when, at seventeen, I was handed the keys to a fifteen-year-old Volkswagen and threatened with my life if I ever dented it."

At this point the party is underway, and the teenagers are all dancing and shouting. I head into the kitchen to check on Nelson, who has things running with military precision.

He looks at me and says, "You look beat. Sit down, and I'll fix you a plate fit for an herbivore."

I decided to take my meal in the family's private dining room along with the rest of my staff so we'd be out of sight. We still have a long way to go to ensure this party keeps rolling along.

It's clear by midnight that we have a few tipsy teens on our hands.

David taps me on the shoulder and says, "Here's a picture you might be interested in." He has been going through all the snapshots he took, and the one he shows me is of a tall blonde woman in a short dress, clearly handing a bottle of booze to a teen. Her facial features are not exactly clear except for her eyes, which are piercing. They seem to jog my memory about something I can't quite put my finger on.

"She's not with us," he says. "I checked that out." At 2 A.M., after assessing the crowd, Phil tells the DJ to announce the last song.

Phil takes over as usual. Anyone who is even the least bit buzzed is driven home or stays in one of the guest rooms. We will *not* let anyone become a statistic, even though no one seems dangerously intoxicated. However, one drunk teen is one too many, and there are several tonight, including Connor, who has decided to hold off on his test drive till tomorrow. Still, the party has been a huge success, and by 3 A.M. everyone has cleared out.

Phil sends David and me home. He drapes an arm over my shoulders and says, "I can wrap this up with the Denver crew. You must be beat." He is my own personal Energizer Bunny.

I curl up next to David at 3:30 and say, "That went well despite the booze problem, don't you think?"

"Yeah," he says. "Kids will find a way to get their hands on liquor no matter what precautions you take—especially when they have an adult aiding and abetting them."

I fall asleep listening to the wind rustling through the aspens and cottonwoods. My last conscious thought is that there is something familiar about that woman in David's snapshot.

CHAPTER 11

Little Mall of Horrors

After three successful grand openings in six months (a four-star hotel, a children's museum, and a luxury car dealership), word was getting out that we were the new hot ticket in event planning.

"We're on a roll now!" I tell David as I head out to meet my crew at the construction site for a new 350-store mall. "This place will be one of the biggest of its kind in the country."

"As long as they have a camera store and a sporting goods store, I'll be happy," replies my spouse.

"Oh, they will," I say on my way out the door. "They will."

When I pick up Sam, she is wearing a red cable-knit sweater and a pair of $350 "distressed" (read "cry for help") jeans. I know this because I was with her when she bought them.

"You know," I say, "I would have dragged a pair of $10 jeans behind my car for a week for half that much, and then you could just sew a designer label on them. Think of the savings. Half off—which is what they appear to be anyway."

"Very cute," she says as she folds her lanky frame into my car. "Listen, I have something to tell you, and you won't like it."

Oh Lord, I think to myself. The biggest event of my career is coming up, and Sam has bad news. This is all I need! Well, might as well get it over with…

"Okay, hit me with it," I say.

"You remember Gwen, right?"

"Don Juan's mother? Who could forget her? By the way, she's asked me to do the baby shower for Don and Lily."

Don Juan married with a child on the way: Just call me the Accidental Matchmaker! Well, maybe not completely accidental…

"She called me to tell me that some ugly rumors are floating around town," Sam continues. "Apparently, Nancy Charbonneau decided against hiring us for an anniversary bash because she heard we were having 'problems.'"

I see clouds moving in, and I hope we're not in for a gully washer. Apparently, they're not the only clouds moving in.

"Who needs to do business with someone who believes rumors, anyway?" I say with a little fake bravado. "Besides, with the groundbreaking followed by the grand opening, we couldn't have fit her in any way. Not that it matters—but what kind of rumors?"

"Oh, jalapeños in salads, a drunken Santa, crude tattoos, vegetarian meals with bacon. That sort of thing," Sam replies.

After my head spins around twice, I exclaim, "Who would know that?! We stopped all those things before the client even knew about them!"

Sam rummages through her bag for the right shade of lipstick for a construction site. "Someone is trying to take us down," she says while pulling out a gold tube of lipstick and muttering, "Ah, Earthy Clay." She continues: "And I think I know who it is."

As we arrive at Chuck and Bob's place to pick them up, I tell her we'll have to put that theory on the back burner for now because our plate is too full with this new gig. Besides, I'm not big on conspiracy theories.

When we arrive, Phil and Nelson are already on site. We all cram into a temporary office trailer surrounded by trucks, bulldozers, and earthmovers. The receptionist passes out hard hats. Sam looks at hers like it is filled with manure.

"What's the matter?" Nelson asks. "Not 'distressed' enough for you?"

"I'll have you know I paid $350 for these!" She snaps back.

"It's true," he mutters. "There's a sucker born every minute."

Susan, the receptionist, explains that the wearing of hard hats is not negotiable, no matter how much they clash with your outfit. Hard hats must be worn.

"In fact, generally, we tell everyone to make sure their legs are covered and wear 'sensible' footwear, but we'll make an exception in your case, dear."

Sam glares at her and turns to Nelson, saying, "Not a word!" Nelson turns away and tries very hard not to laugh out loud.

We are spared from further fireworks when the construction manager comes in. His name is Duke (wasn't that John Wayne's nickname?), and he stands well over six feet tall. He practically has to turn sideways for his shoulders to fit through the door. His jeans are distressed, too, but they come by it legitimately. His full head of hair is silver, and somehow he makes a hard hat look good. My hard hat, on the other hand, seems to have been made for a pinhead. It looks like a cherry on top of an ice cream sundae. He extends his big, calloused hand to me and smiles. I'm trying to figure out if he's being nice or amused at how silly I look in a hard hat. The lines in his face tell a story of a life of hard, honest labor. I decide that he's being nice. I like him.

Off we go to explore the site in a couple of well-used pickup trucks. Duke points out where everything will be. I can hear the gears turning in Phil's head as he tries to visualize it.

"Right now, all I see are piles of dirt, but it'll come… it'll come," Phil whispers. I believe him.

We stop in the middle of the construction site, which at the moment is nothing but a very large mound of dirt. Duke rolls out an artist's rendering of the completed mall on the hood of his truck. It helps Phil and me immensely as Duke orients us to where everything will go. We all pile back into the pickups and head off to meet with the owners.

An hour later, we are back at the trailer. Sam flings off her hard hat as if it were a giant scorpion that just landed in her hair. Nelson catches it before it goes through a window and snaps, "Grow up, will you?" We all head into Duke's office, a chaotic mess of papers, plans, and empty coffee cups. It looks like a tornado hit it, but Duke can find whatever he needs instantly. I can see Phil is impressed—birds of a feather and all that.

"We want the groundbreaking to happen in the next couple of weeks," Duke says. "The grand opening for the public is a little harder to pinpoint, but I figure around eighteen months."

All of a sudden, the four partners of the organization arrive fashionably late.

Duke had confided to me earlier that they are known as the MODD Squad, their names being Michael, Oscar, Daniel, and Dave. After extremely brief introductions, these four begin talking about the logistics of the event, all at once at high speed. I was unable to make out any complete sentences, just phrases. VIP opening, groundbreaking, gold-plated shovels, tents, food, décor, public opening, different holiday themes on every level, different hors d'oeuvres every day for the week-long public opening, Santas, elves, and on and on ad nauseum. Phil catches my eye and pulls a tiny little digital voice recorder out of his shirt pocket and smiles. I grin and nod back at him. The only way we'll make any sense of this is to replay it about a thousand times and take notes.

"'When everyone's talking and no one is listening, how can we decide?'" Bob whispers to Chuck.

"Amen," Chuck replies. "Compared to what these guys have in mind, Woodstock was a walk in the park."

Fortunately, the MODD Squad is too involved in describing each of its inspired visions to hear them.

Duke finally gets their attention so we can get down to business. How these four egos came to form a partnership is beyond me. It was as though the A-Team had decided to give up crime fighting to become real estate developers. If they were a law firm, it would be called Wine 'em, Dine 'em, Sell 'em, and Sign 'em. If they were in Congress, I might consider moving to Cabo permanently. However, despite the odds against them, it works. Their company is one of the biggest real estate development firms in the country.

The groundbreaking ceremony is our first challenge. I reassure the Fab Four that a groundbreaking ceremony is pretty simple.

"You gather a few community leaders together, contact the media, and buy some shovels. A few short speeches and shovelfuls of dirt, and, *voilà*, you are done."

Oscar looks out the dusty window at the barren landscape on which he and his partners have to work their magic over the next few months. "Been there, done that," he sighs. "The press tends to give short shrift to these things. Not exciting enough."

Chuck and Bob snap into action.

"And that's exactly why you hired us!" says Chuck.

"You're thinking of an ordinary run-of-the-mill groundbreaking," Bob continues.

"And...," Chuck and Bob say in unison, "we don't do normal!"

MODD, Inc. gives me a look as if to indicate, "Okay, dazzle us."

I stall by rifling through my purse for my reading glasses. They always make me look more on top of it and in charge. Before enough time goes by to make things awkward, Sam jumps in.

"Beautiful people," she says. Now, everyone is looking at her. "I have a friend who is a firefighter" (my inside voice says, "I'll bet you do") "and his team is putting out a calendar for charity in six months. They've been looking for a way to publicize it." She lets that sink in and continues, "It's got everything. Six buff men and six buff women, all wearing part, but not all, of their firefighting outfits. The profits from the calendar go to the Children's Hospital. They lean on their gold shovels for a few mildly sexy shots and hand off the shovels to the mayor and other dignitaries. Now, *that's* a photo op!"

I follow her with some logistics about catering, PR, and parking, but the MODDs have heard enough. They huddle by themselves, and all I can hear is a lot of grumbling and muttering. I'm frantically thinking of other ideas in case this gets shot down. They break their huddle, and Dan (or Dave?) proclaims, "It sounds fun—just don't make it *too* sexy. Go for it."

"Two weeks," says one of the partners.

Sam, standing behind me, jabs me so hard in the back I think she may have punctured a lung. I do my best to catch my breath and blurt out "Four weeks."

Another partner offers "Three weeks!" and Phil sticks out his hand and says, "You've got a deal."

With that, the partners are off in a whirlwind of briefcases and overcoats. We wait until they are well out of earshot before we all exhale and exchange high fives. We might have even jumped up and down a little and hugged each other, but none of us will ever admit to that.

Three weeks pass in the blink of an eye. Chuck and Bob have decided that their theme will be "Under Construction" since this is groundbreaking, and they have outdone themselves. Chuck and Bob give me a tour of the tent we've erected for this event.

"You'll notice the tablecloths are splattered drop cloths," says Chuck. "And I think the burlap sashes around the cocktail tables help pull the whole look together."

"Notice the steel girders framing the stage," Bob points out. "And the orange cones combined with yellow-and-black caution tape on the bars just scream 'Men at Work,' don't you think?"

They also have artificial turf leading from the tent to the restrooms. Above the three bars is a sign that says, "Cement Mixer." The best part of the décor is the vending trucks (or gut trucks, as Phil affectionately calls them) used for the catering. I'm a little nervous about how the MODD Squad will receive them, but I think it's a brilliant touch. There's some debate about whether the servers should be in character or courteous and professional. Sassy wins out as long as they don't go overboard.

Sam has her servers in coveralls and hard hats.

"I thought you hated hard hats," I say.

"On me, darling, on me," she replies with a slightly wicked smile. "On everyone else, they look simply divine."

Nelson has heavy hors d'oeuvres, including small servings of grits and dirty rice. And for dessert? Mud pie, what else? Phil has everything else humming as usual. The sound system is in place and tested. The runway is all set for our firefighters, who will be parading around signing calendars for all their fans. We set it all up the night before, and Phil ensures the overnight security guards will be supplied with food, TV, and a deck of cards. Always take care of your security team; it pays big dividends.

The partners are the first to arrive, and they are clearly impressed. I give them the grand tour. Michael thinks the drop cloth tablecloths are a hoot, and the gut trucks for the catering are also a huge hit. What a relief that is. It's an hour before the event. The valets are in place, and Nelson has his crew putting the final touches on the display. I am walking around with a clipboard, checking things off, when a tiny woman who can't be a minute over twenty-one bursts through the door.

"The restrooms!" she screams at no one in particular.

Everybody stops and looks at her as if she's about to have an emergency of a personal nature.

She points at me and says, "You're in charge, right?"

"Yes, I am," I affirm.

"Well, someone has spray painted 'For a good time call Donna' on the walls!"

The woman finally introduces herself as Shelly, the PR person for the partners. She takes a tiny break from the panic to glance around the room, and I can tell she likes what she sees.

We have contracted for a couple of restroom trailers that are infinitely more elegant than your run-of-the-mill portable toilets. I have the crew check out the situation, and, sure enough, the message, complete with my phone number, is on every wall.

"Why not just change the number to mine?" jokes Chuck in his best Paul Lind voice.

Bob gives him an exasperated look and heads out to find some white spray paint. Luckily, the construction crew has an abundant supply of spray paint in every color of the rainbow, and in short order the offending graffiti is covered. I gather the crew members together and do my best to calm them down. They are all pissed off as if their mother's name was the one mentioned in the felonious message. I imagine them all with torches and pitchforks, rampaging through the streets in search of the ne'er-do-well responsible for this travesty.

By the time the guests arrive and walk down the red carpet, all traces of the prank are gone, and our blood pressure is back to normal. The crowd is also quite impressed. Everything comes off in grand fashion. The scantily clad firefighters hand the mayor and VIPs the gold-plated shovels, and the photographers' cameras create a blinding lightning storm with their flashes. The speeches, décor, and food are all a huge success.

THIS CEREMONY, THOUGH, is only the tip of the iceberg. I meet with the partners the next day to discuss the grand opening, even though it is a year and a half away. The meeting starts with another huddle of the MODD Squad, with plenty of muttering and grumbling. My stress level starts peaking as my imagination runs wild with all the terrible things that can happen here. Success breeds confidence, but no matter how long I'm in this business, I'll never be able to get rid of this little bit of insecurity that starts to bark at me like one of those little yappy-type dogs when I get into situations like this. They finally break their huddle, and Oscar seems to have been designated to assume the role of spokesperson for the corporation.

"You and your crew did a good job on the groundbreaking," Oscar starts, trying to be as stiff and professional as possible.

"…a great job," adds another partner, which sparks a few seconds of muttering that fades quickly.

"We are quite satisfied…"

"…impressed," adds another partner.

"…with your attention to detail and professionalism," he pauses for a beat and continues, "but we'd like to…" *Oh, God, here it comes!* "…make sure you are willing to do the grand opening for us."

Okay, so my head is about to pop off, and it takes a couple of seconds for me to process the last part of his sentence. I mean, really, you can't lead me down the "but we'd like to… *hire somebody else*" or "*go in a different direction*" or "*take some time to think about this*" road and then spring something like "*make sure you are willing to do the grand opening*" on me.

All the gears in my head have just ground to a sudden stop, so I take a deep breath to make sure my voice doesn't crack in the middle of "Absolutely, we'd be honored to work with you again."

The MODD Squad takes turns shaking my hand as they file out of the trailer, leaving only Oscar behind to discuss the details of the budget.

Time to start planning!

The grand opening isn't just one week-long event. It's to be three events a day on every level of the mall for seven days, plus a VIP grand opening party. That's twenty-two or twenty-three events. Or twenty-four? I don't know—I'm too tired to think, and my glass of Merlot is doing a great job of sending me off to La-La Land. As I drift off, I tell David to let me know if we get any strange calls.

"What kind of strange calls?" he says.

"It's kinda hard to explain," I reply with my last bit of consciousness. "But if anyone asks 'if I'm looking for a good time,' let me know."

And zonk, I'm out.

Fun flies when you're doing time or frantically putting together the biggest event in your career (with what seems like an infinite set of sub-events), but my amazing crew has worked endlessly to pull every event together, and we are ready for the madness to begin. After a year and a half of craziness, temperamental models and vendors, décor from hell, and drunken Santas, the time has finally arrived. Ready or not, the moment of truth has arrived.

The opening event, the VIP party, is the kickoff for the mall. The crème de la crème of society has begun arriving for this black-tie event. Life is good, I am thinking, when Sam sidles up next to me and says, "He refuses to get rid of her, but I'm keeping my eye on her. I don't understand why he can't see through her 'Oh me, poor me' act."

She's referring, of course, to Cara, the major suspect in our string-of-mishaps mystery.

"Have you ever considered the fact that Nelson may be keeping her on as a way of yanking your chain?" Sam is a bit taken aback by my statement. "Don't get me wrong. She needs to be watched," I continue. "Too many weird incidents have been occurring lately. She admits to the Great Bacon Incident of 2009. I know they said ketchup is a vegetable—but bacon? That's what you call pushing the envelope."

Sam and I have studied David's photo from the teen birthday party, and we agree that the woman handing a bottle of booze to a kid bears a more-than-striking resemblance to Cara. I take a deep breath.

Only the strong will have survived by the end of this week. One day at a time, Dear Lord, one day at a time. Fifteen hundred people are in attendance at the grand opening, and from the top level of the mall, it looks like tiny penguins in tuxedos everywhere.

Dinner is served on the first level, but we have dancing music and desserts on every level and in every wing of the mall. The event is to go until midnight, after which Phil has hired the brute squad to tear down everything from the black-tie event, tables, catering, etc. Chuck and Bob have hired their own crew to transform the mall into the next event before morning. It has been total madness, and no one has gotten much sleep. Fortunately, we don't have to go too far as we all have trailers in the back of the mall where we live during the mayhem. We have rented motor homes and an office trailer for our staff. We have become our own city.

Each event throughout the week has a different theme, which means changing décor and the menu on each level of the mall every day. The VIP event has valet parking. The public events have shuttles from the parking lot to the mall.

We have spent months on menus for breakfast, lunch, and formal events. For the kids we have clowns, inflatable bounce houses, games, and prizes. And, of course, since this is mid-November, we cannot forget Santa. The effort involved in keeping a line moving of hundreds of kids ready to tell Santa what they want and have their picture taken is staggering all by itself.

Phil and I are handling the logistics and the choreography. Nelson is expertly handling all the menu changes throughout each day. He has several trailers out back, along with trucks that hold perishables. Everyone checks in with Phil and picks up their radios and the list of duties for each shift.

Phil is saying things like, "Okay, you've got the atrium breakfast shift. There are breakfast sandwiches, coffee, and juice all setup. If you start running low on anything, radio Nelson. He'll have what you need up there in seconds. And if you're keeping Santa's line moving, check in with Sam for your elf costume. The candy cane stock is behind Santa's throne. It looks like a big present with a bow, but the lid is on a hinge. Just lift and grab."

Sam has everyone's measurements and has spent months with a team of seamstresses putting together all the outfits.

She is saying things like, "Okay, who are you today? A server? Fine, what's your name?" She then goes directly to the correct outfit with that person's name pinned to it and hands it to the person. "Try not to spill anything on it," she admonishes. "I've got enough to do without running a laundry."

I can hear Chuck and Bob in the background. "No, no. red bows with green bunting goes on the south side of the second level. Green bows with red bunting are for the food court. That wreath has to move about five inches to the left!" This to a crew member up a twenty-foot ladder whose look screams, "You've got to be kidding me!"

We truly are a well-oiled machine despite the ongoing friction between Sam and Nelson.

As I said, it is mid-November, so the major theme is Christmas. Chuck and Bob manage to make the place look both festive and classy. A fifty-foot spruce graces the entrance to the mall, and twenty trees, each with a different theme and color, are spread out among the different levels.

"I've never seen such big wreaths," Phil tells the boys. "You are truly amazing!"

"You are the conductor, and we are but the orchestra," says Chuck. "We couldn't do it without your guidance, mon Capitan."

Bob clutches his heart, and they have a group "man hug."

This is the grand opening for the public, one of the last events! The mob has waited for hours to get in, and they are getting restless. I guarantee they will be constantly entertained. We have a high-wire act in the atrium, rock climbing walls with professional teams giving demonstrations, mimes, performance painters painting on ten-foot canvases, and performance artists, including a fire-breather, with whom the fire department is unhappy. It is almost overkill, but the crowd loves it.

The MODD Squad had its property management in place long before the first store moved in. Every store is having some sort of giveaway, and some are staging their own events, which is causing a bit of a stir. For instance, a national lingerie store called Ursula's Underworld is staging its own fashion show with scantily clad models walking up and down the corridor, handing out coupons. Normally, this wouldn't be that big of a concern for me, except that Ursula's models are parading right across from where we have Santa set up. How did we not see that happening?

This is apparently not going over well with the parents of the long line of children waiting to have their photos taken on Santa's lap. I manage to redirect the models away from Santa's area before the wives get too upset and the husbands get too overheated. I decide to speak to the manager of Ursula's and see if they will go along with the redirect just while Santa and the children are there.

"Hi, my name is Donna, and I'm the event manager for this whole thing. I need to ask if you could refrain from having your models out here in the atrium while Santa is taking photos with the kids."

"Well," snaps Ursula's manager, "we were told we could have models out here all day."

"I'm sure you were, but when you got the okay for that, did you tell them that your girls would be half-naked?" I ask, trying to maintain my equanimity.

"They are *not* half naked," she replies with utter disdain. Then one of her girls walks by in a peach-colored camisole and tap pants outfit that's sheer enough for me to see the pattern on her thong. The model looks down her nose at me and sneers.

"Uh huh, right," I say. "That's so appropriate to have out here with a few hundred kids. Get them out of the hall now." I reach for my radio and say, "Phil, can you meet me in the atrium near Santa?"

"Sure, I'll be right there." Mere moments later, I see him round the corner.

"I need your help getting the lingerie models out of the atrium," I say.

"Oh, beat me, hurt me, but don't throw me in that briar patch," he says with a wide grin, and off he goes.

Sam glides up next to me and asks, "Is there anything I can help with?"

"Sure, you can ensure the manager at Ursula's Underworld gets her models out of the atrium. She's unhappy about it, but we don't need them out here while Santa is doing his thing," I say. "Phil is out there somewhere rounding them up."

"I bet he is," she says with a wry smile.

No sooner have I put out that fire than a group of overly buxom waitresses in impossibly short shorts, claiming to be from a "family" restaurant called Beau Dacious Bob's Bar-B-Que, shows up to hand out coupons for free Buffalo wings. I see one of the MODD Squad making a beeline right for me.

"Donna! We can't have these girls out here!" he says while his face turns a shade of red rarely seen in nature. "This is a family event for cryin' out loud."

"Yes, sir, you're absolutely right. We are rounding up all of the lingerie models, and I just now saw the barbeque girls. We'll get them back to their restaurant as quickly as possible."

Just then, a gaggle of the lingerie models saunters by, followed by Phil. They are not at all happy about the situation and make no attempts to hide it as they glower at me. Suddenly, Ursula's girls notice the throng of barbeque girls. It is as if matter and antimatter had spotted each other from across the room. The tension is palpable. I excuse myself from Mr. MODD Squad and hustle over to intercept the bodacious babes.

"Ladies, ladies," I say to get their attention. "I can't have you out in the corridor right now."

"And who are you?" asks the tallest and apparently the oldest of the group.

"Hi, my name is Donna," I say as I extend my hand to shake hers. "I'm the event planner for this grand opening. This is a family-oriented event. I can't have you out here, at least not while Santa is here with all these children."

"Well, you're just going to have to talk to our manager about that. We have all these coupons that we have to give away, and that's not going to happen with us stuck inside our restaurant."

"Rest assured, I will talk to him…"

"Her…" she interrupts.

"Okay, I will talk with *her.*" I am now surrounded by eight or ten angry girls, and I'm beginning to think this is about to turn into a tag-team wrestling match, except I don't have any team members here to tag team with. "All right, ladies, back to the restaurant. I'll talk to your manager, and we'll see what we can do about getting the coupons out after Santa and the kids are gone."

The response is nothing short of chilling. Not a word and no indication that the girls are going to move. "*Now!* I'm not kidding. You either get back to the restaurant now, or you'll never see the outside of that place again. Is that understood?" *Wow, where did that come from?* Their glares turn to looks of pure shock, and they, ever so slowly, make their way back to Beau Dacious Bob's. Just then Phil exits Ursula's and joins me.

"That wasn't quite as much fun as I thought it would be," he laments.

"How so?" I inquire.

"They just aren't the warm and friendly type," he says.

"Well, just be glad you didn't have to deal with the barbeque babes. One of the MODD Squad spotted them and told me to get them back to their restaurant. They were not at all happy about it either. In fact, I need to go speak with their manager. Wanna come with me?"

"Sure, I think everything else is under control," he says, glancing around the expansive atrium.

We meet with the manager at the restaurant, and she seems very nice and understanding. We assure her that, after all the family-type events are over and done with, her girls can take to the walkways and hand out their coupons. It's obvious that she's quite taken with Phil and offers us both a free lunch. After explaining that there probably isn't much on her menu for a vegan, I sit with Phil while he downs a generous portion of ribs.

It's not much later that all of the family-oriented events wrap up and we are able to get the word to Beau Dacious Bob's and Ursula's that it would be okay for their girls to resume their activities out in the public areas. Meanwhile, I take the opportunity to stop by and thank Santa for all his hard work. He is one of the truly professional Santas and comes equipped with his own very real beard and belly.

As I make my way over to the stage where the jugglers and magicians are performing, I notice a bit of commotion out of the corner of my eye. It looks very much like a scene right out of *West Side Story*. It seems that the girls from the lingerie shop and the restaurant want to pick things

up where they left off the first time they saw each other. I was right: It's matter and antimatter, and they are bound and determined to destroy each other. On one side, you have the Skeleton Gorillaz from Ursula's, and on the other, the Bad Ass Bumper Bullets from Beau-Dacious Bob's. They've managed to get into a staring contest, and there is a general circular motion to the whole mob. This isn't really happening, is it?
I reach for my radio.

"Phil, Nelson, meet me in the atrium now! Grab any security guards on your way," I squawk over the two-way.

"On my way," says one.

"Almost there," says the other.

I run over to the battlefield and wade through the ring of spectators that have gathered (mostly men, of course) and into the middle of the girls. As I approach, I can hear some unflattering things being said. I can make out things like "anorexic," "flat," "short," "fat." I need to stop the insults before the fur flies. I reach the center of the mob, and there's one girl from each gang face to face, which is really difficult since the barbeque girl is the same height as I am, and the lingerie girl in heels towers over her.

"Okay, girls, break it up," I say while wedging myself between them.

"Yeah, well they…" one of them starts.

"Oh, shut your pie hole…" retorts the other.

"Both of you need to chill. We aren't going to have a smackdown during this grand opening," I say to both of them. "Got it?" One of Ursula's girls has a handful of one of Bob's girls' tank tops. Two of Bob's girls have culled one of the weaker models from the herd, and they look like they are trying to pull her apart, limb by limb.

Just then, Phil and Nelson arrive with a couple of security guards. They start the process of separating the two factions to a chorus of "Hey, get your hands off of me!"

"Quit pushing!"

I tell Phil to gather the barbeque babes and tell them to stick to the two floors on the north wing. I corral Ursula's gang and tell them they are restricted to the floors in the east wing of the mall.

"And, if I catch any of you in this central atrium or near each other again, I'll throw all of you out," I say loud enough for both gangs to hear me. At this point, I'm shaking from my adrenaline high. I allow myself a few moments of solitude by the fountain in the atrium before I confront the managers of the warring factions. Sam, Nelson, and Phil all join me by the fountain, and I take them along as backup.

"WHAT THE HELL was that about?" Sam asks.

"I have absolutely no idea. It must have been some sort of turf warfare thing," I say while shaking my head in disbelief. "But, ya know, when this is all over with, I'm going to have a good laugh over it. It truly was one of the funniest things I've ever seen. I just can't imagine what would have happened if they'd have started swinging at each other."

"Well, Ursula's girls would have had a definite reach advantage," says Sam like she knows what she's talking about.

"Yeah, but I'd have to put my money on the Bob's girls. Some of those models looked a little spindly," says Phil, grinning at her.

"Maybe short, curvy girls and tall skinny girls are just natural enemies. Maybe it's an evolutionary thing," posits Nelson. Sam, Phil, and I look at him like he's lost his marbles.

"Well, I don't know about that. Sam and I get along pretty well," I say to rebut his theory.

"I'm not sure you two fit the model. She's not all that skinny," says Nelson, pointing at Sam. "And you're not all that curvy," he says, poking me in the shoulder. Phil groans, knowing full well that there will be swift retribution for that statement. Sam and I look at each other and then at Nelson.

"Would you like to explain to Nelson the error of his ways?" I ask her.

"I would be *more* than happy to do that," she exclaims.

"My darling Nelson," she starts. The verbal tongue-lashing that ensues is fast, furious, and quite thorough. By the end, Nelson is a beaten man. I think he learned his lesson.

Meanwhile, back at the ranch…

As the piano players and various other musicians I have stationed around the mall do their thing, the finale of the public opening is in full swing. Every store is staying open late with huge sales. It's *Shop Till You Drop* on steroids. A little while later, Nelson tracks me down and informs me that he has let Cara go. He has finally gotten it through his head that she is bad news.

"You have to know that this isn't a huge surprise for me, right?" I ask him.

"Yeah, I know. It was pretty bad, though. I don't know why I didn't see it before, " he says.

"What'd she do to finally get you to see the light?"

"I caught her putting cayenne pepper in the artichoke dip. A *lot* of cayenne pepper. And…" he hesitates, "she was pretty trashed."

"Wow," I say, shaking my head. "Maybe there is something to Sam's theory."

"She was crying like a baby and blubbering, 'I was just trying to make some money to pay my bills.'"

"I've got too much on my plate right now to worry about that, but when this is all over, we'll have to piece all this together and see what we can come up with. This business is hard enough without someone trying to sabotage us."

The charity fashion show is the climax of the whole weeklong event. All the clothing stores have donated outfits, and the charity-enlisted sponsors have paid for the models we hired from the local talent agencies. In addition, we have Sophie Taylor, one of the top models in the country. Sam is really excited to meet her. The local models pose a bit of a problem, though.

"They are all devil spawn," Sam hisses at me the next morning. "They're complaining because cosmetology students are doing their hair and makeup. I told them they could take a hike if they didn't like it. There are plenty of girls out there willing to take their place. The brats!"

It must have worked because, from that point on, the show ran smooth as silk. The band Phil hired was amazing. The local TV anchor who hosted the show was more than gracious. The crowd was wowed by the fashions.

I catch up to Sam and Nelson, who are whispering to each other at the back of the crowd. "Who would have known there were any problems an hour ago?" I ask, but they don't seem to be aware of me. Apparently, they have patched things up.

I catch up with Phil, Chuck, and Bob a bit later. They are completely exhausted but happy. The crowds are gone, and the cleanup brigade has taken over. I gather my crew together. Sam and Nelson reluctantly agree to stop whispering sweet nothings for a while.

"This is the biggest event we've put on so far," I say as I hand out their holiday bonuses. "The MODD Squad is very impressed and wants to talk about doing events all over the western half of the country, and it's all because of your professionalism, talent, and, most of all, teamwork. I'm very proud of you all."

Phil produces a bottle of champagne and hands around glasses for a toast.

"And it's all thanks to Donna, who brought a bunch of rag-tag circus performers together," he says. After a dramatic pause, he continues, "Here's to the biggest event of all…Life. May we always be friends!" We clink glasses and share hugs. Nelson and Sam are the last to hug, but oh my, what a hug.

Okay, now the laughter can begin…

CHAPTER 12

Members Only

The bright lights in the bathroom of my suite are not flattering. I'm squirming like a bad child.

"Sit still," Sam tells me, grabbing my chin firmly and studying my face as if she were an archaeologist gazing upon a great find from a dig in Dinosaur National Park.

"You can't possibly spackle any more makeup on me unless you use a putty knife," I say, pushing her hand aside.

"After the false eyelashes, we're done!" she snaps. "Then we'll shove you into these skin-tight pants, leopard-print top, and six-inch heels. You'll be good to go, so if you can behave for a few more minutes, we can get through this without any bloodshed."

I slump back into the chair and behave, but only because I owe Sam in a big way. She found me Funny Freddie, the actor playing my husband for this gig. He's everything she promised: an intelligent and, best of all, long-time stand-up comedian in nightclubs. Improvisation can be brutal, so it's important to have someone with Freddie's skills to pull this off.

"So, did you ever date Freddie?" I pry. It's difficult to speak without cracking a layer of the plaster Sam has painted on my face. My lips have so much goo on them that it's a struggle to move them, and I fear if I blink, I won't have the strength in my eyelids to lift the fake eyelashes, which seem to weigh a pound each.

"No," she responds. "He doesn't really do it for me. I mean, he's wonderful, but there's just no spark."

"He's a great guy," I mutter, speaking as if my jaws have just been wired shut. I have to practice this whole speaking thing before I take the stage. What's not to love?" She shrugs, packs up her makeup kit, and looks pensively out the window.

"He's funny, but he's not...well, tamed. He can't cook, and he's way too neat for me. I'm a slob compared to him, and that just won't do. Every time he came over to my place, I got this feeling like I was failing an inspection."

I choose to keep my mouth shut and then head off to rendezvous with Freddie, my accomplice.

The two of us have spent weeks writing our back story and rehearsing for this gig. Creating characters is like giving birth, a long and arduous process, or so I've been told. When we finish, Gladys Jo and Earl Ray Cooter have been born.

Even Liberace would draw the line at the amount of bling Chuck and Bob have amassed for Earl Ray.

"Think of these as talismans meant to ward off the blue bloods," Chuck tells Freddie.

"And nothing says 'I live in a trailer' like a sky blue, double-knit leisure suit with bell-bottom pants," Bob chimes in. They've also found a rayon shirt decorated with cocktail glasses and a pair of short white patent leather zip-up boots like Elvis used to wear.

"The boots and the pin-hole cigarette burns on the front of the shirt pull the entire ensemble together," Chuck states proudly.

"Where did you guys find all this stuff?" I ask, but not really sure I want to know.

"We never reveal our sources," Bob says. "It would be unprofessional." With my blond wig, which adds three inches to my height, and my white trash costume, we are quite the sight.

Our ages, fifty for Freddie and forty for me, are only the first thing that set us off from the crowd. I've been hired by the head of the Millionaires Alliance of North America to liven up the initiation of the new prospects. This year, their meeting will be held at a five-star resort off the coast of South Carolina. To get into this group, applicants must be under thirty and own a business that grosses ten million or more a year.

The applicants are to take the stage and address the audience, saying something like, "My name is Thurston Howell IV, and this is my wife Penelope Stanton Robles Howell. I am the President and CEO of Inflated Ego Enterprises. We make silver-plated widgets, and our company grosses twenty million a year. My wife Penelope is head of the Snobby League of Bored Women and a member of the First Cousins of the Southern Revolution. We have five children. Thurston V, Prescott, Miles, Tyson, and our darling baby Samuel. Our children attend an overpriced private school in Birmingham, and we get to see them every Christmas. We want to be a member of this prestigious organization as we feel it is our place to belong with all of you…" or some such story as that.

There are other rules, but, in short, we are the polar opposites of what they are looking for in their members. Only six of the dozen applicants taking the stage will be accepted into this exclusive club. My client, Jack Meyers, is the president of the Millionaires Alliance.

"Here's the deal," he told me when we met weeks before. "This annual dinner is supposed to be the highlight of a week of conferences, socializing, and activities." He explained that the candidates had fifteen minutes to convince the board they deserved to be members.

"Tell you the truth, the whole thing kind of drags," Meyers said. "We need something to spice it up."

"Spice," I say, "is our middle name."

One of his stipulations upon hiring us was that no one could know who put us up to this. This was to be a complete and total surprise. My faux husband and I are to show up as the last couple to step up to the microphone that evening and explain to the crowd why we simply are the perfect candidates to join their club.

"Our treasurer, Harlan Haskels, won't get the joke, but the rest of the crowd will," Meyers said with a grin. "In fact, mention him by name, just to tick him off. And make sure you say you want to join the club. Nothing angers him more than for somebody to call this organization a club."

Harlan, he said, was not only humorless, but the board of the organization was weary of his endless complaints and arrogant attitude.

"The Alliance is primarily about pooling assets and brain power for philanthropic purposes, though there are a few members who use it solely as a social clique," Meyers said. "Haskles is so cheap he married a skinny girl just so he could buy a smaller ring."

The evening of the escapade we use Phil as the driver for our getaway car. "I feel like we're on a caper," Phil says, doing his best Jimmy Cagney impersonation as we pull up to the hotel. Phil and Sam have flown in on their own dime to be part of this prank.

"Phil, baby, I think you've got a real future as a wheelman," I say, patting my buddy on the back. "Keep it close, and don't let it get cold," I whisper with my best Mae West impersonation and slide a twenty over his shoulder as a tip.

The doormen help Freddy and me out of the back of the car as Phil mutters, "I wish I had a nickel for every time a woman has said that to me," under his breath. I feel the wadded up twenty bounce off the back of my head as I steady myself and make the necessary adjustments to my costume.

"You seem to have dropped this, Ma'am," says the doorman as he picks the twenty off the ground and holds it in his outstretched palm.

"Bless your heart, Sweetie, you can keep that," I say as I teeter off in these God-forsaken high heels. I have a vision running through my head of me laid out on the floor, croaking, "I've fallen, and I can't get up…"

We creep into the banquet staff kitchen area and hang out until we know it's our time to go on. I admit that I'm a little nervous about this performance because of the price I charged for the prank. I need this to go off without a hitch.

We arrive just in time to see the final couple go on. Before they take the stage, they give us the once-over and couldn't be more shocked at our appearance.

"Would ya'll like to go ahead of us?" the young wife offers in a sweet Southern drawl.

Earl Ray, hair greased back, cigarette behind one ear, and a toothpick in his mouth, says, "Trust me, Doll, you don't want to follow us."

Then, the announcer calls their names, and they're off.

"We don't stand a chance, Gladys," Earl Ray says, draping an arm around my shoulder.

Getting into character, I slip into a syrupy, sweet Southern accent. "Now, never say never, Earl," I say, grinning up at him as we wait. "Thurston Howell IV and his wife, Penelope, can't hold a candle to us, Sweetheart. Who cares about their silver-plated widgets? Who cares if they pull in twenty million a year? Who cares if their five kids attend private school? We got somethin' better! We got class, Baby. We got class."

Thurston and his wife finish up their speech, step away from the podium, and nod to the five hundred people offering up polite applause from their tables. As they exit the stage, Penelope scowls and gives us a wide berth as if bad taste is contagious.

"You look a little pale, Sweetheart," I say in passing to the sophisticated-looking brunette. Do you want to borrow some of my blush? It's called Passion Ignited. It looks like you might need this." Penelope stiffens up straight as a board, and her husband hustles her off before she can say something un-ladylike.

We take a look at the crowd. Clearly, they're weary from the week of festivities—tennis, polo, yachting, and the like. The applicants are stressed out: The decision to accept or reject these applicants, worthy or not, rests in just a few hands.

Our mole has put us last on the agenda. He's assured us that he will have added our names to the teleprompter after the final rehearsal that afternoon. All we need to do is step into the spotlight, and the clueless announcer will have no choice but to introduce us.

We hear our names and step out from the darkness. A very confused master of ceremonies does a double-take and says, "It seems we have a last-minute addition. Please welcome Mr. Earl Ray and Gladys Jo Cooter."

We step on stage, and all the conversation stops. You can tell that a few people in the audience weren't paying attention as a smattering of applause ends abruptly. Even the wait staff appears to be frozen on the spot. It's clear from the horrified looks that this crowd has no clue that this is a joke.

Above the murmur of the crowd, I hear a lone voice say, "Dear God, what is this? Get them the hell off stage."

A short, round man about to bust the seams on his tuxedo lurches to his feet and starts toward the stage. His wife, who is, in fact, a wiry little thing, snatches him back into his chair and glares at him.

I'm betting my bottom dollar that the heckler in the audience is the terribly unpopular Harlan Haskles. I'm thankful his wife has a good hold on him because I'm sure he'd be up here dragging us off stage if he could.

I CHEW HARD on my bubble gum, stretch some of it from my mouth, then chew it back in. I make a big deal of picking the stuck-on gum from my fingers, grin at the crowd, shrug, and wipe offending fingers on my skin-tight top.

My new favorite actor swaggers back up to the microphone and announces, "My name is Earl Ray, and this here little lady is my wife Gladys Jo." He pauses to chew on his toothpick before continuing. "We're the proud owners of Cooters Rooters, the most successful septic system service company in the entire state of Alabama. We cleared almost a million dollars last year. We never figured there would be that much money in sewage, but it turns out it was a damn sight easier than diggin' for gold."

Slowly but surely, the crowd starts to realize that this is good fun, and we hear a sprinkling of laughter. It's time for me to jump in.

"We're the proud parents of ten of the best dang children God coulda blessed us with. Five are from my previous marriages, and Earl Ray is the proud papa of them other five critters." Laughter fills the room, and I know we're going to be a hit. Just like any proud parent, I continue to brag about my children.

"Bobby Sue just got engaged to be married and finally make it legal. Billy Ray, our oldest, is due for parole before the end of the year, and Billy Jack just received his GED." Choking back faux tears, I continue: "We are so proud of him. Maggie Mae was just released from rehab and has decided to turn her life around and work in the family sewage business with us. Finally, our baby Ernest Joe, who lives at home with us, has just started his own motorcycle gang. We're so proud of him. He's a natural-born leader. I just know he'll go far in life."

By this time the crowd is howling, and we have to pause often between comments for the crowd's roar to die down.

We had been given information on some of the long-time members of the group who took yacht trips and sailing trips and spent time playing polo, so we worked some of those names into our routine so that the crowd would realize we were in the right place. But Earl holds back for a bit before dropping the big name.

"I'm honored to have been yachting with Harlan Haskles, the treasurer of this really great club ya' got here. And the networking has definitely paid off," Earl says. "It was on account of knowin' ol' Harlan that our company got that contract for that Polo Club over there in Tuscaloosa. Apparently, they got some mighty big sewage problems they don't like to talk about."

"That's right," I chime in, "and apparently several members of that club can get pretty backed up, if ya know what I mean."

Harlan utters a curse word simply unsuitable for such a classy event. He escapes from his wife, and I see him make his way to the back of the room, where he stops the room captain and waves at the stage. Oh yeah, he's going to try to stop us. Good luck with that, I think, as we wrap up the routine, performed with flawless backwoods Southern accents that even the Grand Ole Opry would be proud of.

We've been in the spotlight for fifteen minutes, as we've had to hold for extended laughter. Part of our contract is that we have to get out of sight before anyone in the group can get to us, and that includes Harlan. Earl wraps up with, "We'd like to thank ya'll for contemplatin' lettin' us into your club."

The crowd is doubled over with laughter as we start for the exit. We know we have to run with Harlan hot on our heels. This isn't an easy thing to do in six-inch heels. I pull them off and sprint barefoot to the car that's still under the portico at the front door.

Sure enough, as we fly through the front doors, the humorless treasurer rounds the corner of the building and yells, "I'll have you arrested, you trash." We dive into the back of the car as the red-faced man makes a lame attempt to grab me.

"Step on it," I say as Freddie and I pile into the back of the car.

Phil pulls away from the main entrance to the hotel, and Harlan is left pounding on the trunk as we drive off.

"Who the heck was that?" Sam asks.

"Somebody who still doesn't get it," says Freddie with a chuckle.

"Someone I predict will be booted from that club for bad behavior very soon," I add. "In fact, if I was a betting woman, I'd say within the hour."

"For all this, shouldn't you be lugging a briefcase full of hundreds?" Phil asks as Freddie and I settle into the backseat. "I half expect a cop to be in hot pursuit."

"We did it!" I say as I grin and hug Freddie.

"How did it go?" begs Sam.

"Flawless," I reply. "When we walked on stage you could've heard a pin drop."

"They didn't know what hit 'em," adds Freddie.

"I was a little nervous at first, but they started to catch on pretty quick," I continue. "We actually had to hold some of our lines because of the laughter."

"That was more fun than rolling around with pigs in a mud puddle," Freddie says, still stuck in character.

"Sam, you have to chisel this stuff off my face," I beg her. She starts to answer me, but her cell phone goes off.

"Hey, you," she says into the latest and most expensive gizmo she could find. "Yeah, it went well. I'll tell you all about it later, okay?" She pauses, and I see a sweet smile pass over her face. "And me you, too," she murmurs.

"Who was that?" I ask, being the ever-nosy friend.

"Just Nelson, checking to see how it went," she replies while gazing fondly at her phone.

It's interesting that he didn't call me, I think. Then something dawns on me: "What's this 'And me you, too' nonsense?" I pry as only I can. She's clearly flustered as we pull up to our hotel.

"Oh, he was just saying have a good night," she stammers.

"She may be a great costumer, but that was a terrible acting performance. She's holding back on you, my friend. Sounds like she's stuck on whoever was on the other end of that line," Freddie whispers to me as we pile out of the car.

I raise an eyebrow and nod. "Yes, she is, Earl Ray," I tell him with my backwoods accent. "And I think I know who she's stuck on. Trust me; it'll take her a half hour to scrape this stuff off my face. And in that half hour, our little Sammy's going to spill like one of those overflowing septic tanks we're always having to fix up."

Just then, my cell phone beeps, and I dive into my purse, looking for it. Jack Meyers's text is short and sweet: "Crowd still laughing. Haskles having stroke. You guys were great! Thanks."

CHAPTER 13

Under the Big Top

While relating to David the perils of raising the Big Top, another call comes through. "Phil's on the other line; I'll call you back later," I say. "I love you."

I push flash, and before I can utter a word, Phil says, "Turn on your TV. Channel 9. Don't hang up." I turn on the TV to pandemonium. The local Wyoming news reporter is talking a mile a minute.

"Folks, this is the most amazing thing that has ever happened here in..." The camera pans over from him to show six elephants thundering down the main drag, holding each other trunk to tail. All traffic has pulled over, and most cars are abandoned. Parents are running down the street with children in their arms. It's like an episode of *The Twilight Zone*: *"Picture if you will a sleepy little town in Wyoming where nothing much happens..."*

These behemoths aren't doing a circus act. They appear to have a mission.

"Who's the clown that allowed this to happen?" I ask. I am not speaking metaphorically. There really *is* a clown running alongside the elephants, tossing candy to the kids. This ain't *Bozo*. This is for real.

This being my first circus gig, I'm not aware of the quirks inherent in circus people or animals. I have no idea why elephants would make a break for it. We've been hired by a local charity organization to provide a circus event for the benefit of a new children's hospital. While the circus had its own management team and internal event planner, it was our job to arrange for all of the tents, food, and entertainment that wasn't being provided by them.

I'm thinking of all the problems this event has presented so far as I jump in my car and race through rush hour traffic, managing to hit every red light along the way. I think they have sensors that tell them when you're in a hurry. I'm heading for the "scene of the crime." There are fugitive elephants on the loose, and I am desperately hoping they won't hurt anyone.

I've never studied animal psychology or even watched the National Geographic channel, so I don't know how a five-thousand-pound pachyderm might react to some idiotic road-rager trying to make it home in time for dinner. *"Next on the five o'clock news, when circus animals go bad."* I groan at the thought.

When I arrive, there are police cars, fire trucks, and a small crowd of rubber neckers. The trainers have corralled the rogue elephants and are riding them (yes, riding them!) back to the circus. By that point, the principal area of concern for the police and of entertainment for all the kids who have gathered are the prodigious pachyderm pies our large friends have left behind. They had just been doing what anyone would do on their first day in a new town, taking in the sights, I guess. Only in this case, *they* were the sights.

"Well, at least it wasn't the big cats," Chuck says, standing next to a shell-shocked Bob.

"No doubt! That tends to drive attendance down when they eat the residents," I say while we walk back to the car.

"It eats into the profits, too. Pun very much intended," quips Chuck as Bob groans. "And look at all the gifts they've left! Too bad they didn't have time to wrap them."

Always on top of things, Phil interrupts Bob's circus stand-up routine.

"I made sure the circus knows they are responsible for cleaning up this mess. If this is an indicator of things to come, it's gonna be the gig from hell. I've called a meeting with the circus staff to find out how this happened and to make sure we don't have any more stunts like this."

Oddly enough, the circus staff did not seem as concerned as we were. Once I got to know some of them, I began to see why. Not only do these people march to the beat of a different drummer, but they're the ones playing the drum! How many of us dreamed of running away from home to join the circus? Well, these people have actually done it. It was fascinating to talk to some of them. All of them had a story to tell, each with a different mixture of humor and sadness. But they had all found a home and a family here, a very accepting family made up of performers of vastly diverse lifestyles and backgrounds. I thought I had experienced every type of performer, from illusionists to psychics, comedians, and actors with every type of personality disorder possible. I was wrong.

Circus folk are a breed apart. It's as though residents of one planet were performing for residents of another. Management provides them with retirement plans and health insurance, but these are definitely not nine-to-five cubicle dwellers. They live in a perpendicular universe. Also, I had a distinct feeling that a few of them were 'on the lam,' as they say."

At the meeting, we learn that the elephants made their break sometime after the trainer had locked up their enclosures for the evening. Jack, the circus manager, seemed to take the whole incident in stride. He was neither alarmed nor upset. I began to wonder whether this wasn't all just a publicity stunt to make sure everyone knew the circus was in town. It was only because of his obvious respect for Phil that he agreed to the meeting of the troops at all. Most of them are busy practicing for tomorrow's performance.

"We'd never let our big babies out alone. One of them could get hurt," yells the elephant trainer from atop Rosy, the star elephant, who takes a bow, accentuating his statement.

The Amazing Clyde, the lion tamer, takes his head out of Leo's mouth just long enough to say, "They're part of the family, and we look out for our own!"

"Not a chance," says a tiny performer in a little pink dress, hanging from her knees high overhead on the trapeze. I am truly touched at how these people vehemently defend and support one another. I don't know that many "real" families who are as supportive.

"My main concern is who that clown was dancing down the street handing out candy," I tell Jack as Phil brings the meeting to order. By this time, my crew and most of the circus staff are in the room. They all claim ignorance of this stunt.

"We've never seen that clown before," says Clyde. "He's not one of ours."

"Well, like Bob said, thank God it wasn't the big cats," I say with more than a little irritation in my voice. Great, now we have a mystery clown. That's the last thing I need right now.

As I have said, this is a charity event for a local children's hospital. Not only were we handling the smaller tents, food, and non-circus entertainment, but we were also providing the red-and-white striped Big Top. Eliminating the transportation of that large tent, plus the crew necessary to put it up, allowed the local gala peeps on the committee to hire the circus at a reduced rate. For us, it has been a real test of perseverance. Most tent rental companies have, long ago, eliminated that kind of tent in favor of more modern tents that look nicer and are easier to put up. It took a few hours on the Internet and a couple of exasperating phone calls, but we finally found our Big Top.

There are a lot of tents involved in this gig, more than my stalwart crew and I had ever managed before. For the circus performers, there are two tents. One is a dining hall, and the other is an Internet café/game room/lounge. As well, we have a tent that provides a lounge area for our crew. No problem with these tents, but the Big Top is another story.

Tents of a certain size require permits from the city and fire department. They also require an inspection upon completion. They must be habitable with exit signs and fire extinguishers placed every so many feet. A Big Top takes a week to erect and have the wood flooring installed. It had been arranged that we would set up everything on some unused acreage on the grounds of the old golf course. The groundskeeper had agreed to have his crew shut off the sprinklers in our area. The five-foot stakes holding down the Big Top had to be extremely secure, and wet muddy ground would make that impossible.

The 2 A.M. call jolts me out of a deep sleep.

"He could tell the sprinklers were on because he heard the water hitting underneath the flooring," Phil reports of his call from the security guard.

I throw on some sweats and pile my hair up under a baseball cap, and Phil and I head down to the site. After an hour of finger pointing and blame shifting, we finally get the sprinklers turned off and extract an iron-clad agreement from the grounds crew that it will not happen again. I think the prospect of seeing me again at two in the morning without any makeup on was just the leverage we needed to cement our agreement. Our contract has a clause specifically addressing sprinkler systems, electric and sewage lines. All lines are to be marked, and sprinklers are to shut down. For the next two days, the grounds crew stays true to their word, and we are able to dry out.

The day before the inspector arrives, Phil gets another call from the security guard.

"Dude, I can feel the sprinklers under my feet again, and I can't get anybody from the grounds department," he says after apologizing to Phil for the early A.M. phone call. This time Phil is seriously pissed off and more than a little worried. He calls the managing pro, demanding to know why this is still happening.

"Apparently, there is a huge language barrier with the grounds staff, and we are not getting through to them," he tells me as we head for a meeting with the golf course management early the next morning. The vein in his forehead is throbbing, so I make sure I do all the talking. Phil rarely ever gets mad, but this is just the sort of thing to make him go volcanic. I'm hoping a feminine touch will help make the point.

I stand at the head of a long conference table and look at everyone to make sure I have their attention.

"Gentlemen, let me make myself perfectly clear," I say. "If the Big Top does not pass inspection, this fundraiser will go up in smoke. I'm not sure how much clearer I can make this. The show will *not* go on. I don't know what the problem is, nor do I need to know. I just need it to be resolved. End of story." Okay, so much for the feminine touch.

As we are leaving the meeting, Phil says, "I don't think I have ever seen you get that tough."

"Well, this really chaps my ass," I say, borrowing a phrase from my husband's verbal arsenal and still shaking from having to have been that assertive. "Once? Okay, I can understand that. Twice? That's just wrong. And besides, I think the fear of not passing inspection took over."

But my strategy works. The golf course management stays on site for the next two nights, threatening to draw and quarter anyone who even gets close to the sprinkler controls.

The day before the inspection, though, the water has not dried up. Instead, it had pooled, and the stakes on the backside of the tent are not going to hold. Bart Mallard, the head of our tent company, comes out to check all the stakes on the Big Top.

"Three stakes need to be removed," he says to Phil. "There is no way to dry up the ground, so we need to bring in dry dirt and redo those three stakes. Otherwise, you will not pass inspection."

Phil calls me immediately. "Houston, we have a problem," he says. "Meet me at the Big Top in thirty minutes."

With Chuck and Bob in tow, I head for the Big Top. I arrive to see a crew of fifteen with a small earth mover being supervised by Phil and Bart. Three of the tent stakes have been removed, and they are digging out the muck and replacing it with truckloads of dry dirt. Phil gives me the lowdown in his pragmatic way.

"We can't re-stake tonight," he says. "We have to let the dirt soak up the moisture overnight. Then, Bart and his crew will show up three hours before the inspector is due to arrive. Hopefully, we'll have this mess cleaned up in time."

Chuck and Bob, who are watching from a safe distance, can see I was about to snap.

"Let's get back to our tent," Bob says, looking at me all worried like. "Nelson has dinner ready, and I strongly suggest you have some wine with your meal."

"Yes," Chuck adds. "You look like you could use a drink or ten."

But I can't eat. My head is pounding, and my stomach is churning. What more can possibly go wrong? Phil walks in forty-five minutes later.

"They've done all they can for tonight," he says. "Everyone pray to whatever deity you believe in that the ground will be dry enough to hold those three stakes in the morning."

I know Phil is stressed, but he's hiding it pretty well. Considering what a control freak he is, I can just imagine what is going through his mind.

"I'm really worried that we won't pass inspection," he states flatly. "They put a layer of sand and gravel down under the topsoil that will do a good job of soaking up the moisture, but those inspectors are extremely nitpicky, and three loose stakes are not something you can cover up."

As promised, Bart and his crew are on the job early the next morning. We are three hours away from inspection. Everything is working like clockwork until, while hammering in the last stake, they hit a water line that feeds the irrigation system for the golf course. I am driving onto the site when I see the geyser. My crew, the grounds crew, and the tent crew begin working in full overdrive to get it to stop. Phil estimates that around five hundred gallons have been released by the time they shut it off. The whole area resembles a Louisiana bayou.

All I can think while frantically searching for a tranquilizer in my purse is, "Well, it was fun while it lasted. I wonder what I can do now that my career as an event planner has been buried in the mud?" My next thought is, "When will I ever learn? I need to find some work boots that I don't mind getting muddy."

Phil is in total control. He directs everyone from The Amazing Clyde to the head groundskeeper.

One hour before the inspection, I was trying to figure out a way to tell the client that all of his planning had gone for naught. The thought of arranging a conference call with our liability insurance agent and our attorney made me wonder whether there is enough antacid on the planet to settle my stomach.

"Look at the bright side," Chuck says as he and I are wrestling a huge sheet of plywood into place.

"And that would be….?" I snap.

"How many people can say they spent the morning hauling plywood with The Amazing Clyde?" Before I can place my hands around Chuck's neck, Phil announces that the inspector has arrived.

"Act casual and leave it all up to me," he proclaims.

Moments later, Phil is escorting the inspector through the circus area while all the circus folk try to distract him by performing their specialties. The contortionist bends over backward to get his attention, but it's clear that the inspector and Phil are deep in conversation. I thought Phil would surely take him through the front entrance of the tent, but he goes directly to the back, where thirty mud-soaked men are working.

"What the hell is he doing?" I let slip with my out-loud voice. Earlier, Phil had thrown a sheet of plywood over the hole. I hold my breath as the inspector crosses over it. "This is it!" I think. "We're circling the drain."

Offhandedly, the inspector looks around and sympathizes. "Looks like you have a bit of a mess here," I hear him say while stepping over a small river draining from underneath the plywood floor. "I'll just check the exit signs and fire extinguishers and get the paperwork started." This man has had a severe head trauma! Nobody can be that oblivious to the situation. After he checks the inside of the tent, Phil brings him over to meet me.

"Donna, this is Bill," he says. "He was just telling me that he's going on vacation to Boston tomorrow, and I was telling him about that event we did at Faneuil Hall."

"Nice to meet you," I say. When you first talk after holding your breath for ten minutes, it sounds like you're having an asthma attack.

"Oh, you must visit the Aquarium while you're there," I say, still a bit breathless. I am still in my "end of the world" mode when the inspector and Phil shake hands and walk out the front entrance of the tent. Phil comes back and hands me the permit with a grin. I rip the permit out of his hand and stare at it in total disbelief.

"Would you mind explaining precisely what the hell just happened here?" I demand, my voice trembling from the spike in my blood pressure. "He didn't walk in here with a seeing-eye dog, so I know he's not blind."

Phil can't hide the glee with which he is now beaming. "I started out by mentioning what the event was all about, and he was a little disappointed that he wasn't going to be here to enjoy the circus. That's when he mentioned that he was going to Boston in the morning, and I just started flooding him with places to go and things to do. Mentally, I think he was already on the plane headed east."

Jersey barriers are those lovely hunks of concrete the highway departments put on the center line of the road to prevent head-on collisions. They also surround road repair sites with them so no one dumps a car into a big hole. They are very, very heavy. Bart brought in eight of these big boys on a flatbed truck and fastened them to the back of the Big Top, just in case the five-foot stakes don't hold in the muck. The funny thing about tents is that they can become gigantic kites under the right circumstances.

THE CIRCUS "FAMILY" has its own issues, as well. Sampson, the ringmaster, is very "handsy" with the ladies. When he's not commanding the center ring, he's constantly giving unwelcome neck and shoulder massages to our female staff. He comes up behind them and starts rubbing. Well, he's rubbing Sam the wrong way. After three days of his unnerving antics, she replaces most of the female staff with men, effectively ending what has become known as "The Sampson Situation."

The Amazing Clyde, the lion tamer, has a seemingly endless number of flamboyant outfits. Also, he is absolutely infatuated with Chuck and Bob, which makes them uneasy.

"They should call him 'The Fabulous Clyde,'" said Chuck.

"Oh, it's what all the animal trainers are wearing this season," Bob retorts. "I wonder, if a gay lion outs himself, is he coming out of the cage?"

They finally end Clyde's overtures by having a conversation within earshot, during which Bob remarks, "Chuck, refresh my memory. Was it the late seventies or early eighties when those kind of outfits were in style?"

Clyde gives a little gasp and shoots them a "Well, I never" look, but it ends the problem.

There is a contortionist whose entire act consists of getting into and out of a very small box. Then, there is a Mongo type who lifts huge weights on stage and huge éclairs off stage. His costume consists of a tiny swimsuit that is barely visible.

There are sword swallowers, fire eaters, juggling unicyclists, happy clowns, sad clowns, lions and tigers and bears. Oh, my! There is a giant of a man who, although he is extremely nice, seems medicated most of the time. They have trailers that open up into shooting galleries, dunk tanks, and dart-throwing contests. I'm sure we have all been to the circus at one time or another as spectators, but working at a circus event gives you an insight into a world that outsiders rarely get to experience.

Before the public opening, we host a private reception in the Big Top for the benefactors of the hospital's foundation. Chuck and Bob have expertly added to the circus paraphernalia that is already there. Nelson has provided the usual circus fare, such as a popcorn machine, a cotton candy machine, plus bowls of animal crackers and peanuts.

Additionally, he got creative with things like Big Top cupcakes, Carousel Cake, Tiger Paws (slightly altered Bear Claws), little finger sandwiches shaped like animals, balloons, tents, and elephant ear cookies.

As I circulate through the crowd, making sure all is well, I run into my favorite client, Joan Prentice. She is hands down the most approachable and warm person I have ever met.

"Donna, how are you?" she asks, giving me a big hug. "People are still talking about that amazing anniversary party you put together for us last month."

"The most important thing is that you had a good time," I say.

Then, she gets a little closer and lowers her voice a bit.

"I'm a little surprised you've hired Brenda Smith from Sassy Events," she says. "She tried to underbid you for the anniversary party, you know. She was very unprofessional and said some terrible things about you and your company."

"No, I didn't hire her," I say. "I've never even met her."

"Well, she's right over there in the corner," Joan says. "So, I thought… well, never mind."

As Joan gives me a big hug and wanders off to mingle some more, I glance in the direction she pointed to, trying not to be obvious. "So, that's Brenda Smith," I think. "She bears an uncanny resemblance to Cara."

I quickly gather outside the tent with Nelson, Sam, Phil, Chuck, and Bob.

"Nelson, I think your Cara is our saboteur," I tell him.

"She's not *my* Cara!" he protests, looking at Sam, whose face is fixed in a grim expression.

"Well, she managed to get you to hire her, and I'm pretty sure she's responsible for all of the mishaps from the bathroom graffiti to the tasteless tattoos to the vegan bacon."

Sam, who has been dead serious this whole time, suddenly looks like the cat that ate the canary. I swear I see a light bulb appear above her head.

"Okay," I say to her, "what's your bright idea?"

"You," Sam snarls, poking a finger into Nelson's chest. "You are going to get little Miss Brenda into our tent for a friendly little chat."

Nelson winces at the jab and realizes there is no sense in protesting. Trying his best to be nonchalant, he makes his way over to our villainess.

"Phil, darling, can I borrow that cute little voice recorder you always use in meetings?" Sam coos. Her change of personality is scary. Phil gives himself a thorough pat down to find which pocket the recorder is in. He fishes it out and hands it to her. "Thank you," she says. "Now we wait," she whispers. As we do our best to be inconspicuous, we watch as Nelson approaches Brenda and starts a conversation. A few minutes later, they slip out of the Big Top, and Sam turns to us and snaps, "Follow my lead." I'm starting to wonder how many more personalities she has rattling around in that pretty little head of hers.

"Uh, Sam? You know someone will surely notice if she suddenly goes missing," I gently advise.

"Oh, don't be silly—I'm not going to inflict any pain," she responds demurely, "but she doesn't know that."

As we arrive at our staff tent, Sam peaks inside, turns to us, puts a finger to her lips, and lets out a tiny "Shhh." She slips into the tent, and we stealthily follow her. Sure enough, Nelson has managed to lure Brenda into our tent, and they have their backs to us while they chat and enjoy what's left of our lunch buffet. With ninja-like deftness, we close in behind them. When Sam clears her throat to announce our presence, both Nelson and Brenda nearly jump out of their skin. I didn't know we could slink that well. Brenda whips around and is clearly made nervous by the sight of the angry mob now confronting her. She stammers a weak hello and looks to Nelson for help. Sam steals a glance at the voice recorder and punches the record button.

"Why?" Sam demands. "Whatever possessed you to try to ruin our business? What sick thrill were you getting by being a malicious little snake?"

Brenda is visibly stunned and trying desperately hard not to dissolve into tears.

"What are you talking about? What do you want from me?"

"Just the facts, ma'am," says Phil, who has slipped into *Dragnet* mode. "Just the facts."

Nelson has turned furious, his face just inches from hers.

He yells, "You put jalapeños in my salads! You served bacon to vegans! What if someone had a food allergy and died!?" Sam continues the list of transgressions up to and including the elephant escape and the sprinklers.

Brenda suddenly spews, "I was just returning the favor. All I ever wanted to be was an event planner, but every job I bid on was ripped right out from under me by you," she hisses, pointing at me. "You ruined my life," she screams. "I got evicted from my apartment. I've got no money, and now my parents won't even talk to me."

"Well, Missy, doing all of this will end you up in jail, and you won't have to worry about all those other things," Chuck chimes in.

At that moment I actually feel sorry for her. No, I can't forgive her for trying to undermine my business. She has done some damage to our reputation, and it will take a while to recover from some of her sabotage efforts, but I can't see her doing jail time for what she's done. By now, she has confessed to everything, even stuff we somehow missed. Suddenly, she switches from being on the brink of a breakdown to her former arrogant self.

"You have no proof," she says, flicking her hair over her ear. "You don't have a legal leg to stand on."

Sam pulls out the recorder and says, "Oh, really?"

"That won't stand up in court!" Brenda snaps.

"We don't really need it to," says Phil. "We'll just file it away as insurance to ensure you never do it again. And besides, now that we've connected the dots, we have plenty of witnesses to call if this ever does need to go to court."

At this point I shoo everyone out of the tent, and I sit Brenda down at one of the tables. I get her a bottle of water and tissues so she can blow her nose and wipe off the mascara that's running down her cheeks.

"Did you really think that by destroying my business you were going to gain some sense of satisfaction?" I ask.

"I don't know. I don't know what I was thinking. I was just so mad," she says through her sniffling.

"Look, it took me a long time to get to where we are now. I was outbid hundreds of times along the way. You just have to persevere."

"I know—I just let it get the best of me," she blubbers.

"Well, just know that whatever you do now, you can't revert to sabotage when things don't work out. You are lucky, though; I could take this to the police, and you'd never have to worry about being an event planner ever again," I say, trying to be intimidating. She looks up at me, and the waterworks start all over again.

As we leave the tent, my angry mob is outside still and in no mood to be merciful. Brenda's apologies soften them up a bit, but it's clear it will take a while for them to move on from this.

All's well that ends well, I guess. Turns out that the event planner for the circus company got caught with her hand in the cookie jar and was summarily fired. By the end of the day Brenda had, literally, run off with the circus. I made a pact with her that I wouldn't mention her antics as long as she promised to return to the straight and narrow. She agreed, and from what I hear she's doing a great job for them.

After all our trials and tribulations, the event turns out to be a major success. The charity exceeds its financial goal by a good deal. The charity organizers, the golf course crew, and the circus management love us. Like I say, you learn something from every event. Phil and I have a couple of pages of lessons learned from this one. This has indeed been an event I will always remember. I have met so many talented and diverse performers who were each special in their own ways. The circus is one big family of misfits. Every family has at least one member who doesn't quite fit in, but not the circus. Somehow, they are all there because they want to be; they all fit.

Thinking about myself and my path, I realize I am the odd one in my family. Who else is auctioning off miniature donkeys one week and chasing down rogue elephants the next?

CHAPTER 14

You Can't Buy Happiness

"Well, this should be fun," I say to Sam and Phil, who are lazing in the chairs in front of my desk.

"What's that?" asks Phil, staring blankly out the window. It's a hot August day, and our air conditioning is on the fritz. The ceiling fan is doing its best to circulate the hot air in my office.

Well, this should be fun," I say to Sam and Phil, who are lazing in the chairs in front of my desk.

"What's that?" asks Phil, staring blankly out the window. It's a hot August day, and our air conditioning is on the fritz. The ceiling fan is doing its best to circulate the hot air in my office.

"We got that gig in Telluride," I answer, trying not to expend any energy.

"You mean the one with Happy?" Sam clarifies.

"Yeah."

"Sweet," she says. She is sprawled out in a very un-lady-like fashion, and I get the idea she has no intention of moving anytime soon. "When is it?"

"First weekend in October," I answer.

"Well, at least it will be cooler there," says Phil.

"I saw him a few years ago, when he was just starting out," says Sam. "He's hilarious."

"What's his rider like?" Phil asks, seemingly entranced by the clouds rolling by.

"Not too bad," I answer, flipping through the pages of his contract. It's standard stuff: a five-star hotel, one suite, and two regular rooms, a limo to and from the airport, and lots of water and fruit backstage. And it specifies what kind of wireless mic he uses and how many backup mics are to be available."

"Yeah, that's not bad," Phil says with his eyes closed.

"*Zoe!*" I holler. She appears in the doorway, and I notice she has changed out of her skirt and blouse into running shorts and an airy tank top. She's also barefoot.

"Yeah?" she answers.

"Did you call the building manager?"

"Yup."

"What'd he say?"

"They're working on it."

"Did you tell him we are dying here?"

"I did. He didn't seem all that concerned."

"That's it; he's off the Christmas card list."

"I'll make a note of that."

"Thank you."

And with that the conversation dies. I have been working on this for months. It's a never-ending battle with the board of this nonprofit about the cost-benefit analysis of bringing in a star for its annual conference. Then, once the board decides to bring in a high-priced comedian, the members have to fight over who it will be. The list started with about twelve names. Scheduling conflicts brought the list down to six immediately. Price pared it down to three. Then, it came down to a matter of taste and popularity. Since those are very subjective matters, the debates became very contentious. After a few too many meetings, it became clear that the board was at a stalemate. The members asked me who I would pick, and I came up with a list of pros and cons for the last three comedians on the list. The best reasons I could come up with for choosing Happy Noyes were that he worked clean and was riding a tidal wave of popularity. He would be a big draw for the conference. The board agreed and gave me the green light to get him under contract.

The hard part of this process has already been done. Calling the agencies for twelve different comedians is not a pleasant chore. The first step in this process is to call all the agencies and get rates and availability for each comedian. Most big-name stars are represented by agencies in either New York or L.A. A few are represented by offices in Nashville (more about that later). You have to be fluent in two different languages if you are going to interact with these people. When you first start out, you never, ever get to the actual agents. You get to talk instead to their assistants. These devil spawn practice for the day when they will finally get to be real agents by treating you with as much condescension as is humanly possible.

When you talk to the agencies in New York, you have to know how to speak Rude. It's a language that is curt and abrupt. You also have to be able to speak very fast. They don't have time for any hesitation on your part. The first time you utter an *um* or an *uh*, you are banished to a vortex of unending voicemails.

For L.A. you need to be able to speak Snotty. This language is very similar to Rude but not quite as fast. The most important aspect of Snotty is you have to speak it with tons of attitude. When speaking to an agency on the West Coast, you must take great care not to show any weakness. The assistants can smell fear and apprehension over the phone. The first sign of weakness here, and you'll be consigned to a life in the seventh level of hell.

If you are lucky enough to need somebody represented by an agency in Nashville, all you need to know is how to speak Southern. You have to be able to speak slowly and know the proper use of phrases like "Bless your heart" and "That dog won't hunt." You must also be prepared to hear a fifteen-minute dissertation on the latest antics of somebody's grandbabies. It frustrated me too much to deal with these people, so I handed this responsibility to my darling husband. He's blessed with an overabundance of patience and a pretty good flirt on the phone. He found one female agent in each of the big agencies on both coasts who is actually very nice. We send them gifts every so often, just to keep on their good side. Bribery is an accepted part of the game. If we need anything now, he calls them directly. Luckily, the process of letting the agencies know that their comedian has not been selected can be done via email. David calls his contact at Happy's agency in L.A., and in no time I have his contract and his rider in my email inbox.

On something as big as this I always have my attorney look over the contract. Christine, a.k.a. Cujo, usually puts a contract through a shredder, then subjects it to a few minutes in a blender, and finishes it off with a couple of seconds in the garbage disposal. She never likes these contracts what I get back from her bears little resemblance to what we originally received from an agency. We then enter what is commonly known as the negotiation phase of the deal. I read through the contract rider, which contains all the requests and necessities for the entertainer, and I start X-ing out whole paragraphs of what is normally referred to as outrageous bullshit.

Individual performers aren't as bad as bands. Their riders can get way out of hand. Riders for comedians aren't usually too terrible. But we're trying to save our client some money so, no, we aren't going to provide three bottles of Dom Perignon, a fifteen-hundred-dollar bouquet of flowers, or a fruit basket big enough to feed Michigan. One thing that does catch my eye, though, is the part about his signing autographs. The paragraph in question reads that Happy will only sign autographs on things that are to be left in a box outside his dressing room. That seems a little odd to me, but I don't think much about it at the time. We have made sure that the local press will be allowed access to him and that he will participate in a meet and greet before the show. All in all, it's a fairly pain-free process.

The agent agrees to most of Christine's changes to the contract. The ones he doesn't agree with are inconsequential. We have to acquiesce to a couple of them just so he can maintain his ego. He doesn't argue with any of the changes I've made to the rider requirements. I notice that there aren't any red herrings in his rider. Normally, a contract rider will include a requirement for something stupid like "Artist will not perform unless there is a poster measuring three feet by four feet of Yosemite Sam affixed to the wall of the dressing room." Those sorts of things are put in to ensure the client has read the contract and, especially, the rider requirements.

With all the contracts signed and all deposits paid, all we have to do is wait. We have arranged a private jet to fly him in the afternoon of the event and then take him home the next morning. Arranging the hotel rooms, limo, and microphones has been easy. Now, all we have to do is worry about the weather. We tried to get him in a day early, to have a little breathing room on the schedule, but he was doing a gig in Las Vegas the night before, so that was out. Weather in the mountains around Telluride in October can be spectacular—spectacularly beautiful or spectacularly bad. We, of course, are hoping for the former.

We have a few events in the meantime to take our minds off of the Telluride event, but there's a lot of money riding on this, and it has to go off without a hitch. Consequently, I could be in a coma and still manage to be nervous about it.

There's one little thing that keeps nagging at me. Somewhere in the process of hiring a band or comedian, I always ask the agent about what he, she, or they are like to work with. There are three ratings. The very best is he/she/they is/are great. Piece of cake. This means not too fussy. He/she/they will show up, perform, and be fairly pleasant in doing so. The next lower rating is he/she/they is/are fine, which means he/she/they will show up and perform but bring a little ego along. The lowest rating an agent can give a performer is okay. This means you'll need to be prepared for a range of things, from alcoholism to belligerence to supreme arrogance. This is the first time an agent has answered that question with, "You might want to call his manager."

Typically, managers or any number of assistants provide another line of defense that you have to navigate to get to a performer. They are paid to answer all questions and to take care of anything that will keep the star from having to talk to peons like me or be bothered with trivial details. Normally, I would have blown this off, but my curiosity got the better of me. It is too much of a mystery to let that go. I think of a legitimate reason to call Happy's manager and reach for my phone.

"Hello," says the voice on the other end of the call, with just the right amount of annoyance.

"Hi, Leslie—Donna Vessey from Colorado. How are you?"

"I'm good. How can I help you?" Oh, good, I think to myself; I'm glad I've brushed up on my Snotty before calling her.

"From what I understand from reading Happy's rider, we need to have everything that is to be autographed in a box outside the green room?" I ask, matter-of-factly.

"That's right," she answers flatly.

"Then what?" I ask, with an extra dose of Snotty. "When do we get it all back?"

"Once he gets to the green room, I'll bring the box in, and he'll sign everything, and I'll get it back to you," she says as if she's talking to an insolent six-year-old.

"So, the time line goes something like this: Press gets him at five, meet and greet from six to seven, dinner is from seven to nine, and he performs from nine to ten."

"He doesn't do meet and greets," she mumbles.

"Excuse me?"

"He doesn't do meet and greets," she says, this time loud and clear. I scramble to find the file for this event. Locating it on the table beside my desk, I grab it and flip it open.

"Um, okay. Do you have the contract with you?" I ask.

"Yes."

"Paragraph W, page twelve. 'Artist agrees to make himself available for a meet and greet with VIPs for one hour, from six o'clock P.M. to seven o'clock P.M. on the evening of the performance,'" I read to her with a thick, shiny coating of attitude. "Is that Happy's signature and his agent's signature at the bottom of that page?"

"Yes," she stammers. "But he never does them. I don't know how that got into this contract."

"Well, I tell you what—you have my cell number. You can make sure he knows that he's doing one for this event. We're paying ten thousand dollars for a one-hour performance. I think he can subject himself to a meet-and-greet for an hour for that price," I say, pressing my advantage.

"I'll see what I can do," she says and hangs up her phone. I guess I never did get around to asking her what he's like to work with. I get the feeling I didn't need to.

I lean back in my chair and do some deep breathing exercises to bring my blood pressure down from stroke level and pop a few aspirins to head off the inevitable headache. I look at the clock on the wall and start to figure out how long it will take to get a phone call about this. She won't take this to Happy; she's already on the phone to his agent. He'll have to get one of his assistants to find the contract and then read and reread paragraph W a few times. If he doesn't call Happy, I'll get a call in about ten or fifteen minutes. If he calls and talks to Happy, it will be closer to half an hour or forty-five minutes. I'm glad nobody is in my office to make a bet with because I would have lost. I'm more than a little shocked that the phone rings within a minute from the time Happy's manager hung up on me.

"Okay, he'll do the meet and greet, but he won't be signing any autographs," Leslie says, bracing herself for my reply.

"You're kidding, right?"

"No, that's what he said."

"Well, I'm so glad we got that straightened out," I say facetiously.

"Is there anything else I can do for you?" she asks. Translated, that means: "You've completely screwed up my day. Do you want to try for the entire week now?"

"No, no. That's all," I say rather sweetly, just in time for her to hang up on me again. I rest my elbows on my desk and let my head fall into my hands. I hear somebody coming down the hall and look up in time to see Zoe pop her head in the door to my office.

"There's a guy on the phone, and he asked for you. He said his name too fast, but I think it's Happy Noyes' agent," she says sheepishly.

"Okay," I say as I reach for the phone. "Thanks, Sweetie."

"He didn't sound very happy," she says with a grimace.

"It's okay; it'll be fine," I say, trying to be reassuring. Zoe stands in the doorway to make sure I'm telling the truth. I pick up the receiver and punch the flashing button on my phone.

"This is Donna," I say as chipper as possible.

"Donna, this is Bill at KMA." (All big agencies have a three-letter name...)

"Hi, Bill. How can I help you?"

"I just had to convince Happy that breaking this contract would be a bad thing. I also had to tell him that firing me wouldn't be a good thing either."

"You're kidding. What brought that on?"

"The meet and greet thing. He never does them. I missed it in your contract, and he's not, well, happy about it."

"He's doing this one, though, right?" I ask hopefully.

"Yeah, but I don't appreciate you calling my client and almost getting me fired."

"Okay, first of all, I didn't call Happy. I called his manager, and if you'll recall, you're the one who told me to call her. In case you forgot, we are your client, too. We're paying you a boatload of money to get your guy here and perform for my client. If you missed this in his contract, that's your problem. I've got a client that I'm looking out for, and that's my job. I don't care what you have to do to make this right, but I will be at the Telluride airport in a week and a half, and Mr. Noyes had better be there with a smile on his face and a song in his heart. One more thing, Bill: He gets his check *after* he performs for the full sixty minutes. Okay?" I glance over at Zoe, and her eyes are as big as saucers. She's never heard her aunt speak harshly to anyone. It must have been quite a shock to her system. I smile and wink at her, and I see the stress melt off of her shoulders. There's dead silence on the other end of the line. "Did I lose you, Bill?"

"No, I'm still here. I'll take care of it, and he'll be there."

"Good, I'm glad…" he hangs up on me before I get a chance to finish my sentence.

ONE AND A half excruciating weeks later—ten whole days, eight hundred and sixty-four thousand seconds later—I'm standing on the tarmac at the Telluride Regional Airport. It's 2:30 in the afternoon, and I'm waiting for the private jet that is to deliver Mr. Happy Noyes to us. The charter jet company is in contact with the plane, and its representatives have agreed to call me when the plane is fifteen minutes from landing. If everything was going according to plan, they should have called me fifteen minutes ago, and I should be watching a beautiful sleek private jet landing in this gorgeous mountain setting. But, alas, no. I wait. With every minute that passes my heart sinks just a little lower into my gut. I wait for about an hour before I decide to call the jet's home base. I dig through my purse for my phone.

"Hi, Alice, Donna Vessey. I have one of your planes bringing somebody into Telluride, Colorado, from Las Vegas. I was wondering if I could get an update on their ETA." I love it when I can speak the lingo.

"Hey, Donna," she says all friendly like. "Let me put you on hold for just a minute, and I'll get back with you."

"Okay, thanks," I say doing my best to sound calm. Less than a minute later she comes back on the line.

"Hon, I've got good news and bad news. Which would you like first?" she asks.

"I think I'd better get the good news first."

"The good news is they are on their way. The bad news? They just took off."

"How long does it take to get here?" I ask, my mind racing.

"They should be there in just over an hour," she says reassuringly.

"Oh, okay. That's not bad. That gets them here around 4:30 local time. Thanks, Alice, I appreciate it.

"No problem, Hon, glad to help."

Okay, so we'll be a little pressed for time, but we should be able to make it to the hotel and get Happy down to meet the press. At least they are on their way. Before I called EJC Charters, I was trying to figure out how I was going to break it to my client that their expensive star entertainer wasn't coming.

With nothing better to do, I head over to the coffee shop in the main terminal. Sure enough, about fifty minutes later I get a call from Alice letting me know that the plane is about fifteen minutes out. I gather my things, stoke up my courage, and head back out to the tarmac. There, I find the limo and the big black SUV side by side but no drivers. A quick check of the time lets me know I have about ten minutes to find my drivers. Luckily, I remember I had the limo driver's card. I call him and am relieved to find they have just stepped into the general aviation terminal to use the restroom. As the drivers join me by their vehicles, the limo driver notes a plane on the horizon.

"That must be our plane," he says with some enthusiasm.

"Where?" I ask, squinting to the west.

"Right there," he says, pointing out the dot now catching a glint from the sun.

"I sure hope that's ours," I say. Moments later, the beautiful white Gulfstream G200 touches down on the runway, leaving a tiny puff of blue tire smoke in its wake. After slowing down, the plane taxis over to a parking spot not too far from where we are.

"Come on," say my drivers in unison. I jump into the front seat of the limo, and we're off. We pull up to the side of the plane just as the engines are winding down and the cabin door opens. I jump out of the limo in time to see the male flight attendant and the pilot climb down the steps. I walk over and greet them. I pride myself in being a quick read on people, and I notice that these two people are not in the greatest of moods. They open the cargo hold and start unloading what seems to me to be an inordinate amount of luggage. The drivers help them load it all into the SUV. After all the bags have been stuffed into the vehicle, we wait. And wait. And wait. After what I deem is long enough, I turn to the flight attendant and give him my best "What the…" look.

He climbs the steps to the cabin and peeks in. He comes back and stands beside me.

"It shouldn't be too long now," he says. Finally, a young man and a middle-aged woman exit the plane. The woman I'm assuming to be Leslie, the manager. I walk over to them and extend my hand to the woman.

"Hi, I'm Donna; you must be Leslie," I say as chipper as possible as we shake hands.

"Hi, Donna; this is Justin, Mr. Noyes' assistant," she says while shifting her gaze between me and the ground.

"Hi, Justin, nice to meet you," I say, shaking his hand while he studies the tarmac. It doesn't take a genius to see that these people aren't the happiest creatures on the planet either. That must've been some plane ride!

"Leslie!" hollers the voice from inside the jet. It catches my attention, and I glance at the plane in time to see a small, soft-sided briefcase fly from the rear of the plane and land beside the cabin door. Leslie hustles up the steps and disappears into the plane. She suddenly reappears, grabs the briefcase, and, again, climbs down the steps of the jet. She passes right by me and climbs into the front seat of the Suburban. Justin follows her lead and climbs in the backseat.

"Do the drivers know where we are going?" Leslie asks.

"Yes, they do, but I'll be…" and before I can finish Happy appears in the doorway and descends the stairs. He passes right by me and folds himself into the back of the limo. They're never as tall or as good looking as they are on TV. Happy looks a lot older and more wizened than I expected, and the glaring sunlight does nothing for his ruddy complexion. His trademark mop of blond hair and dark roots are about the only thing that would make him recognizable in a crowd. At least he's dressed well. He'd never have had the time to change before he has to meet the press.

"Let's go," he says to the two drivers. I may as well have been invisible. The drivers jump into action, and I'm left standing on the tarmac with the flight crew. It takes me a few seconds to realize I've been abandoned! I look around and find the pilot and the flight attendant looking at me sympathetically.

"What the heck was *that* all about?" I ask the pilot incredulously.

"Well, let's just say that Happy doesn't quite live up to his name," he answers with more than a little disdain.

"And what was the hold up? We had you scheduled to be here at 2:30."

"Well, they were a half hour late showing up, and then he spent another half hour fighting with his girlfriend. It was quite a spectacle," he answers. By that time the female copilot has joined us, and she just shakes her head in disbelief.

"If we didn't have such strict contractual restrictions regarding what we can say about our passengers, I'd have videotaped it and sold it to one of the networks," adds the flight attendant with a snap of his fingers.

"Well, I have to find a way to get to the hotel. I suppose I'll see you tomorrow when they leave," I say as I take my leave of them.

"Okay, have a good night," they say in unison. I walk over to the main terminal to see if I can find a taxi. No luck there. Telluride has a small regional airport, and it's not like it has lines of taxis waiting to pick up passengers. Finally, I reach for the limo driver's card and dial his number.

"Hello?"

"Otis, this is Donna Vessey; are you at the hotel yet?"

"Naw, we're still a few minutes away."

"Okay, once you've dropped them off, one of you guys needs to come get me."

"Okay, I'll call you when I'm on my way."

"I'll wait for you at the main terminal. I'll be at the main door."

"Okay, Miss Donna. It'll be about twenty minutes, but I'll be there."

"I'll see you then." I glance at the time on my cell phone, and it's a few minutes before five. Time to call Phil.

"Hey."

"Hey, they are on the way to the hotel. Leslie, the manager, and Justin, Happy's assistant, are in the Suburban. I think they'll get there first. Grab her and tell her we need to get Happy to the press room so they can have their time with him."

"Gotcha. They're pulling up now."

"Good, and as soon as the limo dumps Happy, send the driver back to the airport for me. They left me standing on the tarmac."

"You're kidding," he says with a chuckle.

"I wish I was."

THE CARAVAN PULLS up to the front of the hotel, and Happy swings the door of the limo open. He gets out, and Phil is right there to greet him.

"Hello, Mr. Noyes. I'm Phil, Donna's event manager." Phil extends a hand, and it becomes obvious that Happy has no plans to reciprocate. "We need to get you down to the press room."

"I need to check into my hotel room first," says Happy, gazing past Phil into the lobby. Just then they are joined by Leslie and Justin.

"No, sir, you and your staff are already checked in. We really need to get you down to the press room. They've been waiting," says Phil respectfully but firmly enough to get his point across. Phil has Happy's contract rolled up in his left hand, and he starts tapping it against his leg. Happy looks at Phil, the rolled-up paper in his hand, and then at Leslie. Happy then takes off into the lobby of the hotel.

"You, get back to the airport and pick up Donna," says Phil, pointing at the limo driver. "You can help the bellmen unload the bags," he says, pointing at the driver of the Suburban. "You two, come with me," he says, pointing at Leslie and Justin. He hands them the keys to their rooms. "Your rooms are right next to Happy's. Here are your keys. I'm sure you can find your way to the press room once you get settled in." With that, Phil runs to find where Happy has gotten off to. He finds him in the lobby bar, trying to get the bartender's attention.

"Mr. Noyes, I know this is a bit rushed, but we really have to get you to the press room," say Phil, waving off the bartender.

"You have no idea what I've been through today," Happy spews at Phil.

"You are absolutely right—I don't have the slightest idea what kind of day you've had," Phil says while laying the contract on the bar and letting it unfurl. "But I do know this: You are a professional, and you didn't get to where you are today by blowing off your commitments. You see, I know all the guys you used to hang with when you were on the club circuit. You rose above all that, and that's why you're here and they're still sleeping in smelly condos and driving from town to town in somebody's car that will inevitably break down just outside of some podunk town."

Happy looks at Phil and starts drumming his fingers on the bar. He lets out a massive sigh and gives in.

"Okay, where's the room?" asks Happy.

"Come on; I'll show you," answers Phil and guides him down a wing off the main lobby. As soon as Happy enters the press room, his whole persona changes. He turns from a petulant, morose brat into a gregarious, fun-loving guy who speaks in one-liners and has the whole place laughing and loving him in no time flat.

BY THIS TIME the limo has come back to the airport to retrieve me, and we break the land speed record getting back to the hotel. I rush down to the press room and enter just as Happy says something hilarious and the whole room is gripped with laughter. Wow, what a relief. Phil is at his side, and he looks at me and grins. The press is done with interviews, and we have a few minutes before the meet and greet.

Phil looks at his watch and announces, "Okay folks, that's all the time we have. We need to get Happy off to his next engagement." With that,

Happy gets up from his chair and shakes every guy's hand and hugs all the female reporters. Phil guides him out of the room, right past me, and down to the room where the VIPs have gathered for the meet and greet.

Again, he reveals his public persona. He's gregarious and accommodating. He meets all the board members from the foundation, and they in turn introduce him to their VIPs. At the beginning he's fine. But, minute by minute, I can see the façade wearing thin. About fifteen minutes into the meet and greet we are joined by Leslie and Justin. Justin has brought with him a large stack of autographed photos of Happy and hands them out to anybody who wants one. I try to engage Leslie in conversation, but evidently she's still mad at me from our last conversation. Some people can really carry a grudge! She simply watches her boss with a blank stare on her face.

Still, I'm a little worried as the minutes pass and Happy starts to look lost in a crowd. Just when I was starting to think we were going to survive this part of the evening, I notice a shy young mother with her seven-year-old son. They are both just as cute as they can be. She's standing off to one side of the room, trying to judge the best time to approach the star of the night. Finally, after a group of admirers walk away from Happy, she makes her move. She walks her son over to him and introduces herself and her boy. This happens at the precise moment Happy runs out of patience with the current situation.

"Hi, Happy, my name is Kathy, and this here is my son Zack," she says with immense pride. Happy is looking around the room to find Leslie. He catches her eye, holds up his left wrist, and taps a finger on his watch. Leslie rushes through the crowd with Justin in hot pursuit. Happy then notices the two strangers in front of him.

"Oh, yeah, hi." He now looks like a drowning man waiting for a life preserver.

"Go ahead, ask him," prods the young boy's mother.

"Happy," he says, "can I have your autograph?" he asks while holding up one of Happy's early CDs.

"Leslie?" Happy cries out, now desperate for his very survival. He looks down at the boy and says, "Son, I don't do that." At that instant, Leslie reaches him and whisks Happy away. Justin gets the boy's attention and tries to interest him in a signed photo. Zack is having none of it. His mom is incensed, and the crowd has stopped talking. You could have heard a pin drop. No, check that. You could have heard a pin drop in a room down the hall. I didn't think he had said it loud enough for everybody in that room to hear him, but I guess people have extra-sensitive hearing when somebody morphs into an asshole. I approach the mom and put my arm around her shoulders.

"I'm so sorry," I say as a tear rolls down her cheek. You can see her son's disappointment is killing her. Justin is still trying to interest Zack in a signed photo, but the boy is consumed with his disappointment. Kathy takes her son by the hand and leads him out of the room. The room is still dead silent, and all eyes are on them as they exit the scene. I hadn't noticed that Phil has come up beside me.

"You stay here. Take care of your client. I'll go have a chat with our performer—and, don't worry, he'll be on stage at nine sharp," he says with an intensity I've never seen before.

Once Phil leaves the room, people start to murmur. The whole room is a hush of whispers that get louder and louder until you can't hear yourself think. I'm glad there isn't a fresh supply of torches and pitchforks anywhere close by. If there were, I'm afraid Happy would never have made it to the gig. I approach my client, who seems to be rather philosophical about the whole thing.

"You give somebody that much money and attention at such a young age, and these things are bound to happen," he says very sagely.

"Yeah, but there's still no excuse for treating anybody, much less a little child, like that," I say.

"Very true, very true. Say, have you given him the check for the balance of what we owe him for the evening?" he asks.

"No, I was planning on waiting to do that until he's finished his performance," I reply.

"Would you mind if I had the pleasure of doing that?" he queries with a twinkle in his eye.

"No, sir, I'd be happy to relinquish that duty to you," I say, opening my folio and retrieving Happy's check.

Meanwhile, back at the ranch, Phil walks down the corridor to Happy's suite. From the very end of the hallway, he can hear the angry voices. As he approaches the suite, it comes as a bit of a surprise that he can hear all three of them—Happy, his assistant, and his manager—shouting. Phil gently raps on the door and waits. The voices inside the suite go silent. He knows he knocked loudly enough for them to hear it, but it's fairly obvious nobody is making a move to answer the door. He knocks again and waits a suitable amount of time. Phil fishes around in his pocket and produces the second set of key cards for Happy's suite. He flips through them and extracts the key card for Happy's suite out of its protective paper sleeve. He knocks one last time as he slips the key in and out of the slot in the door handle. He slowly opens the door and finds Happy on one side of the room and his assistant and manager on the other. All three of them have their arms crossed, and they are all red-faced with anger.

"No, no, I don't want to hear it," Happy says with a wave of his hand, glaring at Phil. "I did the best I could down there. I went way beyond what I agreed to."

"Leslie, Justin, can we have the room?" asks Phil, looking them both in the eye. Happy looks at them in a panic but does nothing to prevent the inevitable.

"That's okay—we were just leaving anyways," says Leslie through clenched teeth. Justin and Leslie leave the room and close the door behind them.

"Shit," mutters Happy to himself, then looks at Phil. "What? What are you going to do?"

"I'm not going to do anything. We're just going to talk—you and me, man to man," says Phil in an eerily calm voice. He sits down in one of the comfortable chairs in the spacious suite's living room.

At the appointed time, I escort our client and all the VIPs to the main ballroom for dinner. It's the typical fare for one of these dinners. A thousand people eat filets or salmon during a speech by the head of the foundation, and a few awards are handed out. The big shock for me comes when the president of the board calls the guests of honor up to the stage.

"Ladies and gentlemen, please welcome to the stage our guests of honor, Kathy Nowitzky and her son, Zack."

As Kathy and Zack make their way to the stage, they are illuminated with a spotlight and given a standing ovation. I can't help it. My eyes well up with tears, and, damn it, I don't have any tissues.

The foundation hosting the dinner and the conference is the Thank the Troops Foundation. Each year at the annual dinner it honors a handful of veterans and the spouse of a soldier who paid the ultimate price for serving his or her country. The thunderous applause gets to Kathy as well, and you can see the tears streaming down her face as she steps up to the podium.

"We know that nothing we do here tonight can sufficiently convey our condolences and our appreciation for what you, your husband, and your family have sacrificed for your country," says the head of the foundation into the microphone. "But, as a token of our appreciation, here is a check in the amount of ten thousand dollars for you, and a check in the amount of ten thousand dollars will be presented to the Thank the Troops scholarship fund in the name of Zachary Nowitzky to help with his college education when the time comes."

Kathy dissolves into tears, and the crowd gives her another standing ovation. A member of the honor guard escorts her from the stage, and she and her son are smothered with hugs on their way back to their seats.

Realizing that the time for our performer to take the stage is drawing near, I rush around to the stage entrance and find Happy and Phil watching the proceedings in the wings. Happy's head is hanging low, and Phil has his arm around his shoulder. I keep my distance, and as Happy is being introduced, I see Phil give him a pat on the back and whisper something in his ear. Two stagehands pull the curtain apart at center stage, and the spotlight illuminates Happy bounding from the darkness to the applause of an appreciative audience. I watch as he transforms into his public persona and brings down the house.

"What'd you say to him?" I ask Phil as we sit in the green room during the performance.

"Oh, not much," he says with a wry grin. "I just made sure that we were here for the foundation's awards."

"How did he take it?" I ask.

"At first, he wasn't, er, happy," replies Phil. "He was a little steamed that his agent hadn't let him know who this gig is for. He calmed down a little when I pointed out that it's all spelled out in the contract and the main reason he was chosen was because his act is clean."

"I was blown away that the young mom and her son were the guests of honor," I say.

"How did Happy react?"

"I think it completely devastated him. I think he felt like a raging moron."

"At least he recovered before he had to go on."

"Yeah, he's a pro. I think he's got a little surprise in store for our client."

"I hope it's a good surprise," I say with some alarm. "I'm not sure I can take any more bad ones."

"Oh, I think you'll be pleasantly surprised."

AT ABOUT THE fifty-minute mark, Phil and I go to stand in the wings and wait for Happy to wrap up his show. I check my watch and am amazed that the hour has come and gone with Happy showing no signs of stopping. The audience either doesn't notice or doesn't mind. He's on a roll, and the crowd loves him. A full half hour later he does his trademark routine that he usually uses to close his show. When he gives his signature punch line and bows deeply to the audience, everybody there jumps to their feet and gives him a long ovation. He then asks for quiet, and that's when I get nervous.

"Mrs. Nowitzky, would you mind if Zack joins me here on stage?" Happy asks the guest of honor.

Zack looks at his mom, and she pushes him toward the front of the room. Zack bounds up the stairs and joins Happy at center stage.

"Not many of you know this," says Happy, surveying the audience. "Maybe none of you know this, but I lost my dad in the Vietnam War." He puts his arm around Zack and says, "I know what you're going through, Little Brother."

Happy fishes a piece of paper out of his pocket and hands it to Zack. "This is my phone number. Anytime you need to talk, give me a call." He digs around in his pocket again and brings out a coin. "My dad gave me this Liberty Silver Dollar when he left for Vietnam to remind me what he was fighting for, and I've kept it with me to remind me what he died for. I want you to have this now, Zack. Keep it with you as a reminder of what this is all about." He hands the coin to Zack and gives him a big hug.

At that moment there isn't a dry eye in the house.

Happy continues, "I appreciate all that this foundation does, and I especially appreciate all that our soldiers and their families do for our country." The room is silent, and he holds their rapt attention. He stands center stage and stares out at the audience for a few seconds. "I understand you have a silent auction going on to raise money for all the great things that this organization does. Well, here's another thing you probably don't know. Before I became a comedian, I was a chef. Well, not really a chef. I never completed any of the courses I started. But I did manage to learn a few things along the way, and I eventually became a pretty good cook. Judging by my waistline, I think I like my own cooking a little too well. Here's my point. I am willing to auction off my services as a chef at the house of the winning bidder. I will cook dinner for you and eight or ten of your closest friends. With the help of my trusty assistant here, let's see if we can raise a bunch of money right here, right now."

Phil looks at me and grins. "The best is yet to come," he says. Happy starts the bidding at twenty-five hundred dollars, which quickly shoots up to ten thousand. Zack walks back and forth at the front of the stage to help identify the bidders. The bidding gets to twelve thousand five hundred, and there it stops.

"Twelve five once, twelve five twice," he pauses for dramatic effect. "*Sold!*"

Amid the applause that follows, Happy hops off the stage and guides Zack back to his mom. He proceeds to autograph everything and anything he can find for Zack. Both mom and son are beaming by the time Happy leaves them. He spends another half hour greeting and talking with his adoring fans. It's hard for me to believe he's the same guy I saw at the meet and greet. I'll never know what Phil said to him, but it obviously worked.

After a while, Phil and I wade through what's left of the crowd and rescue him. We can tell he's exhausted, and we need to get him to the airport fairly early in the morning. He seems genuinely pleased to see us and says good night to the crowd around him. Just then the head of the foundation finds us and presents Happy with the check for the balance of his fee.

"I'd like to thank you for what you did tonight. That was amazing, and the money you raised will go for a good cause. Here's the check for the rest of what we owe you. It was worth every penny," he says as he hands Happy an envelope.

"I should really be thanking you," says Happy. "I apologize for the way I acted earlier. I'll never be able to take that back. My girlfriend dumped me this morning before I got on the plane to come out here. My manager and my assistant quit after my stunt at the meet and greet, but I think I might have had an epiphany." Happy then grabs the lapel of the foundation director's suit jacket, stuffs the envelope into the inside pocket, and then pats the director on his chest. "You need this a whole lot more than I do. Just don't tell the press or my agent anything about it. A bad reputation is a hard thing to live up to."

I'm stunned. The director is in shock. Happy stands there for a moment, then turns and walks away. Phil is grinning from ear to ear.

I NEVER DID see him the next day. He checked out early and took the shuttle to the airport. I never saw Leslie or Justin either. They never stayed in their rooms. Happy's career took off after that. He broke into movies and did a series of tours at the biggest venues in the country. He also became very generous with his time and money and became the national spokesman for the Thank the Troops Foundation.

CHAPTER 15

A Walk on the Wild Side

"Good morning, please do come in," the butler says as he swings the door open.

"Good morning," I stumble, my voice trailing off as I make my way through the door.

It's not the butler that's caught me off guard; it's what's standing behind him. My mouth is agape as I stare up in wild wonder at the spectacle of a Chewbacca look-a-like poised like a church greeter. The sight of an eight-foot-tall brown bear in the foyer has startled the rest of my crew as well. I hear somebody whisper, "Holy crap!" and the butler gives us a wry smile. It's not the first time he's seen this reaction.

The butler shows us into the massive living room before disappearing to fetch the lord of the manor. *What fresh hell is this?* I ask myself. Chuck counts thirty-five "trophies" above the colossal stone fireplace. Phil notes the various foxes and wolves standing lifelessly near one wall.

"We're standing on a zebra pelt," Bob whispers.

"I believe elephant tusks are holding up the glass on that coffee table. Is that even legal?" Sam hisses.

I can't take my eyes off of the lifeless lion, posed in attack mode with one huge paw up as if to lunge; it breaks my heart. Why would anyone kill such a beautiful beast? The taxidermist who stuffed this regal beast must have had a dark sense of humor, though. It appears as though he left the lion's eyebrows raised, ever so slightly, lending him a faintly comical expression of surprise, which, no doubt, accurately reflected the moment of his untimely demise.

"If there ever was a time when you've had to rely on your acting skills," I tell everyone, "It's now."

"You too, Donna," Phil says, "You need to pinch a little color into your cheeks. You're as pale as that mountain goat over there."

David and I have been to the Serengeti and Massai Mara. We have shot hundreds of animals…with a camera! Having seen these creatures running free and wild (and alive!) in their natural habitat, the sight of them stuffed and glassy-eyed in someone's den is truly disheartening. It took all the strength I could muster to remain calm and remind myself that we're here to bid on a job. I am reminded of an old Ellen DeGeneres routine in which she asks people why they have deer heads on their walls, and they always say because it's such a beautiful animal. To which Ellen replies, "I think my mother's attractive, but I have photographs of her."

The butler returns to let us know that Mr. Evans will be with us shortly and invites us to make ourselves comfortable. It would take a truckload of tranquilizers to get me to relax in this room.

"I can't imagine how they are going to want this place decorated," Chuck says to no one in particular as he surveys the room. The first thing that comes to my mind is to get rid of all these dead animals.

"Nothing like a few carcasses to bring a party down," Sam says.

"Oh, I don't know," says Bob, "I can think of a few festive things we can do with that gun collection. Maybe we can load them and hand one to each guest as they arrive. The last one standing wins the door prize!"

"Maybe not—the neighbors would probably complain about the noise," adds Chuck with contrived disappointment. I shush them and start to imagine their heads mounted above the fireplace.

One entire wall is covered with a map of the world. Push pins affix photographs to all corners of the map. Upon closer inspection, the common theme of this display is somebody proudly posing with some very dead animals. This room clearly made some taxidermist a millionaire.

Phil points to the lion that's breaking my heart and adds, "I can see a party hat on that guy there. Think we can wedge a noisemaker in that snarling mouth?"

This causes some snickering among my crew that ceases abruptly as we hear footsteps approaching. I stand and compose myself in anticipation of our introductions. I'm not sure, but I think it was a mixture of

Wild Kingdom, and Crocodile Dundee that made me think I was going to be meeting a tall, tanned, rugged individual. I could have been more wrong, I'm just not sure how. At that very moment, the embodiment of Elmer Fudd enters the room. He is followed by his faithful yellow lab, who appears to be eyeing the heads mounted on the wall. He must live in constant fear of ending up like the rest of the animals in this house.

Elmer is eye level with me, and I'm only five foot two. Predictably enough, he's sporting khaki clothing. A khaki safari jacket clings to his enormous belly, and he removes his Aussie Bush Hat to reveal the most impressive comb-over I've ever seen. He extends his chubby little hand, and I expect him to say, "Sshhh. Be vewy, vewy quiet. We're hunting wabbits!"

"It's nice to meet you, Elm…Mr. Evans," I say, barely catching myself. I introduce the gang and am impressed at our professionalism. To see the forced smiles on our faces, nobody would know we were all about to burst out laughing.

Mr. Evans invites us to take our seats and dismisses the butler.

"So how does it work, this party planning business?" he asks with more than a little dose of condescension. He seems a bit nervous. I notice his eyes are darting back and forth, and his hands are twisting in his lap.
I don't think he likes to be outnumbered. I go into my canned speech that I use with male clients about us being just like general contractors.

"If you need catering, décor, entertainment, or anything else, we make the arrangements and then manage all the details for you," I explain.

"Now, we're going to have forty or fifty people here for this thing. Have you ever done a party that big?" Elmer asks, still not looking me in the eye. *You don't get out much, you little dung beetle, do you?*

"Oh, yes sir," I respond demurely, "we've done some pretty big events." I feel Phil getting ready to embellish on my last statement, and I calmly pat his arm to prevent what I'm sure would be a harsh retort to Elmer's ludicrous question.

I retrieve a list of clients and contact info from my briefcase and slide it across the table to him at the very moment our pompous little host proclaims, "I'll need to see a list of references before we can sign any…oh…" he says, looking down his nose at the list I just slid under his pudgy little fingers.

Phil jumps in. "What we'd like to do is get an idea of the purpose or theme for the event," he says as he slips into his manager zone.

Our host holds up his hand to stop the conversation and announce that his daughter will have all of those details. He stops fidgeting and twitching long enough to explain that this is to celebrate a "big kill" one of his friends has bagged in Africa. He then proceeds to bore us with every little detail of his friend's adventure. I must have checked out at that point because I don't remember hearing any of the details about the poor beast that will soon be frozen in some "natural" pose, staring glassy-eyed in someone else's living room. I don't even remember what kind of animal it was.

When I come back to reality, Mr. Fudd is saying, "The guest of honor is a good friend of my daughter's. She should be here shortly to go over all of the details with you."

Suddenly, a tall, willowy brunette appears and introduces herself as Kenya. She is attractive in a pale, sickly way, kind of like Morticia Addams but without all the makeup. She must take after her mother because the only thing she shares with Elmer is that loud, irritating voice and arrogant, take-charge manner.

"Named her Kenya 'cause that's where she was conceived," says her father with a chuckle. "The day she was born, her mother was out hunting with me and just about to bag a duiker when her water broke." I cringe at the thought of my father talking about my conception and birth in front of total strangers.
I would be especially mortified if he did it in front of me! Judging by the lack of expression on Kenya's face, I get the idea that this isn't the first time she's been subjected to hearing this. After our quick introductions to Kenya, we do our best to get down to business.

"So, Nelson and Sam will need to know a little about your plans for the menu," I say as I direct Kenya's attention to them. Kenya hands them a menu, and I wander behind them, peeking at the list. Thank God there are no illegal meats on this menu. At least, nothing that jumps out at me.

"I'll be having another friend bring in some more exotic dishes, as well," she adds.

Oh, God! *The Department of Wildlife SWAT team breaks through the windows sporting assault rifles and tasers. It takes surprisingly little time for them to have everyone face down on the floor while one of them reads us our Miranda rights. "But,*

but…" I hear myself stammering. "*Save it for the judge, Lady,*" says one of the commandos while a couple of the other stormtroopers are poking Elmer with their rifles. "*Didn't think we'd find out about the Brazilian merganser pâté, did you, you little…*"

"We'll need tables and chairs for fifty," Kenya adds, rudely interrupting my daydream. "We want a hunting motif."

"What does she think *this* is?" I hear Chuck whisper to Bob as they look around the room.

"What was that?" Kenya says with one eyebrow raised.

"Oh, I was just saying to Bob," Chuck says nervously, "that leopard and tiger print linens would just make this room come alive."

Kenya nods while the irony of Chuck's statement goes whizzing right by her.

Kenya mentions the Aboriginal band she's hired to perform. She's flying them in from Detroit, of all places, but they'll need equipment. Phil takes down their contact info to get a list of equipment they'll need.

Chuck asks if he can take a few pictures of the room for planning purposes, and father and daughter agree.

"But keep that coffee table out of the picture," Elmer says. "And that Ethiopian wolf right there. He's a beauty, but some folks are giving me grief. Nearing extinction, my butt. I saw dozens of 'em in one day. Only bagged the one."

Suddenly, Elmer's jovial expression contorts and turns red with rage. He bellows, "Down! Get down! On the floor, right now!" My gang has the same reaction as me. We all duck before we realize it's not us to whom the command has been shouted.

The poor Labrador has his front paws on the couch next to Elmer. The dog is now cowering in a corner, and I feel Nelson tense up. He has two chocolate labs, and I can tell he's having difficulty witnessing how this poor dog is being treated.

Kenya immediately rushes out of the room. She returns quickly with what appears to be a cup of tea.

"Here, Father," she says, rubbing his back. "Sip this. It will calm you down. You know it's not good for you to get excited."

It's then that I notice that we've not been offered anything to drink, but I figure it's just as well. It probably would have been concocted from yak blood or something.

Kenya offers a tour of the house, and we leave her father in the living room, sipping his tea and muttering to himself.

"Great," Sam whispers in my ear. "We're in the house with Mr. Crazy and an arsenal of guns. What's to worry about, right? I have a feeling I can kiss my wedding plans goodbye."

Ah, it's been a while since Sam has managed to make something all about her. I'm glad she didn't waste this golden opportunity. When Nelson first proposed to her, Sam was very casual about the wedding. "Just a brief ceremony and a small gathering of friends," she said. Then, without warning, she transformed into just another bridezilla. She has dragged me to more than a dozen bridal shops, and after she tried on her twenty-fifth wedding dress and whined about it not being "the one," I decided I would no longer keep track. Now, as we walk through this game preserve disguised as a house, she is still obsessing about her nuptials. I continue through the house, taking notes of everything Kenya requests.

"I'm thinking we should give expensive hunting knives as party favors," she says, wandering through the halls. Kenya continues as I keep scribbling. "They're big and sharp. My thought is that we set the table with them. People can cut their steaks, wipe them off, and then bring 'em home. Heck, if it can gut a deer, it sure can slice into a juicy steak." At this time, we enter the kitchen, which stops Nelson in his tracks. It's huge. It would make a restaurant kitchen green with envy. Poor Nelson has the look of a person who just walked into the Sistine Chapel for the first time.

We are about to flee, when Kenya suddenly decides to be hospitable and invites us all to lunch. Great, I think. Now, she decides to be the polite hostess.

I hear Chuck behind me whispering, "I don't think I'm in the mood for baby seal ka-bob."

Phil is muttering, "No way in Hell."

I offer a lame excuse, but Kenya will have none of it.

"Then it's settled. You're staying," she says. "The cook has some elk stew that's been simmering all morning, and his alligator appetizers are out of this world!"

I stammer an excuse, and then Elmer Fudd proclaims we *will* be staying for lunch.

"I won't take no for an answer. It's settled," he says.

I'm envisioning a firing squad assembling when I explain I'm a vegan. I'd be better off walking into the Vatican and proclaiming that I'm an atheist.

"Actually, we'd love to, but we have a big meeting with a group of veterinarians for their annual dinner," Nelson says.

Mr. Creepy's eye is twitching as if he knows Nelson is telling a lie. I want to hug my buddy.

"Where's your meeting?" the creep asks, directing the question at Phil.

"As Donna probably explained to you, all the details of her clients and their parties are held in the strictest of confidence," my right-hand man explains.

This seems to satisfy him, and we beat a hasty retreat to the van, piling in with the speed of gazelles being hunted by a pack of lions. Or hunters.

Back at the conference table in my office we hold a planning meeting for the great white hunter and his daughter. There have been events I'd have loved to turn down. I don't have a real good feeling about this one, but it's the slow season, and I've got rent and payroll to worry about. Nelson and Sam run through the menu again and assure me there's nothing illegal on the list. Fearful of the extra menu items Kenya's friends plan to bring, I call my attorney. She advises me to list every item on the menu we are to provide as per the contract and add a clause that will protect us, stating that we're responsible solely for the food we're supplying.

"WE ARE NOT going back in that house without a strong, attractive bodyguard," proclaims Bob. "Those two are about as homophobic as they come."

"I can just envision us," says Chuck, "stuffed and mounted in some secret room with a plaque that says 'The Rare Colorado Queens.'"

"And worse than that," continues Bob. "Within six months, our clothes would be out of style."

Homophobia notwithstanding, Chuck and Bob have done an amazing job coming up with the decor for the room. They found fabric prints representing the cheetah, zebra, tiger, and leopard.

We have one final meeting at the house before the party to confirm everything we've discussed, sign the contract and collect a deposit.

The butler lets us in and seats us in the trophy room. To this day, I can't hear the word "trophy" without getting nauseated, thinking of those "great hunters" killing a wild animal that has been cornered by their hired "guides." What kind of grubby, delusional person sees that as a "sport" that should be honored with a "trophy"?

The man of the house enters, twitchier than ever. Kenya follows behind him, pushing a cup of tea into his hands.

"Here you go," she says with a smile at the rest of us. "Tea calms him down. I have other affairs to attend to. Daddy, will you be a dear and handle this for me?" With that, she's off before she sees the look of disdain on her father's face.

I hand over the contract, hoping he doesn't notice the "mystery meat" clause. He barely glances at the words before signing with a shaky hand. I politely tell him we need to secure payment before the event.

"I'll get a check," he says flatly and shoves his teacup behind a stack of books on the coffee table. As he stumbles from the room, I wonder if the caffeine in that tea might be doing more harm than good. Fifteen minutes later we're still waiting.

I decided to stick my head into the kitchen hoping to track down the butler, the maid, or Kenya, but no luck. There's not a soul around. As I wander back through the house, I'm anxiously looking for some signs of life. I want to get this wrapped up so we can get out of here. I don't want to be here any longer than I have to.

SUDDENLY, I HEAR the sirens getting louder and louder. A fire truck, accompanied by an ambulance, has pulled up in the front driveway, and there is a storm of activity as firemen and paramedics dismount from their vehicles. Soon, the foyer is filled with the emergency crews who are quickly escorted by the butler to a back room. Within a few minutes, Elmer Fudd is being wheeled off on a gurney.

"You have *got* to be kidding me?" Phil says, shaking his head in total disbelief. "Can this get any more bizarre?" he says under his breath as we all watch the paramedics tote Mr. Crazy off to the ambulance.

Not wanting to sound too mercenary, I suppress the urge to complain about not getting the check before all this happened.

I call Kenya later that evening to find out about her father and to ask if the event is still a go. While I'm dialing her number, I try to figure out a way to ask for the deposit. Asking about her father while at the same time trying to get a deposit from her seems a little crass. Without my even having to ask, though, Kenya gives me the credit card information and tells me the party must go on.

"It's what he'd want," she says.

"So, you expect your father will still be in the hospital then?" I ask her. The party is four days away.

"In fact," she tells me, "he's been checked out of the hospital this afternoon. He's now in the morgue."

I'm stunned, and it takes me a couple of tries to hang up the phone. It's not that Mr. Evans was my favorite person on the planet, but I was just at his house! I was talking to him. And now he's gone. It was all so sudden. It was all so creepy!

David walks into the room and notices the dazed look on my face.

"It looks like you've seen a ghost," he says, not knowing how close he is to the truth. I'm still so shocked I can't even answer him. "Hey," he says softly, "what's up?"

"My client, Mr. Evans, is dead."

He knows exactly how to calm me down. He directs me to my favorite comfy chair and settles my fat tabby cat on my lap. Nothing like a little cat therapy to calm one's nerves. That and a nice big glass of syrah.

"Are they canceling the event?" David asks.

I chuckle and say, "Nope, that's the strangest part of all. That's still a go."

"I know you'll be glad to have this one behind you," he says. "But once in a while, you have to say, 'It's just a job.'" I take a healthy swallow of Syrah, sigh, and pet the cat.

"She showed no emotion at all," I say. "I have to go back tomorrow to be sure the furniture has been cleared out so the team can set up. I dread it, and Phil has asked for the day off so he can volunteer at the twins' school."

David, my hero, pushes a photography session to another day and goes with me to the place I've come to call "Animal House." Nothing has been moved, and the event is tomorrow! Kenya wanders into the room, looking dazed. She introduces me to Jason, a reed-thin man with a scraggly beard. He's trailing her as if he's a loyal dog and she's holding a bone.

"Jason is our guest of honor," she says. David and I exchange glances. He looks barely able to shoot a squirrel with a BB gun, never mind big game.

My cell phone rings, and I step outside to take the call.

"Hello, this is Donna," I say, trying to sound chipper.

"Mrs. Vessey, this is Detective Drake. Do you have a minute to talk?"

"Sure," I say. How can I help you?" I ask, not relating this call to the current situation.

"You were one of the last people to speak with Mr. Evans—is that correct?" Pow that hits me like a locomotive.

"Um, yeah," I hesitate, trying my best not to sound nervous, "I guess I was." My mind is reeling. Why are the police involved in this?

"Did you notice anything out of the ordinary with Mr. Evans' demeanor or his physical nature?" asks the detective.

"Well, I only saw him twice, so I'm not the best judge of what would be out of the ordinary," I explain.

"I understand," says Detective Drake. "I was just hoping you could help us out," he says, as calm and soothing as any voice I've ever heard. "There are some irregularities surrounding Mr. Evans' death and..."

I'm totally checked out at this point. Good God! I'm a friggin' suspect, I think. *"We know you did it, Missy! We know you're a tree-hugging animal rights type, but killing big game hunters won't help your cause." "But, but..." "Aw, save it for the judge, Lady."*

"Do I need to call my attorney?" I ask, not really wanting to hear the answer.

"Do you have a PhD in chemistry?" is his reply.

"Um, no," I answer, remembering that I flunked the only chemistry class I ever took in high school.

"Then no, you don't need a lawyer. We have a pretty good idea of who did it and how. We're just going to have a tough time proving it."

I drift off during his explanation of what they are looking for and how I might help. I'm bathed in relief that I am not a suspect but immediately start to worry about having my company's name associated with a murder investigation. I'm in the middle of a real good worry when the word "poison" snaps me back to the here and now.

"...seems that he'd been given this stuff over a period of time, and it was just lucky that the coroner found it in the autopsy."

"I'm sorry. Can you repeat that?" I ask.

"We wondered if you saw Mr. Evans eat or drink anything on your last visit," Drake asks. "Was he acting oddly?"

"Well, he was shaky and certainly seemed distracted," I say. "His daughter brought him tea to settle him down."

Drake explains that trace amounts of something called tyrosine kinase inhibitor was detected in his blood. And that, apparently, can cause heart failure over time.

After a few more questions about the household, he winds up our conversation by saying, "It's going to be a tough case without hard evidence. All we have now is circumstantial."

I wander back into the house, now fearfully looking at the butler, the maid, and Kenya. David is accepting a cup of tea from Kenya, and I lunge for the cup. "Oh, honey," I tell him with a bright smile. "You *know* what happens to you when you take in caffeine." I wrestle the cup from him and hand it to the maid. I wink at Kenya and whisper, "It does bad things to his lower intestines if you know what I mean."

David looks a bit stunned but shrugs and offers his thanks to our hostess. Only then do I look around the room and realize the furniture still hasn't been moved. I realize there have been a few distractions, but the party is tomorrow, and we need to act like nothing's wrong.

Right before I voice my disappointment, I see it. Remember the screeching violins from the shower scene in *Psycho*? Well, that's what's playing in my head when I see the teacup hidden behind the stack of books on the coffee table. With my blood pressure up around stroke level, I try to think of a way to distract everybody in the room.

"Ya, know, I could use a glass of water," I announce, sounding as unconvincing as humanly possible.

The maid looks at me like I've lost my marbles and takes off for the kitchen. I then look at David and say, "You should see the collection of hunting rifles that Kenya and her father have."

David gives me a look not unlike the one the maid just gave me, but he follows Kenya to the gun locker.

Great, two down, one to go. I fish my cell phone out of my purse and apologetically tell the butler that I need to make a call and turn my back toward him. I push the auto-dial number for Phil and wait for him to answer. I peek over my shoulder to find that the butler has wandered off, and I make my move. I grab the cup, fully expecting there to be some tea left in it, and try to figure out how to get it to the car without spilling any of it. To my utter disappointment, the bottom of the cup is as dry as a bone. I hear the maid's footsteps approaching as I frantically try to decide what to do next. I'm not sure if Detective Drake can still use the cup, but it makes my job a little easier as I drop the thing in my purse and zip it up, just as the maid comes in with my glass of water. I thank her and take the glass from her with one hand, realizing I still have the phone in my other.

I hear Phil saying, "Hello? Hello?" and I fold my phone and hang up on him. I'll have a little explaining to do later. The maid walks off, shaking her head and muttering something under her breath.

Back comes Kenya with David in tow, and I can tell he's totally annoyed with me. The last thing he wanted to see was a collection of guns. We settle on the arrangements for tomorrow's party, she agrees to get her staff to move the furniture, and we take off. We arrive a few minutes later at the police station, stolen cup of tea in hand. I hand Detective Drake the cup and explain my disappointment that there wasn't any tea left in the cup.

"Here's something you probably can use," I say. "I'm sorry, but it's all dried up."

"Where'd you get this?" he asks, suddenly sounding a little less than happy.

"From the Evans' house," I explain. "It's the cup he was drinking out of right before he went to the big hunting ground in the sky."

"Shit! Did anybody else see him drink out of this cup?" he asks with some irritation.

"Yeah, practically my whole staff. Why?" I ask.

"Well, it's just not kosher to gather evidence like this. At least we can test it. The district attorney's office will have to figure out if we can use this or not," he says with some disappointment. "Maybe it's enough to get a search warrant."

"I'm sorry—I thought I was doing you a favor," I say defensively. "Anyway, there isn't any tea in there. You might not get what you need from it."

"Not to worry," he says, "the lab can use this just fine." He stuffs the cup into an evidence bag and mutters something about not booking us for the petty theft.

THE NEXT DAY, everything is in place for the big party. The animal print linens fit perfectly in the décor scheme, and Kenya has dead animals placed as if they are marching around the tables.

Wearing an animal-print caftan and a turban, Kenya looks every bit like Norma Desmond on safari. She makes her entrance into the room, and the crowd hushes. With her Joan Crawford eyebrows and cold expression, she is one scary woman.

In an attempt to make conversation, I approach her and tell her how sorry I am for her loss. She simply stares at me with a blank expression. Is she in shock, I wonder, or is she a cold-blooded murderess?

It's no surprise to me that Kenya does have some of her own appetizers prepared by her assortment of oddball friends. We never ask what those dishes are, and the guests don't either. They gobble it up as they exchange stories of hunting forays and the benefits of various rifles.

"The aboriginal band is wearing nothing but loincloths, beads, and war paint," Phil says as if I'm blind.

"And the downside of that would be…?" quips Chuck.

Phil gives him an exasperated stare and walks off, saying, "We've done some weird events, but this takes the prize… uh… I mean trophy."

One small table in the corner holds a lonely place setting, along with a lone candle and a pith helmet. This is apparently Kenya's homage to her father.

Just before dessert is served, Kenya leads her guests in the strangest ritual I have ever witnessed. After passing out lighted torches, everyone gathers in a circle. One of the guests starts to speak in a language unfamiliar to me, and for the next fifteen minutes, the rest of the group members take turns speaking. Not a word is familiar to us. I zone out after a while and hide in the kitchen to escape the smell of kerosene from the torches.

After the ritual, everyone returns to their seats, and dessert is served.

Nelson and Sam have outdone themselves with individual cheesecakes shaped like animals. The two searched long and hard for molds in the shape of black rhinos, cheetahs, lions, zebras, and the like. There are even elephants with white chocolate curled tusks. Kenya walks up after the party to tell me how pleased she is.

"And my father would have been happy with the party," she says, giving me an awkward hug. It's awkward because I'm stiff as a board and can't bring myself to do more than pat her half-heartedly with one hand.

The doorbell rings just as we're about to make our escape. I spot at least three police cars in the driveway. I hear Kenya loudly arguing with an officer at the door.

"It's called a search warrant, Miss," a sturdy-looking officer says. "In fact, we do have the right to search the house."

A WEEK LATER, I arrived at the office and see Phil behind his desk, reading the newspaper. The headlines proclaim what we've known all along: "Evans' Daughter Charged with Murder."

"Kenya and her former boyfriend, Jason, are being held without bond," I tell them after explaining about the Great Teacup Adventure.

"From what I hear, they're so busy trying to rat each other out; it's most likely a jury will convict them both."

It seemed all those trips to Africa had drained Kenya's resources, and Daddy had refused to fund her lifestyle. The meek Jason was, in fact, a chemist with a gambling problem. The unlikely duo met in a club, and after hearing about her problem, he offered a simple solution: a drug that would slowly kill her father. Jason had no problem creating it.

"So what happens to the house and the fortune?" asks Nelson, draping his arm around Sam.

"You'd better sit down for this, you guys," I say.

Their attention is all on me, just the way I like it. Phil urges me on. I'm grinning like a loon, but I can't help it.

"Their evil plot wouldn't have done them any good, after all," I say, enjoying the anticipation in the room. "It would seem that Elmer Fudd had a conscience after all. He left all his earthly belongings to the World Wildlife Foundation."

Laughter breaks out in the room, and we toast the end of another saga with our coffee cups.

"To the most bizarre party we've ever pulled off," I say, toasting the crowd.

Sam stands up and offers another toast.

"And here's to the woman who pulled it off so brilliantly. To our own super-sleuth, Donna," she says, raising her cup.

"You know," Nelson says. "Maybe the detective business can work into something else. This crew seems pretty good at solving mysteries."

"Yeah," says Chuck. "All we need is a lime green van and a talking dog."

"She would have gotten away with it, too, if it hadn't been for those meddling event planners!" adds Bob.

Nelson and Sam explain that they have to leave to visit yet another catering company.

"I don't think I want any great mysteries at my wedding, okay, boss?" Sam says, giving me a hug.

Nelson captures his bride-to-be in a tight embrace and says,

"The only mystery at our wedding will be why you agreed to marry me."

Phil groans, and Chuck and Bob roll their eyes.

David comes by to take me out for a nice relaxing dinner.

"I hope there's no great drama or mystery at Sam and Nelson's wedding," I say. "I've had about enough of it for a lifetime."

He opens the door for me, the gentleman he is, before jumping into the driver's side.

"You know, you're really a pretty sexy detective." He looks at me, winks, and leans over to give me a quick kiss.

"I'm an actress who fell into an unusual career," I respond. "Solving mysteries? It was a fluke. It will never happen again."

David puts the car in gear and shoots me a look.

"Never say never, Donna. Never say never."

ABOUT THE AUTHOR

Donna Vessey is a multifaceted artist with a varied background in event management, entertainment, and media. As the former owner and creator of Donna Vessey Events, an international event management company, she honed her skills in orchestrating unforgettable experiences.

Donna's passion for performance led her to study improv at Chicago's renowned Second City, laying the foundation for a successful acting career. With over 100 television commercials and 600 theatrical performances, she has established herself as a versatile performer. Her role as host of the adventure TV show "Hittin' the Road" for Rocky Mountain PBS further showcased her on-screen charisma and love for exploration.

Born into a military family, Donna's childhood was marked by global travel, instilling a lifelong passion for new experiences and diverse cultures. This adventurous spirit continues to fuel her creative endeavors and storytelling.

Today, Donna channels her wealth of experiences into writing and public speaking. Her engaging narratives through books, blogs, and speaking engagements captivate audiences. As the creative force behind the popular party blog "Dear Gala Guru," she offers a humorous and insightful perspective on event planning and celebration.

With an unwavering commitment to infusing joy and laughter into her work, Donna Vessey continues to inspire and entertain, drawing on her unique blend of event expertise, theatrical flair, and globe-trotting adventures.

www.thegalaguru.net